# IN THESE TIMES

# IN THESE TIMES

# TIMES

BERNARD LEVIN

JONATHAN CAPE
THIRTY-TWO BEDFORD SQUARE LONDON

First published 1986
Copyright © 1986 by Bernard Levin

Jonathan Cape Ltd, 32 Bedford Square, London WC1B 3EL

British Library Cataloguing in Publication Data

Levin, Bernard, *1928*–
In these times.
I.    Title
082        PR6062.E916/

ISBN 0 224 02405 1

Phototypeset by Falcon Graphic Art Ltd
Wallington, Surrey
Printed in Great Britain by
Hazell, Watson & Viney Ltd,
Member of the BPCC Group,
Aylesbury, Bucks

# Acknowledgments

Once again, I am indebted to the same trio of supporters who have helped me for several books past. Sally Chichester, my assistant, dealt with all the items in this book as they appeared, one by one, in their original newspaper dress; she also helped, as ever, in innumerable and indispensable other ways. Margaret van Hattem read the proofs and spotted many an error. Oula Jones, of the Society of Indexers, was again at hand; because of the tribute I pay her in the body of the book, she figures for once in her own Index; the tribute and the appearance alike are inadequate recompense for her skill and labour, and even more inadequate for her friendship.

I should also like to join my publishers in thanking the following for permission to quote copyright material: Faber & Faber Ltd for the lines from Alan Bennett's play *Forty Years On* (p. 157); Heinemann Educational Books Ltd, London, for the lines from Robert Bolt's play *A Man For All Seasons* (p. 283); Gerald Duckworth & Co. Ltd for the Belloc verses (pp. 25, 182); and A.P. Watt Ltd on behalf of Miss D.E. Collins for the Chesterton (pp. 117-24, 276).

# Contents

# Introduction

This is the fourth anthology of my journalism to be published, succeeding *Taking Sides* (1979), *Speaking Up* (1982) and *The Way We Live Now* (1984). The first two volumes contained between them all the newspaper and magazine articles I felt like preserving out of the immense number I had by then written (it added up to something like ten million words – an alarming thought); the items in the third selection all dated from after March 1982, and consisted only of articles chosen from those I had published in *The Times* and *Observer* since that date. This book therefore takes up where that one left off; the choice was again made from those two sources only.

But if I now begin where I left off, where exactly was I when I did leave off?

It is a truism of journalism that today's striking thought is tomorrow's platitude and next week's cliché; remember, cynical old hands among newspaper staffs used to tell the newcomers, it will wrap the cinders by nightfall. But it is not only in order to escape such an indignity that I have now pressed four collections of my flowers between hard covers; not even the vainest newspaper writer, consumed by the most intense fantasy, can believe that his work is destined to outlive marble and the gilded monuments of princes, though it were bound in Nigerian goatskin and sold in a slipcase of stainless steel. When compiling my first collection, I had a nasty shock at the discovery of articles written with urgency and passion about subjects so entirely forgotten that I could not make out, even in the most general terms, what the point at issue was, let alone why I had felt so strongly about it, and today I dare not open *Taking Sides* lest I should find in it, hard covers or no hard covers, material buried almost as deep in oblivion.

*Tout passe, tout lasse, tout casse*; write it in letters of chromium above every newspaper's doors. And yet a paradox is to be observed. Take, from my own work, an example so obvious as to be crass: my articles about individuals who suffer persecution, wrongful imprisonment, torture or death in lands where freedom is unknown except in the people's dreams. I constantly hear of more such victims; I could fill any number of newspaper pages every day with their case-histories, without discussing the same instance twice in a year. But though I always present each case as an example not of man's inhumanity to man but of particular men's inhumanity to a particular man, there is inevitably a sense in which all victims of political cruelty become one in their oppression, and the cries of the maltreated blend into a single chorus of pain. Very well; but what does that mean for one who presents the abstract and brief chronicles of his day? It means, obviously, that the subject of tyranny, so far from becoming obsolete or even stale, remains alive and ever-present in the minds of my readers, so that provided I find new words each time I say old things (which is a matter of technique), the plea strikes a response – as I well know from the volume of correspondence such articles invariably generate.

The point about tyranny, then, is that it is timeless; it has always existed, and will go on existing until the hearts of all mankind are filled with peace, love and wisdom, which happy day will, I fancy, be quite some time in dawning. Now it is always difficult for any writer to be sure about the springs of his writing, to know exactly why *that* subject loomed so large, why *those* feelings were activated by *these* facts; any explanation on my part, therefore, is offered tentatively. I believe that my wider feelings about tyranny and persecution, beyond the natural reaction of anger at news of yet more injustice, comes from my wonder at the extraordinary complexity of the human heart, which can encompass the peace, love and wisdom I have referred to, but which can also contain the most monstrous wickedness, as this very century can testify more forcefully than most.

Since it is obviously true that there are far more good people in the world than bad ones, I find myself increasingly fascinated by the nature and motives of the exceptions, and at times I can almost persuade myself that if evil could be explained it could also be ended. Of course, I know that what I seek is not to be found. Even if we could pull evil out of the ground and show the roots to those who live by it, we would have changed nothing. And yet I cannot deny that when I hear of another case of oppression and cruelty, my first thought after the rage has subsided is: how, and why, do people behave like this?

How difficult it is for anyone to answer that question can be gauged by reading some of the items in this book: 'Stone dead hath no fellow', for instance, or 'Crime and punishment'; it is much easier, and more comfortable, simply to tell the story and leave the questions to the reader, as in 'From the house of the dead'. But my failure to answer a question that has baffled the human race for upwards of a hundred centuries does not preclude my searching for an answer; on the contrary, it makes the search more urgent.

*Felix qui potuit rerum cognoscere causas*. Most of us, however, have to content ourselves with asking the questions, and are obliged to leave the answers to the experts. What, though, if there *are* no experts? For it is not only the origins of evil that elude explanation; it seems to me, more and more, that virtually nothing of importance has been explained. I began with the cruelty of political oppressors, but I might just as well – better, actually – have tried to discover where goodness comes from, what altruism is, what animates those who resist unrighteousness for righteousness' sake.

I have often pointed to one extraordinary and heartening fact of tyranny; the way in which men and women living in a closed society, with no access to truth or even to enough knowledge from which the existence of truth might be deduced, have nevertheless worked out for themselves the difference between right and wrong. This can only mean that the distinction is innate in human beings, and if that is so, it raises a question more tremendous than any, though I cannot answer that question with any certainty, and many apparently convincing answers fail to explain *how* we get that knowledge, let alone – much more important – *why* we get it.

This may seem to be making heavy weather of the task before a journalist on a daily newspaper with a brief to write about anything that interests him and nothing that doesn't. But it would be very strange if I did not want to know why the things that arouse me do so, and why some things that used to arouse me no longer do. I wrote a series of articles of which I have included three in this book (pp. 40–53), in which I discussed the nature of personal responsibility, following the theme through many of its guises. Why did I say, in one of the series, that I think responsibility may soon become the crucial question of our time? That question is not nearly so far as it may seem from the question about the springs of intolerance; at any rate, the link seems very clear to me. An hour or so before I embarked on this paragraph I read a newspaper report of a speech by an archbishop (once, I suppose, it would have been a sermon), in which he sharply criticized the individualism of modern society. Reading his remarks, it struck me that I had not for many years heard any exhortation, clerical or secular, urging self-betterment, nor had I lately seen any of those books, once so numerous, from which the reader would derive instruction for getting on in the world; getting on in the world had, I realized, long since been re-classified as sin. What perplexes me, and it is why I wrote the articles here reprinted, is the apparent belief, now very widespread, that self-help is not only unnecessary, but to be condemned.

Whatever view may be taken of this question, few, I think, will deny that it is an important one. To me, however, it is much more than important, if by important is meant (as today it usually is) *politically* important. The level of unemployment, the rate of inflation, the revenue from North Sea oil – all these are important in that sense. But if unemployment fell to a negligible figure, if inflation could be contained at a modest annual rate, if North Sea oil could be guaranteed to keep the balance of payments healthy for ever, such problems would cease to matter. There are other problems, though, which continue to matter even when they are solved, and those are the problems that interest me most; it is hardly too much to say that they are the only ones that now interest me at all.

The articles about responsibility deal with just such a problem; I cannot imagine a more fundamental one. Are we or are we not responsible for our own lives? If we are, are we not culpable if we do not strive to make the best of them? If we argue that we are economically disadvantaged, and that it is not our fault, have we thereby conclusively answered those questions? Does *that* question need revising if our claim to be incapable of improving our material conditions should turn out to be false? If not, how do we account for the fact that there are, and always have been, millions of people much worse off than we are who nevertheless demonstrate in every waking moment that they are the captains of their fate and the masters of their souls? All these questions beg a more important one. Why is it so frequently assumed that 'to better ourselves' means only to do so economically? I specified that meaning, but others rarely think it necessary to do so, taking it for granted – rightly, most of the time – that the idea will be conceived and examined in that sense alone. Yet I can think of a dozen different meanings for it, all of them much more important and potentially satisfying – and more easily attained, too, for any but those so desperately poor that all those energies have to be directed to survival.

As I have said (see p. 42) I stopped bothering to think about the problem of free will when I noticed that nobody who denied its existence *ever* failed to look for the traffic before stepping off the pavement. But my certainty that we *do* have real choices every minute of our lives, however and whyever we got them, has led me not only to ask those questions about responsibility, but to ask also the much more fundamental (and, to me, interesting) questions about the *nature* of responsibility and the widely different attitudes to it that are encountered in our time and place. And I continue to insist that what distinguishes human beings from stones is that we are not the passive objects of forces outside our control; the only experience that, once we are fully conscious, resists our desire to affect it is death. And even with death we have a choice in the matter of how we meet it; it is open to all of us to accept it as a defeat or to turn it into a triumph. Nor need death come in any dramatic form for this to be true; even to face it unafraid is to defeat it. As Pascal pointed out, if we lose the wager we shall not even know that we have done so; how many punters could say as much?

What I am saying (I think) is that it is not only necessary but easy to distinguish the questions which affect *what* we are and *why* we live from those which concern only *who* we are and *how* we live. I do not believe, and would be a fool to believe it, that the way in which Mozart has become a huge and still increasing part of my life tells me nothing about myself other than news of changing musical tastes. There is not much about Mozart in this book, but the discussion of the art of Francis Bacon says much of what I would want to say whichever artist I was discussing; it is, after all, extremely unlikely that such meaning as the universe holds for human beings does not also permeate art. Throughout all history, almost all artists have been yea-sayers, on the side of life, to such an extent that the test can be used as a definition of an artist; is anybody so silly as to believe that that astonishing fact is nothing but a coincidence?

The article on Francis Bacon is not the only one in this collection in which I become immoderate on the subject of art; 'The empty Grail' is a sustained curse on the Pre-Raphaelites and all the work of their hands. But there is method, or at least purpose, in my madness, and it is signposted clearly when I say that my chief objection to the work of such painters as Millais, Holman Hunt, Burne-Jones and Ford Madox Brown is that *it is not true*. Truth is more easily defined and discovered in art than in any court of law, and to know this, we do not have to go to Rembrandt's 'Self-Portrait as the Apostle Paul', or to *Fidelio*, or *The Idiot*; something much less elevated will serve, namely the work of Richard Strauss. Strauss was a deeply flawed man, and every now and again the flaws can be heard clearly in his music; I really do not think that I shall ever again be willing to hear *Die Liebe der Danae*, and I go to *Salome* with the greatest reluctance and usually only to hear some promising new singer in the part. The grossness, the spiritual ugliness, of these works is palpable, but the subtler worm of cunning, of heartless artifice, can be heard in *Rosenkavalier* and even in *Capriccio*, for all the ravishing beauty of those works. But listen to the great hymn to married love that closes Act Two of *Die Frau ohne Schatten*; we are listening, as we know beyond any doubt, to the naked truth clothed in art.

Freedom; the individual personality; art; these are three pillars substantial enough to hold up any journalist's attempts to shed light on matters of public concern, and what they have in common is their timelessness, their universal applica-bility, the shock of recognition they provide and, above all, the fundamental nature of the way in which they define what it means to be human, and what duties being human entails. At any rate, these are the themes I now return to most often; I always did write about them, but they now make up a greater, and still increasing, proportion of my writing. And since my journalism consists largely of comment on the behaviour of our society today, it must follow that the themes most prominent in my work are those which loom largest in the world around me. After all, my regular column in *The Times* has been appearing, whatever the subject, under the heading 'The Way We Live Now', and it is the way we live now, whether I like it or not, that inevitably fills my prose as it fills my thoughts.

There are simpler tests, some of them quite dramatic in their simplicity; take 'The odd copper'. It is given to few of us to find that, overnight, we have become richer than Croesus, and with no barb, like Midas's, hidden among the riches. The policeman in my story had precisely that experience; but he was simultaneously faced with a choice that he could not avoid and would not evade. If you read the story, you will see what the choice was, and how he chose. But the details are less important than the principle that was involved, which was no less than whether he and his soul would have to part company. And there are two morals in the story, not one; the first, as I say, concerned the immortal part of himself, the part which tells us, always and infallibly, when we are doing wrong. But the second is that it is not necessary to be clever, or well-born, or educated, or devout, or committed, or happy, or beloved, or respected, or indeed anything but human, to hear that voice. The most ruthless criminal can hear it as clearly as the purest-hearted saint, the illiterate beggar as the most profound philosopher; and to every one of these, and to everyone else, is given the choice: to heed that voice, or to ignore it.

A few years ago, I bought a set of the Nonesuch Dickens, the most beautiful and desirable edition of his works ever created; it was in twenty-three volumes, and limited, by the

publishers' decision, to no more than 877 sets.* I cleared a
complete shelf for my new treasure, and determined to read
right through everything that Dickens had ever written, both
those works which I had read before, and those I had not. For
a year, there was always a volume beside my bed, and when I
had finished my other nightly reading, for work or pleasure,
I would read a few chapters of Dickens. It was a remarkable
year, for many reasons; the discovery of such masterpieces,
previously unread, as *Dombey and Son* and *Little Dorrit* was a
literary revelation to compare with any I have ever had. But
reading some Dickens *every day* brings the reader face to face
with the mainspring of Dickens's genius: the implacable
pencil with which he drew the line between right and wrong,
good and evil, saved and damned. Dickens, of course, was a
great artist as well as a great moralist (and would have been
no use as a moralist if he had not been an artist); some of his
characters start on one side of the line and end on the other,
some go back and forth across it, some even straddle it. But
the line is drawn for all of them, and for all of us. Other
artists draw that line, too; Dostoevsky with a dagger,
Shakespeare with an opal, Beethoven in a train of fire. But no
one draws it more clearly, more unashamedly, more passionately, than Dickens, and no one makes clearer the
universal applicability of the choice the line offers and the
ability of every human being to comprehend the offer and
make the choice.

Choices can be painful; they can be dangerous, even fatal.
There is a good deal about Germans in this book, and most of
the Germans referred to were faced by one of the starkest
choices in all history; to bow the knee to unqualified evil or

* The curious number, which could have been over-subscribed many
times, was arrived at because the publishers had acquired from Chapman
and Hall (Dickens's publishers in his lifetime) all the wood and steel plates
from which the original works had been illustrated, and they included with
every set sold one of the blocks, in a box made to the same format and
binding as the volumes. There were exactly 877 illustrations. (Mine is a
scene from *Martin Chuzzlewit*.)

to put their lives into the hazard by resisting it. The Germans in 'Vons and rebels', and those in 'They also served', offered their lives to bear witness against the terrible thing that had seized control of their country; but they knew, to the last moment of their agonizing deaths, that it had taken possession only of Germany's body, and it was into their hands that their country's soul had passed. Many years later, some of their countrymen had a far less brutal choice; what it was, and how they decided, is told in 'These Germans and those Germans', but I have no doubt that if the crucible had been as hot for them as it was for their fathers, many of them would have made their decision just as bravely; it is a pity that murder, hate and persecution bring out the finest qualities in human beings more readily than the piping times of peace.

The piping times of peace face us with gentler choices, but these may be no less meaningful than the ones generated by battle, murder and sudden death. Take 'Catalogue aria', which is little more than a list of things nobody in his right mind would imagine wanting, or 'Ars brevis', which shows how some celebrate that which is not worth celebrating. I suppose there has always been rubbish cluttering up the world; Fool's Gold and Dead Sea Fruit were not invented, or even dubbed, in the twentieth century, and there has always been an ample quantity of false art masquerading as true. I dare say Noah wondered, at times, whether he really needed *all* those animals. But he did not have an electrically-operated nail-varnish drier in the hold, nor yet an earring caddy, and if he did have a luggage-strap it did not bear his name on it. You may say that Noah's choice was as stark in its way as the choice faced by the German Resistance, but my point is that there is a sense in which all choice is the same, and no one has to be brave in order to be wise.

We must face the fact that there are twin forces in our society which seek to deprive us of choice altogether. One of these is comparatively easy to fight; it is the totalitarian threat posed not only by an aggressive and hostile foreign power but more closely and perhaps more dangerously by the threat from within, from the fanatics described in 'And what rough beast', 'Liberation theology', 'Seal of disapproval' and even 'Big person is watching you', where the threat is to nothing more corporeal than the language. (But see also 'Hold your tongue', for an argument that a nation's language is its most precious possession.)

But the other danger uses no threats and no force; it seeks to deprive us of choice over our own lives with the argument that we really have no choice, and that even if we have we may hurt ourselves by exercising it. Those who press this view upon society insist that enterprise in business may lead to bankruptcy, and is therefore better avoided; if this view is rejected, it is replaced by a sterner one – that enterprise is inimical to society, because not all members have the ability, energy or resources to indulge in it. We have seen, in recent years, an intensifying assault on competitive children's games, which demonstrate that one child can run faster, or jump higher, than another, or – worse – that one team can score more goals than their opponents can. We have seen the English language come under fire for encouraging the belief that individuals are not identical, that, indeed, some are of the male sex and others of the female. We have seen libraries purged of books that stress the diversity of peoples or the femininity of women, school curriculums emptied of history that speaks of noble deeds, even concepts of art rejected that allow for the possibility that some forms are better than others. And step by step, these views come closer to the day when it is suggested that perhaps it would be better if nobody ever did or thought anything different from his fellows, and that perhaps it would be best of all if nobody was allowed to.

And yet we can still live, if we so choose, very differently. We can live by timeless standards, rejecting the moral relativism that has already half-drowned us, repelling those who tell us that choice is neither necessary or desirable, and insisting that freedom is, contrary to so many arguments, still worth having and if necessary dying for.

There are different kinds of choice, different kinds of freedom; for that matter, there are different kinds of dying. The most different kind of all is described in 'Tell me the old, old story', and my comment on it there is not affected in the least by the fact that I am not a Christian; the first Christmas and the first Easter hold a lesson for all mankind, and even if they are both without any historical foundation, that remains true. For the story that unfolds in the plays I describe in that article shows what the truest choice and deepest freedom can mean, and in that, at least, all mankind is one: there is something in all of us which strives towards the light, as our remote ancestors in the swamps and seas strove towards the land.

That striving and its source (at which we can guess but never arrive) seem to me to constitute the most important subject any writer can deal with, in which conclusion I am by no means alone; most of the world's religion, philosophy and art has dealt with it. But it seems to me that a journalist with a platform like mine, on which I may say anything, would be neglecting his duty if he did not think, and write, about that subject, no matter how ephemeral, mundane, remote or familiar the particular spark that sets off the train of thought. I deal in the questions of the day, and all too often the day is brief indeed. But I can always hope, if the hand is quick enough, to catch the fleeting moment as it passes, and bring it to the ground to make a comment on some enduring thing. Whence this book.

# The odd copper

HERE IS A TRUE STORY; it comes with a warning that there may be a moral in it.

An American policeman was having lunch not long ago at a café he regularly visited; over the time he had been going there he had become friendly with one of the waitresses, who always attended to him. While he was eating, he was filling in his entry in the local public lottery, putting down numbers (there was, it seems, no skill involved) as he thought of them. He turned to the waitress and asked her, presumably on the familiar superstitious instinct that another's guess might bring luck, to call out some numbers at random. She did so, and with them he completed the coupon. As he left the café, he told the waitress that if he won anything with his lottery ticket, he would give her half.

His entry won the first prize, which was six million dollars. The day after he got the money, he went into the café and gave the girl exactly half of it. Rebuked by the cynical for such wanton generosity (there was, of course, no enforceable contract involved), he said that a promise was a promise, and added that anyway friendship was more important than money.

The burghers of Hamelin, faced with the Pied Piper's polite request that they should pay him the money they had promised, demurred:

> So, fellow, we're not the ones to shrink
> From the duty of giving you something for drink,

Or a matter of money to put in your poke,
But as for the guilders, what we spoke
Of them, as you very well know, was in joke.
Besides, our losses have made us thrifty;
A thousand guilders? Come, take fifty!

The Pied Piper did not; and the town soon had reason to
regret going back on its word. But the policeman in the café
faced no such retribution. He could have stood his ground,
maintained that the whole thing – lottery, numbers, promise
– was a game, a trifle, not to be taken seriously. It is indeed
unlikely that the waitress would have thought any the less of
him; if he had given her, say, ten thousand dollars or a fur
coat, she might very well have thought *more* of him. So what
was he worrying about? He was worrying about the same
problem that worried Launcelot Gobbo:

> Certainly my conscience will serve me to run from this Jew my
> master. The fiend is at mine elbow, and tempts me, saying to me
> 'Gobbo . . . use your legs, take the start, run away'. My
> conscience says, 'No, take heed, honest Launcelot . . . do not
> run; scorn running with thy heels . . . my conscience says,
> 'Launcelot, budge not'. 'Budge', says the fiend. 'Budge not',
> says my conscience. 'Conscience', say I, 'you counsel well';
> 'fiend', say I, 'you counsel well'.

Unfortunately, Launcelot spoilt the good impression made
by his initial resistance to the fiend by in the end preferring
the fiend's counsel to that of his conscience; he ran away,
presumably breaking his indenture. The policeman heard the
same two voices. He budged not.

Three million dollars, you may say, is enough for any
man, certainly for a man who could not hope to earn that
much in a century; there is probably nothing in the dreams of
a policeman that cannot be bought with three million dollars
because it costs six. Suppose the policeman had won 100,000

dollars; would he then have given away the half of his green kingdom?

This problem was once put well by H. L. Mencken, when he drew a distinction between the *honourable* man, who always keeps his promises, and the *moral* man, who keeps his promises sometimes but breaks them at other times; at the other times, he defends his breach of promise by reference to a higher morality, a greater good, the avoidance of a greater evil. Mencken, being Mencken, pointed out that these latter instances invariably coincide with what will benefit the moral man most, but it is not necessary to assume hypocrisy, likely though it is; assume that honour is honourable and morality moral, and then say which comes first?

Conscience, and the policeman, are right. The reason is not at all high-flown, but very pragmatic. The moral man's actions can never be free of ambiguity, and his appeal to a higher standard than that of a promise made, a promise kept, cannot be tested in laboratory conditions; the Heisenberg effect will take care of that. For every man has his own ladder of comparative moralities, and every man's ladder will have removable rungs, so that they can be moved about as necessary. 'I would rather lose the election than deceive the people' is never true, but even if it were it would always be subject to a higher truth; 'I must deceive the people because otherwise the safety of the realm would be endangered', 'I am entitled to deceive the people because only I know the full facts, and if they knew what I know they would applaud me', 'I will deceive the people when, but only when, the people will benefit more from being deceived than they would from not being deceived'.

All these things might be perfectly valid; the trouble is that it is impossible ever to be sure. But a man who says 'If X, then Y' subjects himself at once and without argument to a test with unvarying standards. A policeman who says 'If I win the lottery I will give you half the money' has only two choices; more important, he is manifestly seen to have only two choices. They are to keep his promise or to break it, and everybody knows, whatever they may think of him, which it is that he has done.

And the policeman knows it. As it happens, this was an honourable policeman, and kept his honourable word. But if he had been a moral policeman, and had found a moral reason for breaking his word, I believe that he would have known that that was what he was doing. For the test with varying standards only works externally; inside, it is as clear as the test of the promise, as Launcelot Gobbo proved. Launcelot did not, in the end, *listen* to his conscience; but he *heard* it, and unless a man be truly deranged, he is never so deaf that he cannot hear Jiminy Cricket give a little whistle, 'and always let your conscience be your guide'.

That policeman kept faith with his friend the waitress. But he kept another faith; with his own soul (which is the breath that animates the voice we call conscience). If you don't believe me, try a different test, also with only two choices. Here are two tombstones, both with your name and your date of birth on them. Be assured that when the date of your death comes to be filled in also, those in charge of the proceedings will add either 'He *always* kept his word' or 'He *always* acted from the best of motives'. Which would you choose? You would? I rest my case.*

*The Times* August 23rd, 1984

---

* Since this was written a man has won *ten* million dollars in the same lottery. His wife, who had constantly reproached him for spending money on lottery tickets, was asked how she felt now about his habit. She replied 'Better'.

# Post mortem

I AM BEING HAUNTED by a lawsuit I read about some time ago, and must try to exorcise the spectre today, lest I should end up as crazy as, on the face of it, all the parties to the case were at the end, if not the beginning.

But I must warn those of my readers who wish to come along on the ghost-hunt that my phrase 'on the face of it' was not simply employed to ward off the possibility that I might, by a fine irony, find myself stewing slowly in a lawyer's pot. The *casus belli* was, it is true, so small as to be invisible – it was, as a matter of fact, a piece of land 1.3 sq ft in area – but the passions released, on both sides, were such that they could scarcely have seemed greater if the parties were each laying claim to the whole of Texas. And it is those passions, rather than a few ounces of earth, that concern me here.

First, an outline of the facts. Early in 1983, a couple in Kent decided to repair a fence-post on the edge of their land; in doing so, they moved it from its original position, in the direction of their neighbours' ground, and a bit over.

Ha! cry all the lower deck lawyers among you; attempting to pinch land belonging to others, were they? Then they *deserve* to be eaten by lawyers, without butter and without salt. Very possibly; but their march into friendly and peaceful territory, I must now reveal, was somewhat less dramatic than the Nazi blitzkrieg, and they travelled, in the course of it, not quite so far as Mao Tse-tung and his companions on the Long March. They moved the fence-post *two inches*.

*De minimis*, it seems, *curat lex* like billy-o. I have, it is true, often drawn attention to the fact that no one has ever seen a fat litigant or a thin lawyer, but there cannot have been many cases which pointed as clearly as this one to the sinister truth behind that curious phenomenon. For two and a half years the battle raged, even though those who moved the fence-post represented themselves. (If they had hired lawyers too, the case would doubtless have gone on for two and a half decades. The Jarndyces didn't know when they were well off.)

When the hearing was over, the judge took four months to consider his judgment, which took two hours to read. The costs totted up to thousands of pounds, and it is by no means certain, at least to me, who won, or for that matter what 'won' meant in such a case; the only conclusion I have come to on my own behalf is that in my next life I am going to be a manufacturer of those little blue cardboard corners that lawyers fix to packets of documents.

Now if you think that two and a half years of litigation is a fairly steep price to pay for two inches of land, you are right, but I am even righter than you, because I once read of a case in which the dispute concerned not the position of a fence-post, for both parties agreed that it was exactly on the boundary, but the string round the post, which thus entered, feloniously and with malice aforethought, on to the other man's patch, so that the dispute was literally over the thickness of a piece of string.

Shortly after I read about that horror, I found myself talking to a barrister at a party, and invited him, on no more than those facts, to extemporize a closing speech to a jury on behalf of the man who complained of trespass by string. He did so with such conviction and brilliance that I began to make the sign against the Evil Eye, and several of the more devout listeners to his efforts crossed themselves.

Hamlet had views on this problem. When faced with the imminent death of twenty thousand men to decide the ownership of a piece of land that had in it no profit but the name, whereon the numbers could not try the cause and, for good measure, that was not tomb enough nor continent to hide the slain, he decided that rightly to be great was not to stir without great argument, but greatly to find honour in a straw when honour was at the stake.

The people on both sides of the moved fence-post thought that honour was at the stake; so did those who debated the thickness of a piece of string. So did the former policeman, sacked at the time of the Liverpool police strike in 1919, whom I used to see at Speakers' Corner in my youth, carrying a placard about the injustice he claimed to have suffered, and making for the thousandth time the same speech about Commander Locker-Lampson. So was the lady who spent *decades* trying to prove that she had not been guilty of the trivial traffic offence for which she had been fined £5.

I forget who said, of *Othello*, that with a little give and take on both sides the trouble could have been avoided. (Katharine Whitehorn went even further and pointed out that if, when Othello said, 'Lend me thy handkerchief', Desdemona had said, 'It's at the laundry', there would never have been any trouble in the first place.)

Yet people have ruined their lives for sixpence, and the lives of others for threepence; they have murdered for slights invisible to every eye but their own, and committed suicide because the wind changed; they have spent all that they have on what Hamlet, in the same scene, called a fantasy and trick of fame, and gone to their graves like beds.

'Ah, what can God do', cries Mrs Boyle, 'agen the stipidity o' men!', but even she did not get it quite right. Stupidity will take us far towards hell, but not quite into it; what makes the doors fly open without benefit of knocker is obstinacy, and that rock is enough to sink all the world's navies. A few lines later, Mrs Boyle calls upon the Sacred Heart of Jesus: 'Take away our hearts o' stone, and give us hearts o' flesh! Take away this murdherin' hate, an' give us Thine own eternal love!'

A moving plea, and few will wish it unanswered. But I would settle for something much less: a method of getting into the heads of men and women the world over that not everything matters, and that many of the things that seem as if they matter most are among those that matter not at all.

Some years ago, in response to a newspaper article, by a priest, which called for more forgiveness for wrongs real as well as imagined, a correspondent firmly rejected the call, and revealed that he had borne a number of grudges all his life, one of them for *fifty* years, and had no intention of giving any of them up. That forgotten hero, mind you, is being challenged hard by Mr Auberon Waugh, whose immense list of grudges and vendettas, regularly frotted into life, is headed by Lord Gowrie, who has been on it for twenty-four years, for no better reason than that, when they were both at Oxford, a lady preferred Gowrie's charms to Waugh's. (Among the many others on the list are Martin Seymour-Smith, who has notched up thirteen years for indicating that he did not think very highly of Evelyn Waugh's novels; Charles Douglas-Home, who scored fourteen years before death removed him from the scroll – if indeed it has done – for the mere suspicion on Waugh jnr's part that Charlie had been responsible for winding up a terrible weekly column Bron used to write in this newspaper; and David Pryce-Jones, whose stint has so far been some twelve years, though neither I nor David himself can even guess at the reason.)

We all, at times, find our sense of perspective becoming distorted, even though rarely as distorted as that. I cannot think myself into the minds of either party to the fence-post dispute, but I have no doubt that I, too, have sometimes dug in my heels when the game wasn't worth the shoelaces. 'What do you do when you're innocent?' asked the wife in the couple who moved the post, adding, 'You can't just give in, can you?'

Oh, but you can, if what you are innocent of is a two-inch

trespass, and that goes also for those who are *guilty* of such a misdemeanour, ' 'Tis pride that pulls the country down,' sings Iago, and so it is, if the pride is the sort that moved those who moved the fence-post and those who objected to its moving. I don't really begrudge the lawyers their cream buns (some of my best friends are lawyers), and I dare say that many of them try to dissuade clients from entering upon litigation that can bring them nothing but sorrow, if not ruin. But what can they do if the client insists?

I once heard a terrible story of an old man, dying, who had on his conscience the memory of bullying a boy at school. He found his victim's address – both men were by then in their seventies – and wrote to ask forgiveness for his childish cruelty, so that he could die in peace. The other wrote back that he would *not* offer forgiveness for the sin committed six decades before, and the dying man had to find in other thoughts what consolation he could. I hope he died in peace; I wonder if the other man, on his own deathbed, was troubled by his refusal.

Cromwell did not live up to it, but he said it: 'I beseech you, in the bowels of Christ, think it possible you may be mistaken.' But how thick is a piece of string?

*The Times* January 7th, 1986

# Silence in court

THERE IS AN amazing debate going on concerning the question whether judges should be permitted, or even encouraged, to make speeches on matters of public concern, to take part in television and radio programmes, and to write articles in newspapers.

And I call the argument 'amazing' because the thrust of it is *in favour* of such a development, whereas I would have thought that anyone who values his sanity would be concerned to ensure that, so far from judges being allowed to weigh in on any subject which takes their fancy, they should never be permitted to open their mouths off the Bench for any purpose more controversial than to say 'Thank you' to the leader of a Scout patrol which has helped them across the road, and indeed that even when on the Bench they should be obliged to confine themselves entirely to a limited range of the simplest possible expressions, such as 'Five years', 'Costs against the plaintiff' and 'Usher, shut the windows'.

It all began with a circuit judge (he calls himself a 'mere' circuit judge, but there is nothing mere about his views, let alone the language in which he expresses them) named James Pickles, who has more than once been rebuked by the Lord Chancellor for talking out of turn, and is in danger of removal from the bench for 'judicial misbehaviour' – a threat which he met with a letter to Lord Hailsham in which he declared that he was 'appalled' that Lord Hailsham should threaten him with dismissal, and concluded with a counter-threat of making 'representations to both Houses of Parliament and the media'.

Judge Pickles's cause has now been taken up, not only by fools; the prospect of a seething mass of chattering judges seems, even to some normally sagacious observers, to be perfectly acceptable. Well, it doesn't seem acceptable to me; nor does it seem so to Lord Hailsham, who has now formally set out the case against the notion, pointing out in doing so that he was only following in a long line of holders of his office who were opposed to it, and that every time the judges in general were asked their views on the matter, a substantial majority were of the opinion that things should stay as they are.

Before I paint a blood-curdling picture of what would happen if the prohibition were to be lifted, there is one point on which the critics of the present system do have a powerful argument to deploy. It is that although Britain's constitution insists on the separation of the judiciary from the executive, we put up with the anomaly of the head of the judiciary being a Cabinet minister (and simultaneously the Speaker of the House of Lords).

The law officers in the House of Commons are in a similarly impossible position, but these have always solved the problem in a commendably pragmatic way: they behave like the most servile party hacks, and pretend they don't. The Lord Chancellor, however, is a judge, and for all the history that lies behind his dual function, I have never been able to see it as anything but an outrage.

I now find myself in the rare position of agreeing entirely with Lord Hailsham. I am not particularly concerned about Judge Pickles, who seems quite capable of looking after himself (I will lay generous odds, if he is unfrocked, that he will shortly be found standing for Parliament under the banner of the Alliance); the prospect, however, that opens before us if Lord Hailsham or a successor to him should weaken on this point is so dreadful that it must be faced *now*.

Even as things stand, the amount and nature of irrelevant judicial comment from the Bench, usually but not invariably in the form of *obiter dicta*, is enough to cause nightmares. How many litigants in divorce cases have sought a decree and received in addition (and sometimes instead) a detailed critique of their morals? How many convicted criminals have had to listen to a lecture as long as their sentence? How many courtrooms have resounded with the bombination of bees from judicial bonnets, let loose in the knowledge that no apiarist present will dare to take the swarm?

But that is the situation now, and in court; what is proposed is that the judges should have the right to air their opinions up and down the land, to commit them to paper in the form of published articles, and to speak them on television and radio. Have you any idea of what would happen if the proposal were to be accepted?

It would start with speeches at public events. Here, Mr Justice Bun will advocate the return of capital punishment; there, Judge Currant will denounce the idea of a Channel Tunnel; anon, Lord Justice Saucer will urge repatriation of Commonwealth immigrants; next, Judge Teapot will insist upon a complete reshaping of the educational system; sooner or later, Lord Chief Justice Lane will be heard demanding a specially heavy sentence for men convicted of rape who have pleaded not guilty.*

Then, the newspapers. At first it will be confined to complex points of law and judicial reminiscences; but it will not stop there. In no time the judges will be foaming at the mouth about (or even from) fluoride, they will be insisting that compulsory seatbelts are an infringement of our liberties (or that they are not), they will be demanding the resignation of Cabinet ministers involved in Westland controversies, they will be criticizing CND, the repertoire at the National

---

* Unlike the other judges in my list, Lord Chief Justice Lane is real, and so was his demand.

Theatre, the failure of the government to control public spending, the activities of the Militant Tendency, the EEC's common agricultural policy and Prince Charles's taste in architecture, dinner-jackets and slimming diets.

Next, it will be Dial-a-Judge. Just as politicians, eager to get themselves before the public, will answer any question from a reporter who telephones them, so the judges will be reported as saying what they think of the Post Office, Gower's cricket captaincy, Denis Thatcher's feelings about a possible third term for his spouse, the man who kept nine boa-constrictors in his bedroom and Mary Quant's knickers.

But the full horror of the plan will be seen on television. They will infest *Question Time* and drive poor Robin into an early grave with their opinions; they will take walk-on parts as themselves, in sitcoms, like Harold Wilson; they will interview talking dogs and sing with Des O'Connor in Christmas specials; and, most dreadful of all these dreadfulnesses, they will appear on chat shows, where they will make puns, essay risqué jokes, fawn on pop singers whose knuckles brush the ground as they walk, and ask Selina Scott, with a roguish smile, what she is doing after the show.

Stop this horror *now*, before it starts. However much and however often I have criticized judges, I have never wavered from my belief that a visibly impartial and independent system of law is crucial to a free society. But this includes an essential element of remoteness, even of inhumanity, in the judges and their work.

The only excuse for a judge with opinions is that he refrains from expressing them; the moment he steps into controversy, or even indicates that he has views, all respect for the law itself will collapse, as the public abruptly realizes that the august figure, wigged and robed, who embodies the rule of law and its truly vital function as the foundation of our liberties, is only a daft old geezer with funny clothes who thinks that pubs should be made illegal and that all homosexuals should have their whatsits cut off.

Having expressed unqualified support for Lord Hailsham, I may perhaps be permitted to offer him some advice. It is to sack Judge Pickles, *pour encourager les autres*, at once; the opinionated bencher will not suffer, for he will most likely be offered a book-contract for an advance of £100,000. But the cause of justice will be made more secure.★

*The Times* February 28th, 1986.

★At the date of going to press, Judge Pickles had for some time been trailing his coat even more assiduously. But the Lord Chancellor was still biding his time.

# Mincing words

*Fair of Speech: The Uses of Euphemism* Edited by D. J. Enright[*]

WHEN H. ALLEN SMITH, the American humorist, was a young reporter, the word 'rape' was not socially acceptable in newspapers (nor, incidentally, was 'cancer'). Covering a criminal trial, he was once therefore obliged, in summarizing the prosecution evidence, to report that the defendant had lain in wait for a woman neighbour, punched her in the face, dragged her along the street, thrown her down the stairs to the cellar of a derelict building, and there assaulted her.

That was a euphemism, but it was of a particular type: all Mr Smith's readers knew what *thing* had happened, but the danger (real or imaginary) of their being offended by the *word* had been averted. Exactly the same technique may still be seen whenever we come upon 'f —' or 'f★★★' in print; every reader supplies the missing 'uck', but the Whitehousian proprieties are observed. ('Whitehousian', adj. Pertaining to an aberrant form of nominalism (qv), in which words are regarded as deeds, leading ultimately to the belief that it is possible to catch VD off a television screen.)

It is one of the weaknesses of this collection of essays on euphemism that there is no serious analysis of the distinction between the euphemism that is designed, with hope of success, to deceive ('organic food', 'Advanced Passenger Train', 'non-nuclear defence', 'gay'), and those, much the

[*] Oxford, 1985.

more numerous, which fall into the assault/rape category ('senior citizen', 'new Commonwealth', 'public ownership', 'developing country'). The distinction is surely crucial, for the second kind, but not the first, raises the complicated question of why we willingly enter into a conspiracy to pretend, as consumers of euphemism, that we do not know what the producers of it mean.

A further, and more serious, failing of the book is that there has clearly been no attempt to organize the contributions by divers hands into a properly synoptic study; indeed, there has been virtually no editing at all, for apart from the wildly uneven quality, at least three of the sixteen authors cite the same reference from Tacitus ('They make a desert, and call it peace') and three others single out 'the Final Solution' as the final euphemism.

Euphemism is bordered on the north by slang, on the south by cliché, on the west by mendacity and on the east by irony; indeed, it is often surprisingly difficult to be sure of the genuine article. Most of these contributions slip across the frontier from time to time (Richard Cobb's, crammed though it is with fascinating lore, has clearly lost its passport), and several of them are little more than lists.

The lists can be instructive; Derwent May, on 'Euphemisms and the Media', has an easy task when it comes to compilation, and rolls up an impressive muster, from 'sick leave' (which 'allows people to avoid thinking of the power of illness – leave, after all, is taken voluntarily') to 'of special interest to the disabled' ('we hope we can persuade a few able-bodied viewers to watch it too'). He also offers an ingenious theory that brand-names with an 'x' at the end are euphemisms for objects that arouse unease or distaste: Durex, Tampax, Andrex. (There are also Ex-Lax and Amplex, but his theory will not hold water: what about Lux and Weetabix?)

Simon Hoggart, with 'Politics', digs more deeply, and comes up with some examples that are far from obvious:

. . . 'Jews' is thought too harsh and even anti-Semitic, Politicians prefer to say 'members of the Jewish community'. 'Community' is no doubt supposed to soften the blunt 'Jew' and implies an identity of political and social interest which might not always exist.

The professions, of course, are rife with euphemisms; for medicine, Diane Johnson and John F. Murray distinguish between to 'fall' ill (not our fault) and to 'catch' a disease (we co-operated), and might have added the Pronoun Conspiratorial, 'How are we today?' which seeks to bind the sick patient with the well doctor. For the law, David Pannick, himself a barrister, so mercilessly scythes down his colleagues and their jargon that he would be well advised (another euphemism) to commit no murder, for his chances of a fair trial would be slim:

> Barristers prefer to be called *counsel*. This suggests that they act as a friend or confidant rather than in a professional capacity . . .
> *It's your Lordship's point* is a euphemism expressed whenever the judge has shown the slightest understanding of the argument . . .
> *The court did not have the benefit of full argument* – that is, neither the barristers nor the judge saw the crucial point.

Five of the chapters are outstanding: Robert Burchfield on the linguistic history of euphemism, Patricia Beer on some literary uses, Catherine Storr on euphemism in relation to children (she has a vast collection of childish terms for going to the lavatory – and 'lavatory' is itself a euphemism), John Gross on euphemism and death, in which he, almost alone, takes seriously the need for, and virtue of, euphemism, and – best of them all – Peter Mullen on 'The Religious Speak-Easy', a meticulous, learned and savage assault on the Noddy-language of the New English Bible and Alternative Service Book, grounded in profound theological understanding and so concerned to attack the implied theology more than the stated linguistic horrors that it should be put with Orwell's 'Politics and the English language' as demonstrating the connection between the corruption of language and the corruption of thought.

Nobody mentions the expletive 'Shoot!', widely prevalent in the United States, as a euphemistic substitute for its near-homophone, or the airline pilot's sign-off after giving the passengers route information: 'So now just relax and enjoy the flight.' This is a euphemism for 'it's perfectly safe', which must be eschewed lest passengers start to *think* about safety instead of simply assuming it. But Marghanita Laski had the last word years ago, when she translated 'simple inexpensive gowns for the mature fuller figure' as 'nasty cheap dresses for fat old women'.

*Observer* April 21st, 1985

# Liberation theology

SOMEWHAT TO MY own surprise, and doubtless even more to the surprise of my readers, I find myself today turning to the subject of mink. Hitherto, my only knowledge of the subject has been gleaned from those ladies who, when I have offered them yet another diamond necklace at Christmas, have indicated that they would prefer a mink coat, whereat I have naturally hastened to fulfil their wishes (though of course they have always received the diamond necklace as well). But what I did not know until recently was that there is an *animal* called a mink; I suppose that if I concerned myself with the details at all I vaguely thought that the fur came from some more familiar beast such as a bear or a fox (I say, is there an animal called a sable, and is there yet another called an astrakhan?), and beyond taking care to assure the pretty creatures draped in the result that it went well with the colour of their eyes I thought no more about the matter.

Now, however, I am obliged to. For of late there has been something of an epidemic of attacks on mink-farms by people calling themselves the Animal Liberation Front, and just recently they caused sufficient damage to the fences of a mink-breeding establishment to enable many hundreds of the animals to escape. Or so the liberators claim, though as you shall hear, that is not quite an exact description of what happened, and in the inexactitude there lies something of considerable interest.

When the raid was over, and the countryside was swarming with mink, the first thing that happened was that a police warning went out urging the populace not to 'have a go'. It seems that mink are very fierce beasts and will bite anyone who comes near them, even if they are approached with kindness and a knob of sugar; children are specially at risk because, seeing a nice cuddly-looking animal, they are inclined to toddle up and stroke it, only to find themselves, a moment later, short of a finger or two, or perhaps an eye or a nose.

Well, well; no doubt the mink-liberators would say it serves the little bleeders right. Much more serious, however, is that it is not just human beings that mink like for elevenses; they also eat game birds, rabbits and hares, and even chickens. What is more, there is evidence that they do not confine their chicken-eating to broiler fowls (which the Animal Liberation Front would certainly claim was inspired by a desire to help free their feathered friends, the casualties among the chickens being caused by an over-hasty attempt to bite through the wire of their cages); they also think nothing of gobbling any free-range ones that come their way. And mink go further still. They kill fish, ducks and geese, and – as in what followed several previous 'liberations' of the furry slaves – pet cats and dogs.

Now if there is one thing that can be asserted with untroubled assurance, it is that none of this worries the members of the Animal Liberation Front in the slightest. If it could be shown beyond doubt that the favourite diet of all liberated mink consisted of ecologists, protestors against acid rain, nuclear disarmers, whales, *and other mink*, if the first action of every liberated mink were to buy a horse and go hunting with the Quorn, if indeed liberated mink carrying bulging suitcases crammed with mink-pelts could be seen daily trotting through London in the direction of Calman Links, it would make no difference at all. The truth about organizations like the Animal Liberation Front is that their members have no interest in animals of any kind. What they are seeking to demonstrate is their detestation of human beings.

A more *soigné* version of this attitude is expressed by Mr John Aspinall, who has repeatedly said, in so many words, that he prefers animals to mankind, and if we note the human mortality rate at his zoo we shall probably find it easy to believe him. Mr Aspinall puts his case in what it would not be too absurd to call philosophical terms; violent or illegal behaviour, and foaming at the mouth, are not for him. But the actions and words of the Animal Liberation Front, as they break down a mink-farmer's fence or smash up a medical scientist's laboratory or spit upon the guests arriving at a luncheon for some organization that has incurred their displeasure, show clearly that the 'liberators' are so consumed with hatred of people that they have no room at all left for love of animals.

That, as a matter of fact, is what I would have expected; if you do not love your own kind how can you love a stranger? Moreover, it is clear from the fanatic violence and extremist language used by the 'liberators' that they are very far indeed from being at peace with themselves, let alone their neighbours; some of them, to judge by their statements, must be seriously disturbed individuals, in greater need of liberation from their hallucinations than any mink from its cage. But even the fully sane ones plainly take more delight in wishing all the plagues of Egypt on the two-legged creatures than freedom on the four.

This is, I think, a phenomenon very much of our time. St Francis loved the beasts and preached to the birds; indeed, he spoke kindly of the flea. But his love of animals stemmed from his love of mankind, and it would never have occurred to him that the one precluded the other; in his father's house there *were* many mansions. Now, we hear on all hands that man is the enemy, that the planet cannot stand much more of him, that only animals are noble and pure.

I think it is worse than that; I think there is a hatred of life itself somewhere down in the cellarage, an unbearable rage at the very fact that there is a universe and that we are in it, for good or ill, along with the animals. I noticed, for instance, the satisfying relish with which nuclear disarmers describe the impending holocaust and its lakes of molten eyeballs, its forests of instant skeletons, its mountains of roasted flesh.

A far cry, you may say, from the mink, which now roam the Staffordshire countryside, seeking what and whom they may devour. But there is one more loose end to be tied. I mentioned the claim of the 'liberators' that they broke into the mink-farm to let the mink escape. Imagine, however, their surprise when the mink showed no inclination to escape through the hole obligingly cut in the wall of their terrible prison. A passer-by could have feasted his eyes in wonder at the sight of the liberators *chasing* the mink out of the captivity they were plainly reluctant to leave, but which their rescuers had decreed that they must leave, whether they would or no.

If a mink in its natural state and habitat will, as we are told, bite savagely anyone who approaches it too closely, imagine what extra degree of crossness will be felt by a mink which has been forcibly liberated against its will. Unfortunately, we cannot even hope that poetic justice will ensure that the mink's victims will be its liberators. I am sure that long before the question arose they were all back in their comfortable London homes, grumbling that the dustman was late again this week.

*The Times* July 27th, 1984

# Seal of disapproval

FROM MINK TO SEALS. Last week I had much to say on the 'liberators' of animals bred for their fur; today we shall discuss the more widely-felt problem of animals killed to preserve the balance of the herd (among other reasons, most of them more discreditable).

Little white seals, indistinguishable on television from the ones you buy in toyshops to give very small children, are inevitably going to provoke emotion: 'Ah, how sweet!' is the cry that goes up from a million throats on seeing such a creature waddling into vision, its big, round eyes fixed appealingly on the camera for all the world as if it was Mr Wedgwood Benn. (The seal, not the camera.) When the creature, having waddled far enough into view, is then seen having its head bashed in, cries of outrage rapidly replace the billings and cooings.

The first thing to be said, therefore, is that if the killing were of adders, jellyfish or rats no significant fuss would be made. Yet I dare say that these creatures are as much averse to having someone beat their brains out as are the seals; as I have pointed out before, the question of whether it is lucky or unlucky if a black cat crosses your path depends almost entirely on whether you are a man or a mouse.

There is no quibble here. Seals arouse compassion and indignation because they are small, furry and white; anthropomorphism then takes over to ensure that the animals become not just cuddly companions for children, but the children themselves. Do you remember Pipaluk, the polar bear cub born at Regent's Park Zoo? I do; I remember the seething crowd around the enclosure, some of the women waving their own children like tickets of admission, and one or two of them looking as though they would willingly heave their infants over the railings if sweet little Pipaluk expressed a wish for a light lunch. I also remember Pipaluk's mother, tired of being nipped by her offspring's small but sharp teeth, suddenly giving the creature a most unmaternal but vigorous crack across the face with a giant paw, which sent it into a double back-somersault before it landed, squealing, on a rock several yards away. Some of the spectators would have lynched her if they had had the chance.

The Bishop of Quebec, not long ago, was writing to this paper to regret the British boycott of Canadian fish products, a response to the campaign against seal culling. I think the bishop must have been misinformed; I have seen no sign of crazed seal-lovers storming the supermarkets and making bonfires of Canadian tinned salmon, and indeed I was unaware, as I dare say were most people, that any boycott existed. The bishop pointed out that such a boycott would hurt Canadians, like fishermen in British Columbia, who had nothing to do with seal-killing; I have to tell him that logic has never been part of the armoury of animal fanatics, and in any case many of the fiercer ones would say that it serves the fishermen right for catching fish.

But that brings me to the next fallacy in the seal protectors' *Syllabus Errorum*. As I pointed out last week, mink are very fierce and implacable predators; the ones chased into the countryside by their 'liberators' have killed chickens, geese and domestic dogs and cats. That's as may be, the seal-lovers would reply, but you can't pin crimes like that on *our* little furry friends. To which I answer: you can if you're a fish. Seals are very partial to fish, and for that matter polar bear Pipaluk would certainly have eaten any seal it came upon in its natural habitat; the opportunities for bewilderment among the animal lovers grow greater and more numerous every minute. (And the fish eat plankton, remember. What do the plankton eat, the ravening little bastards?)

> He prayeth best who loveth best
> All creatures great and small.
> The streptococcus is the test,
> I love him most of all. .

Thus sang Hilaire Belloc, but it is significant that there seem to be two versions of the quatrain, in one of which the last line reads 'I love him *not at all*'.

Nature is red in a) tooth, and b) claw. What is more, and very discouraging for those most given to going ooh and aah at the sight of a white seal pup, in nature the weakest invariably go to the wall. Nothing preys upon a tiger; everything carnivorous will eat a gazelle that stops to admire the scenery when its wiser siblings are running away.

Some of our more extreme animalists would institute a vast programme of dentistry for beasts which eat other beasts, and would not rest until every one of them had had its teeth removed and its familiar diet replaced by bread and milk. The less extreme, if there are any, would say that nature might be cruel, but that is no excuse for man to add his own cruelty to hers, and as a matter of fact I would have a great deal of sympathy for such a view if they were content to leave it there. But they aren't; there is today a growing cult of hatred of mankind, sheltering behind love of animals, and it is significant that the animals singled out for most of the loving are those which appeal most to that watery sentimentality that for many of such people has replaced real love. The helpless baby seal provides a safe substitute for the dangers inherent in any real human relationship, and the worked-up anger at the creature's fate is no less an alternative to real human passions, anger and all.

Of course there is a great deal of hypocrisy on the other side; the use of the word 'culling' when what is meant is the near-homophone 'killing' is the most obvious example (cf.

'field sports' for 'hunting', and for that matter 'separate development' for 'apartheid'). But men have always believed that if they succeed in deceiving themselves they will thereby also deceive others; ostriches do not bury their heads in the sand and think they are invisible, but the attribution of such behaviour to them by human beings tells us much about the human beings.

Killing some animals deliberately, distasteful though the seal-lovers may find the thought, is often necessary if far more members of the herd are not to die accidentally very much more wretched deaths, from starvation, for example. That is how the seal-killers defend their annual hunt, and I am not disposed to give the benefit of the doubt to those who foam at the mouth and scream 'murderers' because that is easier (and much more fun, incidentally) than trying to find out the facts. The Bishop of Quebec, in discussing the boycott of Canadian fish, expressed 'a fear that the British people are acting on incomplete information'. They are indeed. But the bishop will have to reconcile himself to the fact that the very last thing that the boycotters want is information. They want a deep, warm feeling that they are virtuous. What they do to acquire that feeling will not save a single seal. But saving seals is the last thing but one that they want.

*The Times* August 2nd, 1984

# Rats live on no evil star

I MUST CRAVE MY readers' indulgence (as we old-fashioned writer-johnnies say) if I quote myself rather extensively this morning before going on to the point; please be assured that when we get to the point the reason for the quoting will become clear. In a column published in this newspaper I wrote the following:

> . . . In the 1950s, a new type of rat–poison was developed, and sold in this country under the name Warfarin . . . There was no known antidote . . . at any rate none available to the rats . . . So they developed a biological immunity to Warfarin . . . The consequence was that within only five years there were types of rats and mice on which Warfarin had no effect, and . . . these strains flourished more and more . . . At the weekend, the men in the white coats unveiled a new poison, called Sorexa CR . . . In field trials on farms, rats and mice immune to Warfarin were each offered a dose of Sorexa CR: before you could squeak, there was another cat out of a job . . . The date today is December 4th, 1973. On December 4th, 1983 (please synchronize your watches) we shall meet on this very spot and discuss the recent spate of reports that rats and mice immune to Sorexa CR have been found . . .

A calendar, a calendar! Look in the almanack; find out moonshine, find out moonshine! It is true that Monday February 27th, 1984, is a little later than our rendezvous, but you must admit that three months' leeway in a full ten years is not unreasonable. And on Monday, ten years and three months after my prophecy appeared, my agricultural colleague John Young wrote, on this very page, as follows:

> Super Rat is thriving . . . in the farms and fields around Sutton
> Scotney . . . Immune to every commonly known poison . . .
> each pair is said to be able to produce 200 offspring a year . . .
> 'We have struggled with all sorts of poisons, including one
> which is still advertised as killing Warfarin-resistant rats', Mr
> Giles Rowsel . . . says. 'All I can say is that it certainly doesn't
> kill ours.' . . . He succeeded in bringing the infestation under
> control by the use of a new poison, Brodifacoum, under a
> Ministry-approved testing scheme . . .

Well, bully for Brodifacoum; but I thought of that, too, in
my column ten and a quarter years ago, and said that when
we had finished saluting the clever scientists who had perfected a poison that could refresh the parts that Warfarin
couldn't reach,

> . . . we shall then adjourn until December 4th, 1993, when we
> shall once again forgather here and drink a toast to the scientists
> who, ever-mindful of our interests, have developed a rat-poison
> as far superior to Sorexa CR as is . . . Sorexa CR to Warfarin.

The open-air life which John Young leads stands him in
good stead; he will therefore certainly be around on the
appointed day ten years hence, and although Ladbroke's will
not offer such generous odds on me, I think I may yet
surprise the actuaries. Give or take a couple of months,
therefore, I look forward to sharing with you all a decade
from now the amazing, unprecedented, wholly unexpected
news that there are rats and mice whose favourite form of
elevenses is a Brodifacoum sandwich, which they swear is
what keeps their coats so sleek and their whiskers so crisp.

It was St Paul who pointed out that God is not mocked. It
did not occur to him (or if it did he kept quiet about it) that
God might be a rat. But even if God is a rat-catcher I suspect
that he is still not mocked, at any rate with impunity. For the

point of the column in which I made my uncannily precise long-range forecast was that the rats and the rat-poison are no different from the people and the people-poison. Antibiotics were discovered, praised, and adopted for general use against a wide range of micro-organisms, which they slaughtered in numbers comparable to the rats and mice which went down under the massive cavalry charge of the Knights of Warfarin and their successors, the Sorexa Halberdiers. But the last laugh was given to the micro-organisms, for many of them developed an immunity, to virtually anything ending in -cin, comparable to the resistance put up by the vermin, and just as it has proved necessary for the agricultural scientists to raise another new regiment, the Brodifacoum Light Horse, so new and more powerful germ-killers have been required to deal with the new and more powerful germs.

I am sorry, but I must quote once more from that prescient column of a decade ago:

> If you feel depressed . . . and go to a doctor . . . he will provide you with a prescription for tranquillizers. If you take the stipulated dose, you may feel less depressed . . . After a bit, however, a puzzling effect will become apparent; the pills will begin to seem less efficacious. Returning to the doctor, you will point this out, and he will recommend a slight increase in the dose. You will be much relieved to find that the increased dose is as effective at dealing with the depression as the old, lesser dose was. But after a bit, a puzzling effect will become apparent . . .

When will we realize that Nature is cleverer than we are? Do you remember DDT? It was hailed as the answer to every problem of the countryside – Colorado beetle, blackfly, locusts, potato-blight, broccoli with hollandaise – there was nothing it wouldn't kill. As, indeed, turned out to be the case, to such an extent that all of a sudden you couldn't get a measure of DDT at the jug-and-bottle for any consideration, not even ready money. I did not follow that story as closely as I did that of the rats and the ratticides, so I do not know where it has got to now. But I am willing to bet that just as there were scientists to hail DDT as the answer for every agricultural problem to puzzle the human race from Cro-Magnon Man to Peter Walker, so there were scientists (the same ones, I wouldn't wonder) to hail the new super-DDT as the answer to all those problems *and* the problems caused by the ordinary, unimproved DDT without the Miracle Ingredient that Makes All the Difference.

How many more times do Horace and I have to say it before the world will listen? Once more? Very well, then: *Naturam expellas furca, tamen usque recurret.* Or, for any rats who know no Latin and are reading this while breakfasting off a steaming bowl of Warfarin with Sorexa CR sprinkled on the top, you may drive out Nature with a pitchfork, but she will always come running back.

Somehow, somewhere, somewhen, we must stop believing that the hair of the dog will heal its bites. Sooner or later we shall have to persuade this imperceptibly but fatally poisoned stream to flow in the other direction. I do not know, and it makes no difference to my theme, whether there is any truth in the legend that dock-leaves, with their soothing juice, are always found near nettles, with their poison that needs soothing. I *do* know that for many centuries country folk who cut themselves with an earthy spade would clap a cobweb on the wound, and were smiled at by all the *bien-pensants* for such superstition, until those spores floated in through Fleming's laboratory window and proved the old folk right.

These things take time. I do not suppose, therefore, that the world's attitude to nature and its slow certainty will have changed entirely within the next ten years. But I cordially invite you to synchronize your watches again and meet on this spot on February 29th, 1994 (no, it isn't Leap Year – make it March 1), when we can greet the scientists' discovery of a new and much improved rat-poison with our thumbs to our noses. Light refreshments will be served, including canapés of Warfarin, Sorexa CR, Brodifacoum, DDT, penicillin and Valium. Rats welcome.*

*The Times* March 2nd, 1984

* The original article was included in *Speaking Up*, which was published in 1982. At the rate I publish these anthologies, I calculate that the prophesied article will be included in the next but three.

# A room without a view

*E. M. Forster's Commonplace Book* Edited by Philip Gardner*

THIS BOOK, FOUND among Forster's papers at his death, is considerably more than transcriptions of notable passages from his reading (the traditional use of such a volume), or even than such transcriptions with his own comments upon them. At times, and particularly towards the end of his life (the first entry was made in 1926, the last – 'How it rains!' – in 1968, two years before his death), it becomes a diary, despite the fact that he kept one of those, too, which has not yet been published.

Forster's commonplace book had been bought in 1804, for that very purpose, by John Jebb, a clergyman who became Bishop of Ireland; at that time the keeping of such a record was common among the reading classes, though it must be rare today. The bishop, however, did not persevere; he filled only a few pages of the book, and when Forster inherited it from his aunt in 1924, there were some 380 left. The editor and annotator, Professor Philip Gardner (who has done his work with exemplary care, thoroughness and tact), quotes Forster's comment on the thought of publishing both the bishop's few entries and his own many – 'It would do his reputation no harm . . . and mine no good' – and expresses his confidence that readers will disagree with the second half of Forster's verdict.

This reader, alas, does not. Indeed, as a devoted and unwavering Forsterian from boyhood on, I am tempted to

* Scolar Press, 1985

wish that his literary executors had burnt the thing. Forster's
self-honesty never falters; would that it had, for he totters
from these pages like a querulous old woman, worn out
before his time, grumbling about the decay of everything,
and his own failing powers, as early as 1928, when he was
still only fifty:

> *Death an escape into the non-human.* That, if consciousness sur-
> vives, will be an adventure worth attempting after roads full of
> cars, skies full of aeroplanes, and the very heart of night
> throbbing with little noises that man has made.

Next year he develops the theme:

> Young people keep me young unless they are the sons of my
> contemporaries; then I regard them as spies. My vitality goes
> more and more in keeping myself young. When I was young it
> went in creating.

Then he begins to depreciate his own writing (and since, after
all, he *is* Forster, it cannot be anything as false as mock
modesty): 'Shaw's St. Joan and Joyce's Ulysses into which I
looked today . . . make me ashamed of my own writing.
They have something to say, but I am only paring away
insincerities.' The author of *Howards End* was *not* 'only paring
away insincerities', and he makes it worse when he says of
that very book ('approaching a good novel') that there is 'not
a single character in it for whom I care'.

*Laudator temporis acti*; not a role we instinctively associate
with Forster. Yet here he is, comparing himself to Voltaire:

> We belong to the cultural interlude which came between the fall
> of barbarism and the rise of universal 'education'.

To one who knows *The Longest Journey* practically by heart,
those quotation marks are agony, and there is worse to come.
Under the heading 'Lover of Danger' is the infinitely depressing comment 'enviable but disgusting; coprophagist'. A
few pages later he writes 'I have always wanted to share my

advantages with others. But I am asked to give up my advantages so that others may have things I don't want . . . it is a severe demand.' And finally, these chilling, killing words: 'I am so ready to delegate things, and they may involve sensations. "Here, feel this for me" do I say to posterity.'

What had happened to him? This is not quite the same as the familiar question – why did he stop writing? – but it overlaps, and, again because he is Forster and no lesser man, he faces it:

> . . . my three nibblers – kindness, lust and fun. My enemies they are not, there is no enemy but cruelty. But they waste me and diminish me – especially kindness . . . Tolerance, easiness, laughter, even sympathy have their leaky aspects, and while exercising them – as I do – something essential drains away.

It is tempting, after that, to see a terrible metaphor in his 'How my life has been encumbered by rubbish . . . By how much am I surrounded which I never summoned and can't manage to throw away', and an even more cruel one in the lament for his inability to get out of the bath.

It is not all like this. There is a long section of notes and thoughts for the Clark Lectures, which became *Aspects of the Novel*, a fascinating glimpse of work in progress. More refreshing are the many moments when the real Forster surfaces. Sterne is caught in three words – 'floppy but tenacious' – and Shelley's 'Defence of Poetry' in seven – 'there are too many hopes in it'. There is also, thank God, the old Forster with the old vigour; here he is at Abinger, wielding the scythe, in 1943:

> Mrs Nicholson wishes that she could be in Berlin for an hour in an invisible cloak, and hopes she could see all the women looking starved and ill. Mrs King suggests that strikes could be stopped by exchanging strikers for our POW in Germany; she did not think that Hitler need be consulted. Listening to these

two village fools, I told myself that they talked in order to be thought clever, and that Mrs Nicholson in particular inhabits a cocoon of self-esteem. Yet it is difficult to grasp that they meant nothing.

And of course it *is* a commonplace book too; the passages of prose and verse he includes and evaluates extend and deepen our understanding of his literary values; anybody can be honest about Tennyson's defects, but it takes a Forster to be clear about his genius, 'the discontinuous glory of Tennyson which must be continually watched for'. It also takes a Forster to say, writing about *Clarissa*, that 'Long books, when read, are usually overpraised, because the reader wants to convince himself and others that he has not wasted his time.'

'Criticisms of me as spinsterish, something in them': these · are almost the last words in the book. If his shade is reading this over my shoulder, let him be assured that as far as the novels, the biographies and the two volumes of essays are concerned, there is nothing at all in those criticisms. Nor is there anything but honesty and courage in his cry, desolate but not despairing, of 'I am at the frontiers of a kingdom but cannot get in.'

*Observer* November 18th, 1985

# Footnotes in the sands of time

IN THE PAGES OF Professor Maurice Cranston's outstanding new biography of Rousseau (only the first volume of two so far) there is lurking a man who I fear is destined to remain an unsung hero unless I sing him.

He (come to think of it, he might be she) is G. R. Havens. This Havens I have never met, and it is unlikely that he is still alive, for he published a book in 1933, and the book was not of the kind likely to be essayed by a youth. Still, if he wrote it in his thirties he could still be well and cheerful in his eighties today, and if any reader of these words is in a position to pass on to Mr Havens my best wishes, I would esteem it a kindness.

The book he wrote is called *Voltaire's Marginalia on the Pages of Rousseau*, and it was published by Columbia University Press. Had I stumbled upon this title before reading Professor Cranston's book, I would have assumed that the marginalia consisted of remarks like 'Tiens!', 'Regardez!', 'Imbécile!', 'Nom d'une pipe!' and – this one would have had to be written sideways down the margin, not horizontally – 'How many more times do I have to point out that it was *not* me who said "I disagree with what you say but I will defend to the death your right to say it" but one of my twentieth-century biographers, who put the words into my mouth?'

Unfortunately, I cannot at present lay my hands on a copy of the book, and the only lines that Professor Cranston quotes directly consist of things like 'Ridiculous supposition!' and 'Ass of Diogenes, how you condemn yourself!' Possibly these lose something vital in translation, but I have to say that 'Ane de Diogène, comme vous condamnez vous-même!' and 'Supposition ridicule!' do not go far towards bearing out Voltaire's reputation as a wit, besides being not much different from the kind of thing I would have envisaged from the title of Mr Havens's book alone.

But it is not the quality of Voltaire's annotations that concerns me today; it is the industry of Mr Havens. For the truth of the matter is: I wish *I* had thought of the idea, and carried it out. I wish *I* had tracked down Voltaire's copy of Rousseau (it is in Leningrad, apparently, of all unlikely places), deciphered his handwriting, elucidated any oblique references, summed up Voltaire's opinion of Rousseau's ideas as indicated in these marginal notes, added an introduction, a bibliography and an index, and sat back, as I hope Mr Havens did, content to have dotted an i and crossed a t for posterity.

Once, it was possible to know everything about everything; the first edition of the *Encyclopaedia Britannica* was completed in 1771 (it included, among much other interesting information, the news that California was an island) in three fat volumes, and there were many men, in London and Edinburgh and Paris, in Weimar, Rome and St Petersburg, who knew everything the book contained, and some who knew a great deal more.

It did not last; Goethe, last of the polymaths, died in 1832, calling for more light. By the time the nineteenth century was into its stride, it was no longer possible to know everything about everything; very well, said the savants, we will henceforth know something about everything and everything about something. The first of these twin aims took sick when the explosion of scientific knowledge began in the second half of the century and was finally laid to rest with the larger explosion after the Second World War. All that was left was the knowledge of everything about something, and when the few remaining exemplars of that

knowledge – Professor Edel on Henry James, for instance
– are gone, there will never be another.

That is where I come in. I would, it is true, like to know
everything about everything, or failing that something about
everything, or failing *that* everything about something. But I
would settle for knowing everything about nothing.

Who fished the murex up? What porridge had John Keats?
These are the questions I would like to be able to answer,
knowing that I shall never learn what song the sirens sang.
Indeed, I once conceived a real project of this kind, based on
Swedenborg's *Arcania Caelestia*, of which I had read or been
told (or dreamed) that the first edition sold precisely four
copies and that one of these was bought by Kant. What I
would like to know, or more precisely to discover for
myself, is: who bought the other three?

I shall never know that. I shall never know how many of
Shakespeare's pentameters have feminine endings, or why it
matters (if it does); I shall never even know whether Dr
Rowse is the Rival Poet or the Lovely Boy. I shall never read
all, or even any, of the plays of Lope de Vega, I shall never
write the comprehensive study of the changing length of
men's neckties between 1898 and 1968, I shall never edit the
final, definitive edition, all cruxes resolved, of Menander,
Colley Cibber, Langland or the man who writes the verses
for Raphael Tuck Christmas cards. But if I had thought of it
first, I *could* have written *Voltaire's Marginalia on the Pages of
Rousseau*, and now I can't.

But I can salute Mr Havens for doing so. You may think,
from my tone, that I am mocking him, but I assure you that I
am not. Scholarship is an admirable profession, whatever it
issues in, and I believe that any work written or conceivable
is of interest to somebody other than the author, even
Swedenborg's *Arcania Caelestia*. Certainly no one can say that
Mr Havens's book is of no interest; Professor Cranston
found it useful for his own synoptic view of Rousseau, for a
start. Besides, the thought of it opens up all sorts of

possibilities; *The Marginalia of F. R. Leavis on the Pages of His Supposed Enemies*, for instance, would probably fill a shelf, and the list of the said enemies, even unannotated, a pretty hefty volume. And surely someone who knows him well must be writing in the margins of the *Collected Works* of Roy Hattersley, with careful instructions about posthumous publication.

My old tutor, still happily with us (I went to his eighty-sixth birthday party only a few months ago), was once conducting a seminar at which I was present. Someone came to a rather too broad conclusion, whereupon the Prof recalled a promising student he had had some years before, who had expressed a wish to work for a doctorate. And had he an idea of what subject he would choose? Yes, he had: 'The influence of the eighteenth century on the nineteenth'. I would not want to write that book; but I shall never cease to mourn the fact that Mr Havens beat me to *Voltaire's Marginalia on the Pages of Rousseau*.

*The Times* March 10th, 1984

# Responsibility: I

THERE IS GOOD NEWS from across the Atlantic for the
anti-smoking industry in Britain, though I rather think
that the difference between the American and British legal
systems will prevent the ASH-fanatics and their friends from
exploiting here the device at present being tested there by
some enterprising lawyers. (On the whole I am against mass
murder: I rarely commit it myself, and often find myself
quite out of sympathy with those who make a habit of it.
One must not, however, be too dogmatic, and if the victims
of the next general *battue* should be the American Bar I doubt
if I would make more than a token protest. Perhaps we could
compromise; there would be no general massacre, but a
bounty could be paid, like that on the tails of grey squirrels,
for anyone bringing an American lawyer's head, not
necessarily smoked, to the appropriate office.)

The wheeze is simple. You bring an action against a
tobacco company for causing the death of users of their
products. What made me take particular notice of the subject,
however, was a suggestion that the lawsuits may now
succeed, though similar pleas have been rejected in the past,
because the courts are now willing to take a fundamentally
different view of the matter of consumer responsibility.

Once, as a judge ruling in such a case put it, there was a
reluctance to 'render Elsie the cow liable for deaths brought
on by cholesterol'. The thalidomide victims were entitled to
massive compensation because the women taking it did not
know, and had no means of finding out, that it was poison; no

literate adult in his right mind can now plead that he is unaware of the dangers of smoking, so if he chooses to smoke he has brought his misfortunes upon his own lungs. A man who falls down the stairs because of a well-concealed hole in the carpet may claim damages for his broken leg; one who jumps merrily out of a window with a cry of 'This is much quicker than the lift' is unlikely to be received with sympathy in the court when he enters it on crutches.

Let us leave the American lawyers at this point, though readers who wish to pursue the study of them should reflect on the recent case in which a man in an American hotel was given the key to the wrong room at the reception desk, and opened the door to find a naked lady in what he thought was his bathroom; he was so startled that he jumped back, bumped his head on the door, brought a lawsuit *and was awarded twenty thousand dollars*. (Perhaps it is American judges rather than advocates who should be attended to next St Bartholomew's Eve.)

Let us also leave, though this will be harder, our own anti-smoking legions and their hectoring, bullying and general intolerance of those who do not share their tastes. Let us concentrate on the very important question that lies at the heart of this matter, which has nothing to do with lawyers or cigarettes.

Are we, or are we not, responsible for our own lives? When we act other than under duress, and in possession of the relevant facts, should we or should we not be held to intend the likely consequences of our action? I say yes, and in doing so I am in the company of practically all mankind's philosophy, religion and law; but in so saying I am, I think, out of the company of the present *Zeitgeist* and its more vociferous admirers.

Those admirers have erected a ramshackle and fraudulent structure of belief which now casts its shadow over practically all modern life. The belief which the monstrous building houses is that we are not autonomous beings, with a mind, a will and even a soul, but the helpless playthings of our upbringing, our environment, our system of economic and political government. (Note that there is no mention of our heredity, and no longer much of Freud; the former is held not to exist at all, and the latter is under suspicion of propagating the wrong kind of determinism altogether.)

In all the argument, throughout the centuries, about free will, those who deny its reality *never*, in any circumstances, behave as though they are right. However certain a man may claim to be of the truth that our every action and its effects are predetermined and wholly outwith our control, he never steps off the pavement without looking to see if there is a bus coming. But the illogical nature of his belief does not prevent him applying it to others, and today's determinists are applying it more and more widely and ferociously. In its political form the application penalizes home ownership and prefers rented council-house helotry, hates small businesses and loves nationalized ones, insists on closed shops and cannot abide a man without a union card, above all is implacable in the retention of flat-rate benefits and the rejection of the principle of a direct contribution to these, for the moment we start differentiating between citizens, on the grounds that those who need more should get more and those who can pay more should pay more, we are making both lots of citizens into independent human beings instead of objects stamped out by a die in whatever quantities are desired.

I have always thought that the 'no-fault' insurance principle (it exists in much accident legislation, and there is pressure to extend it to motoring) is perhaps the clearest example of a benevolent idea with pernicious effects. Why should we not be obliged to look where we are going? Why should we not have to make good that which we have made worse? Why should we not be blamed when we are blameworthy, penalized when we have incurred penalties, compelled to pay when we have run up a bill?

Above all, why should we be relieved of all responsibility over our own lives? What are our lives *for*, if not to make or mar, regret or be content with? 'Who is here so base', asked Brutus, 'that would be a bondman?' Alas, there are indeed some who wish to be slaves, and no lack of those who would oblige them by fastening shackles on their wrists. The trouble is that the men with the shackles wish to fasten them on the wrists of the rest of us, too, and they have already got quite a long way towards their goal. And the man who is posthumously claiming damages because although he knew it was dangerous to smoke he couldn't help smoking is advancing their cause.

*The Times* April 30th, 1985

# Responsibility: II

WHAT IS THE MOST STRIKING difference between Mrs Christina Harrison of Buxted, Sussex, and Mrs Cynthia Caler of Houston, Texas? What does the mother of the Chancellor of the Exchequer have, justifiably, that some 'lords and ladies and baronesses' also have, much less justifiably? What *exactly* did the late John Galbraith (no relation to the economist) of Santa Barbara, California, die from? What do all these questions have in common?

Mrs Harrison has recently been the victim of an unpleasant hoax. A statement was published, as an advertisement, in a local newspaper, purporting to be from her, which 'confessed' to deplorable behaviour; she had never behaved in the manner described, and it transpired that the notice had been inserted by someone else using her name, with malicious intent. 'I feel dreadful,' she said; 'my first reaction was just to hide. Now I'm trying to put on a brave front but it's awful to know that someone out there hates me.'

Mrs Caler has also, apparently, been the victim of a hoax, or at least of a serious mistake or accident. She bought a doll for her infant daughter; it was one of those which, when a miniature tape-recording inside the doll is activated, speaks. This doll spoke in language not common to dolls, viz., a torrent of swear words. Possibly someone in the factory was doctoring the product; perhaps someone had switched the innocent doll for a less reputable brand; anyway, the child was learning words that are normally met with somewhat later in life. Mrs Caler was, understandably, shocked.

So far, the two stories are similar, now they diverge quite sharply. The doll company, apprised of the rogue doll, was suitably dismayed, and promptly offered to replace it with one which would speak only honeyed words. Mrs Caler declined the offer, and sought redress from the law. Mrs Harrison, too, was offered redress by the newspaper that had printed the fake advertisement, in the form of an apology in a subsequent issue. She, too, declined the offer, but on very different grounds; 'I just want to forget the whole thing,' she said.

First question answered; on to the Chancellor's mum. This good lady, well struck in years, is disabled; both hips, it seems, are damaged, and she is therefore unable to use public transport. But she cannot afford many taxis (she does not take financial help from Mr Lawson, because she believes it would be unfair to a man with so large a family of his own to support). To her rescue there comes an unlikely Roland in the shape of the GLC; for disabled people in the metropolitan area a special card is provided, free of charge, which entitles the holder to go anywhere within the GLC bailiwick, by taxi, for an even pound, the rest of the fare being paid for by – well, by you and me, actually, out of our rates.

I certainly do not begrudge Mrs Lawson my share of her reduced taxi rides. But the GLC says that the *only* qualification for the magic taxi card is disability; the 'lords and ladies and baronesses' to whom my old friend A. Spokesman referred are all disabled, but there is no suggestion that they are also all unable to pay the full fare in a taxi. Yet our rates are subsidizing them, too, even if they can afford to *buy* the taxi, never mind flag it down.

The story of the never-to-be-sufficiently-lamented Mr Galbraith has been bubbling along for some time. Not long before he turned up his toes, at the age of sixty-nine, Mr Galbraith began a lawsuit against a tobacco company, which his heirs and assigns are continuing *post* his *mortem*; he knew he was dying of lung cancer, and claimed that he had contracted the fatal disease because he had smoked sixty cigarettes a day for fifty-one years. (I must say that if I were running the accused tobacco company, I would plaster that news over every hoarding and television commercial in the land; to smoke for half a century at the rate of sixty a day – something over *a million* gaspers – before being carried off could well be evidence of quite astounding therapeutic properties in the weed.) To the question that springs at once to mind – what became of the principle of *volenti non fit injuria*, if a man who smoked himself to death can claim damages from anyone but himself? – his lawyer, the inevitable Mr Melvin Belli, has found an ingenious answer. Mr Galbraith argued, and his surviving relatives are continuing to argue (to be precise, all the arguing is being done by Mr Belli, presumably on a cash-and-carry basis), that although Mr Galbraith believed that smoking was doing him in, however slowly, he was so wedded to his poison that he couldn't stop, so it was not his fault but that of the tobacco: the lawyers are thus arguing that although he backed an also-ran, he should have his money back with a good bit over.

Now what is the common element in these strange tales of our strange time? It is *responsibility*, which takes many forms but is of a like nature in them all. Mrs Harrison was unpleasantly defamed; shocked and hurt, she at once took steps to heal her own wound – she refused even the proffered redress, let alone the potentially rich pickings available in the courts. We score one upright and responsible woman, and turn the page. On the *verso*, we find another woman, in her way no less shocked and hurt than her English counterpart. But mark the difference; when the doll-maker offered immediate redress, Mrs Caler refused it, and went off to her lawyers. I would like to believe, but unfortunately am unable to, that they promptly told her to shut up and stop making a spectacle of herself; any day now, therefore, we may expect a nice, plump, brand-new lawsuit, in which damages of anything up to $972,000 million will be demanded from the doll company for teaching Little Miss Muffet to say 'bugger' before she was two years old. Hand on heart, can you say that the American party of the first part has behaved as wisely, to put it no more sharply, as the English one?

Now for Mrs Lawson, proud mother of a real live Chancellor, and her hips. She scores twice; once for refusing to burden Nigel with extra financial commitments, and once for expressing gratitude to those who have enabled her to get about. But would you stake your life that among the 'lords and ladies and baronesses', and for that matter the misters and missuses, who also travel by taxi at others' expense, there is *none* who could regularly afford the full taxi fare? And those who could, but prefer to cadge it from those who in many cases are less well off than they are themselves; what does 'responsible' mean to them, other than what it means in the sentence 'I think somebody else should be responsible for the cost of my comforts'? (It used to be said that the first sentence to be learned in a foreign language by a bad linguist abroad is 'The gentleman over there will pay'. *Autres temps, autres moeurs*; today, it is most useful at home.)

As for the case of Mr Galbraith, his family and whoever thought up their wheeze, it shows much more than the degree of shameless impudence that can apparently be deployed with impunity in an American court. For it must surely mark also the furthest point yet reached in the retreat from responsibility. When a man announces unambiguously that although he knowingly took poison, and went on knowingly taking it for fifty-one years (and, incidentally, enjoying it), somebody else is now to pay for the effects of it on his health, it suggests, among other things, that he has a funny idea of what it means to be human rather than a glove-puppet. (Mr Galbraith claimed that he could not help himself; he was *addicted* to tobacco, so he must be absolved from any duty or responsibility to himself. Nor have those pursuing the claim failed to argue that when he took up the habit, at the age of eighteen, he was only a trusting innocent, quite unaware that smoking can lead to more smoking. It is a mercy that the tobacco company is not being prosecuted for infanticide.)

King Lear had a hand in it, you know; 'I am a man more sinned against than sinning.' But where did *he* get the idea? He got it from Adam, who put it in its purest form, the form in which it has survived intact to this day: 'The woman whom thou gavest to be with me, she gave me of the tree, and I did eat.' No doubt Adam hired Mr Belli for the subsequent lawsuit, but it would be quite unfair to blame those who make a living out of the abandonment of responsibility for the abandonment itself. Somehow, we have got to get back to a condition in which we do not instinctively look to others to pay our bills, in which, when someone treads on our toe, we do not promptly sue for the full amount of an amputation at the hip, just in case, in which we accept censure for our failures and wrong-doings as completely, even if not as cheerfully, as we take praise for our successes and achievements. Somehow, we have got to get back to the realization that although little children must be protected from dangers that they are too young to understand, adults are presumed to be able to protect themselves.

I hope the heirs of Mr Galbraith are non-suited; I hope the taxi-cadgers have their fingers shut in the door; I hope Mrs Caler, if she proceeds with her lawsuit against the doll-maker, becomes the laughing stock of all Texas; and I most fervently hope that Mrs Harrison and Mrs Lawson live long and prosper greatly. More to the point, I hope that they live long enough to see their kind honoured, and the other kind looked down upon. But I fear that if they are to see such a revolution they will have to live very long indeed.*

*The Times* November 19th, 1985

*The late Mr Galbraith lost his case.

# Responsibility: III

SIR GORDON BORRIE, director-general of the Office of Fair Trading, has been complaining that too many people are in debt, and 'thousands . . . are falling behind in their payments'. You may ask what that has got to do with fair trading; the obvious answer is nothing, but Sir Gordon does have an excuse. The failure of Mr and Mrs Higginbotham to keep up their hire-purchase instalments (the 'never-never' it was called when I was a boy) cannot be described as trading, fair or unfair, but the provision of the hire-purchase goods and terms can be, and Sir Gordon has only drawn the family Higginbotham into the net designed for Messrs Vulture and Shark.

He denounced finance companies, building societies and others whose business is credit (of which, I suppose, the plastic credit-card is the most ubiquitous form) for selling so much of their invisible but potent product. Such merchants are 'over-selling', nay, 'irresponsible'; they are exerting 'pressure to buy now and pay later'. (That, incidentally, is a definition of credit; if you buy now and pay now no credit is involved.)

Before everybody faints dead away at the horror revealed by Sir Gordon, let us look a little more closely at his facts. He tells us that Britain's total of personal debt, excluding mortgages, is £22 billion, that is, an average of £1,000 of debt for every household in the country.

That means we are dealing with 22 million households, among which there are 'thousands' of 'worried debtors who've borrowed beyond their means'. How many thousands? 20,000? 50,000? Shall we say 100,000? If we do, we shall discover that these feckless debtors comprise slightly less than half of one per cent of households, or something like a quarter of one per cent of adults.

From this, the only possible conclusion is that the people of this country are almost dangerously fanatical in their determination to avoid being over-indebted, and quite astoundingly successful in making sure that they are not.

For every non-existent problem there is an imaginary solution. Sir Gordon, having convinced himself that the country is drowning in unpayable debts, proposes that 'Finance houses and other credit firms should put their hands in their pockets to support a chain of independent money advice centres throughout the country.' Well, I suppose it would be one way of reducing unemployment among accountants.

Now before I go on to draw a moral from this tale, I must invite you to listen to a variation on a similar theme. There is a practice called 'hacking', which consists of using a computer to get into other people's computer systems; apparently this is quite easily done by those with the necessary skills, who are thus in a position to 'eavesdrop' on others' computerized material. The practice is not in itself illegal. Indeed, the Scottish Law Commission, which has been investigating this curious sport, has just come to some extremely unambiguous conclusions on it, which it has summarized thus:

> If property is not removed it does not count as theft, if records are not interfered with for gain it is not fraud, and if nothing is damaged it is not vandalism, so it does not look as though a crime has been committed.

You and I would think that, after so lucid a summary of the position, there would be nothing to add. We would, however, have reckoned without the Scottish Law Commission. Faced with a practice that makes it nervous, and discovering after exhaustive examination that the practice has the impertinence to be perfectly lawful (for the very good reason that nobody is harmed by it), it has recommended that it should be made illegal, in a brand-new category of crime all to itself, with up to two years in prison as a penalty.

Again, you and I might think that two years in chokey, for no better reason than that the Scottish Law Commission had nothing to do one rainy afternoon, would be coming it a bit strong, but just listen to the words of Mr Gordon Nicholson, QC:

> While a lot of hacking has been done for sheer fun there are undoubtedly people who would seek to use the activity as a form of industrial espionage.

Well, while six-foot lengths of rope are very handy for children who want to play skipping games, there are undoubtedly some people who would seek to use the commodity to strangle QCs with. But to avoid this appalling outcome, would Mr Nicholson make skipping illegal, or even rope? Surely he would do better to buy a very stiff collar? For insofar as industrial espionage is a crime already, no new laws are required to punish it if it is done by a hacker rather than by a cat-burglar, and insofar as it is not, it can hardly become one merely by being done through a computer.

What have both Sir Gordon Borrie and the Scottish Law Commission forgotten? It comes back to that word I have lately been using more and more: responsibility. There is no recorded instance of credit being forced upon an unwilling debtor at the point of a gun; similarly, no ruthless gangs, equipped with electrified cattle-prods and Dobermann Pinschers, are preventing firms from taking their own precautions against industrial espionage.

Let us, suppose that the 'worried debtors' are numbered in their millions, not thousands; let us assume that other millions spend all their time in front of computer keyboards, hacking away 19K to the dozen. The English for both *caveat emptor* and *vae victis* is *serve you right*; in a democracy we do not prevent sane adults from making their own choices, even though we know that some of them will make choices that turn out very badly for them, and similarly we do not turn innocent behaviour into a crime because some people are embarrassed by it and cannot bestir themselves sufficiently to work out ways of avoiding the embarrassment.

I say we do not do these things; but the truth is that we do, and we do them more frequently and more extensively as time passes. Year by year, the Nanny State (I believe I coined the term) embraces us more firmly and comprehensively, tying our hands with the softest of silk cords, and hobbling our ankles with the lightest of aluminium chains, and assuring us – often quite truthfully – that it is not to prevent us harming others, but to prevent us harming ourselves.

But if we do not have the chance to hurt ourselves, we shall not be able to help ourselves, either; if we are forbidden to walk into danger, we shall never be able to walk anywhere interesting; if they take away our power to do wrong, they deprive us of any meaning in doing right.

And these are not metaphors. Nanny no longer confines herself to what we are not allowed to do; gradually, she begins to concentrate on what we *must* do. There are many roads to serfdom, and one of the straightest and fastest is paved with the very best intentions.

It is certainly unpleasant, worrying and painful for people to see the three-piece suite and the video recorder, so cheerfully bought on credit months ago, disappearing round the corner in the recovery-firm's van, and it is not enough to say that that will teach them to do a few sums before they sign next time; there are some who will never learn, and will end up without curtains or a kitchen chair. But despite them, we have got to restore the connection, now almost invisible throughout the country, between cause and effect, action and reaction, purchase and bill.

Sir Gordon Borrie would deal with the problem of debtors by condemning their creditors; the Scottish Law Commission would deal with the problem of hacking by arming the hackers' victims with the criminal law. I would deal with both problems by first declaring that they are not problems at all, but the inevitable result of our now almost universal refusal to let anyone suffer the consequence of his own folly, or even to let anyone tell him it *is* folly, and after that by sending each of the worried debtors, and each of the hack-fearing firms, a handsome pokerworked board, bearing these lines of A. E. Housman:

> To think that two and two are four
> And neither five nor three
> The heart of man has long been sore
> And long 'tis like to be.

And I would send the pokerwork board COD.

*The Times* March 14th, 1986

# *1789 and all that*

*Reflections of a Nonpolitical Man* by Thomas Mann[*]

THE CUPBOARD DOOR has swung open at last, and the skeleton, hidden for seventy years in the decent obscurity of the German language (and a particularly impenetrable variety of it, too), is now dancing and grinning in the daylight of translation. This astounding and outrageous book is the last of Thomas Mann's principal works to be given to the English-speaking world; for decades dark legends have been woven about it, some of them going so far as to suggest that it showed Mann to be an Ur-Nazi, others insisting that it was the cause of his temporary but bitter estrangement from his brother Heinrich, still others that he was so ashamed of it that he tried to suppress it.

Legends are not true; that is why they are called legends. Thomas broke with Heinrich because of Heinrich's words in an essay published before *Reflections*; the Nazis could have derived no satisfaction from it; so far from Mann repenting of his book, he saw it to the end of his life as a vital stage in the continuity of his life, career and political development.

Yet I called it astounding and outrageous, and it is both. Started during the First World War just as the tide had begun to turn against Germany, it is a massive polemic, in places hysterical, against the spirit of the Enlightenment, and a no less uncompromising hymn to the ancient virtues of Protestant Europe, which he identified with German culture. Which is all very well; but in the course of it he justifies (and

[*] Lorrimer, 1986.

with a contemptuous wave of his hand) both the German violation of Belgian neutrality and the sinking of the *Lusitania*, and goes a very long way towards justifying the execution of Edith Cavell. Is this really the Thomas Mann of *The Magic Mountain* and *Joseph and his Brothers*?

Yes, it is, for beneath the molten lava there is a formidable case. Mann's enemy is 'civilization's literary man', a phrase which runs through the book like an incantation. This is the figure, dominant in those lands (particularly France) which 'missed the Reformation'; history's watershed was signalled by Luther's hammer at Wittenberg, history's doom was sealed in 1789. The cosmopolitan intellectual, without roots in hierarchy, blood or art, who looks to Rousseau for guidance and knows nothing of the importance of ancient frontiers, is the enemy; he is usually French (though 'Italy's defeat would be the defeat of Mazzini and of d'Annunzio, of the democratic-republican incendiary orator and of the aesthetic-political clown, both of whom I hate from the bottom of my heart'), and had gone far to corrupt the integrity of Germany (Heinrich, not named, comes in for many a blow), fighting not only for her life but for Europe.

> Art politicized, intellect politicized, morality politicized, the *idea*, all thoughts, feelings, desires politicized – who wants to live in such a world? In a world where freedom means general and equal suffrage and nothing more? . . . Love! Humanity! I know it, this theoretical love and this doctrinaire humanity that is hissed out through one's teeth to show one's disgust for one's own nation.

And in case that did not convey Mann's meaning with sufficient clarity, there was also this:

> The arrogant simplicity with which you other nations base your patterns of thought, judging us by your value systems – why don't you finally give it up! Morals! Domestic affairs! But if the justification of foreign adventures, of war, is to be decided

according to the domestic conditions of a country, according to whether its social *conscience* is in good condition; then Germany would have the right to war *before* France, England and Italy, not to speak of Russia. For the belief in the dignity of the state, in its moral calling, has been more alive here than anywhere else, the idea of the state as an institution for the protection of social justice.

Where, then, is salvation? Long before the reader gets there, he can deduce Dostoevsky, and predict Mann's use of him: 'All disbelief in political revolutionary ideology, all belief in its necessary "inner bankruptcy", all despair of it, is of religious nature . . .' Such distinguished foreigners are welcome allies, but the main defenders of true culture (always used as the antithesis of 'civilization'), as of order and the historical sense, are Luther, Nietzsche, Schopenhauer, Wagner and, above all, Goethe, who saw where the Revolution would ultimately take Europe.

And soon we see why Mann never repudiated this book, which rises to truly Dostoevskian heights of political and psychological insight.

> Do we not know them from home, these lovers of the human race . . . abstract, but 'resolute' lovers and prophets of *liberté, égalité et fraternité* with their civic lamentations and their great concern? Do they not also live quite well, yes, even extremely well in the process, glorious and spoiled, as they nourish themselves spiritually with the thought of their own civic-moral beauty, but bodily, perhaps, with the help of a smart impresario from the capitalistic world system that they curse as they receive the greatest benefits from it?

Mann's *bürgerlich* roots, from which *Buddenbrooks* grew when he was only twenty-six, are evident throughout this book; indeed, there is a chapter called 'Burgherly Nature'. He admired – how could he help admiring? – the virtues of the German *Bürger*, and the national stability that those virtues gave. Yet he never falls into the trap of sentimentalizing the sturdy patriots of his native Lübeck, let alone the PBI of the wars of the Reformation; he quotes with approval a passionate critique of universal suffrage, and with even more satisfaction Nietzsche's condemnation of 'the rise of parliamentary stupidity, of newspaper reading, and of the participation of everyone in the literarylike discussion of everything . . . the growing rise of democratic man, and of the stultification of European man brought about by this rise'.

Mann's profound conservatism was based in his pessimism, a pessimism in turn founded in his contempt for the inadequate psychology of the Enlightenment and of the even greater inadequacy of its historical understanding. Europe's master ironist lived to see the Nazis' simultaneous perversion of thought and feeling, and to chronicle it in *Dr Faustus*.

The translation is by Professor Walter D. Morris of Iowa State University. It is strewn with such infelicities as 'unbridledly' and 'humanitarianly', and with horrible modern slang. No doubt Professor Morris would argue that the prose of Mann's original is ugly, but he can have no excuse for the complete abandonment of his duty of proper editing. There is no index or bibliography, individuals and books are left unidentified, quotations are unattributed, there is no attempt to set the book in its historical context other than a wholly inadequate introduction, crucial allusions are unexplained, and there is no recognition of the need to elucidate the nature of long-forgotten movements, philosophies and causes. For such a book to be put forth in such a condition can be characterized by no milder word than disgraceful.

*Observer* March 2nd, 1986

# Or I'm a Dutchman

I WILL HAVE YOU KNOW that I am very big in Holland. My book *Enthusiasms* has been translated into Dutch (will the gentleman at the back who observed that that is only fitting in view of the fact that I have been writing in Double-Dutch for years kindly leave the room), and I believe that the police there have already been called out several times to control the crowds trying to force their way into the bookshops.

I have just been sent the customary author's copies, and a rather weird experience I have found it. I have seen my words translated into French and German, but these are languages with which I have at least a nodding acquaintance; of Dutch I understand not a word, and in an idle moment I took down a copy of the original and began to collate some passages.

I turned first to the jacket blurb, which begins: 'Bernard Levin is de vaste columnist van de Londense *Times* . . .', a remark which I feel is singularly uncalled for; I know I have been putting on a bit of weight lately, but no one could call me vast. On turning to the book itself, however, I began to realize what an appalling task I had set the translator (Pauline Moody), for the elaborate intricacy of my rhetorical style, seen through the distorting mirror of a language so strange to me (and somehow made more strange rather than less by its distant cousinship with German), seems almost ungraspable in any language but ours.

Take a passage such as this, for instance, which must have put Miss Moody on her guard at once because of the reference to the principal city of The Netherlands:

> In Amsterdam, as in London, whole city blocks have been taken over by the pornography industry, and the property developers lie awake at night wondering what further beautiful old buildings they can pull down. In London, as in many other British cities, there are enormous and obtrusive rubbish bins on the pavements, put there by the municipal authorities or civic-minded shopkeepers and businessmen, but they are painted in such vile colours, and bestrewn with municipal or commercial advertising in such ugly typefaces, that the result is to make the streets worse than if the bins were not there and the litter was thrown upon the ground, which it usually is anyway.

In Dutch (my apologies to Mynheer Compositor) that reads as follows:

> In Amsterdam zijn evenals in London, hele huizenblokken overgenomen door de porno-industrie, en de projectontwikkelaars liggen's nachts wakker terwijl ze zich afvragen welke mooie oude gebouwen ze nog meer kunnen afbreken. In London staan evenals in veel andere Engelse steden, grote opvallende afvalbakken op de stoep, daar neergezet door de gemeentelijke autoriteiten of door winkeliers en zakenlui met burgerzin, maar di zijn in zulke walgelijke kleuren geschilderd, en volgeplakt met gemeentelijk en commercieel reclamedrukwerk in zulke lelijke letters, det het resultaat de straten erger ontsiert dan als die bakken er niet stonden en het afval op straat gegooid, wat trouwens toch meestal gebeurt.

As you so rightly say, *sic*. But to my eye the passage not only seems astonishingly faithful to the original but in places takes on a kind of poetry. I shall never again think of a property developer, for instance, without turning him into a *projectontwikkelaar*, and *grote opvallende afvalbakken* are much more impressive objects than enormous and obtrusive rubbish bins. Other words in the passage cannot be allowed to stand prosaically representing my original ones: *huizenblok-*

*ken* may have been city blocks to Rembrandt, but they will now always be hot blokes to me, and as for *winkeliers*, I am going out at once to buy the biggest I can lay my hands on, with a view to hanging it from my drawing-room ceiling to brighten the winter gloom. (In the chapter on opera, I began 'Some are born to music, some achieve music, and some . . .', well, some *krijgen muziek opgedrongen*.)

Now you may be thinking that if I came here this morning to tease the Dutch for their language it was a pointless intention, besides being in questionable taste. In fact, however, all this is leading up to something quite opposite, an admiring and astonished tribute to the people of that remarkable country, based on an experience that befell me in Amsterdam last March.

Soon after *Enthusiasms* was published in Britain, I had a telephone call from the producer of a Dutch television chat-show, asking me to talk about my book on her programme. I explained that I did not have a word of Dutch, that subtitling a conversation with me would be like trying to dry up the Atlantic Ocean with a single sheet of blotting paper, and that no interpreter would survive more than ten minutes.

That was no empty threat; I believe that Sir Isaiah Berlin is the only man in Britain who talks more rapidly than I do, and even that is a close-run thing. (I once had to give evidence in court; the old-fashioned shorthand-writer had been replaced by the much swifter 'stenotypist', but the hapless girl, after several appeals from the judge for me to slow down had had no effect, simply gave up.) But I was assured that no form of translation would be necessary, because the audience – both the one in the studio and the one at home – would understand my English.

Understand *my* English? I am quite capable of speaking, unprepared, a sentence containing anything up to forty subordinate clauses all embedded in their neighbours like those wooden Russian dolls, and many a native of these islands, speaking English as to the manner born, has followed me trustingly into the labyrinth only to perish miserably trying to find the way out; I had visions of some new de Ruyter, egged on by his infuriated countrymen, sailing up the Medway and sacking Chatham. But intrigued by the absurdity of what was being proposed, and feeling that any excuse for a visit to Amsterdam should be seized upon, I agreed.

Shortly afterwards the producer of the programme, together with the host of it, visited me in London to discuss the details. They both spoke excellent English, but that proved nothing; they both assured me that my fears were groundless, but that proved nothing either. I set off for Amsterdam looking forward to an hour or so of hilarious mutual incomprehension.

At the studio, I learnt that I was one of four guests on the programme and that we would each talk to the host separately. I was to go in first wicket down.

The opening bat was a Dutchman; well, I never suggested that the Dutch can't speak Dutch, and the studio audience, of about eighty, as I recall, were attentive throughout. Then the first guest left, and it was my turn. The host was a genial *huizenblokke*, and his English not only excellent but idiomatic. He introduced me in Dutch, and we were off; I determined that even if only out of international courtesy, I would speak slowly and clearly, use no complicated expressions, and keep my sentences short and simple.

A fat lot of use good resolutions turned out to be; I could no more reshape my manner of speaking than I could, implored by m'lud, slow it down, and in about two minutes I was talking in my normal way. To my astonishment, it was plain that the studio audience was following every word (anyone used to speaking to or before audiences can immediately tell whether what he is saying is being taken in), and a few moments later, I essayed a joke.

Now any joke in a foreign language is the hardest test of

understanding, and my jokes, which tend to be intricately verbal, must be harder than most; astonishment turned to amazement when the audience not only laughed, but laughed with *exactly* the same reaction-interval as a British audience would. From then on I abandoned all thought of making concessions, and spoke as I would speak at home; never once did the audience fail to respond as an audience at home would.

But that did not exhaust the surprises in store for me. When my stint was finished, I was returned to the penalty-box at the side of the studio; the third guest was Dutch again, but the fourth was German, and she spoke no more Dutch than I did. The same pattern, however, was displayed; it was apparent that the audience understood German every bit as well as they understood English (and the host's German was as complete as *his* English). When it was all over, I asked how the audience in the studio were selected; I learnt that they were not – as with many British television programmes, people may simply write in for tickets, and since this particular audience would not have known in advance that a Dutchless Englishman and an equally Dutchless German would be on the programme, it was plain that the audience must have been fully representative of those who watched it at home.

I left in a thoughtful state of mind. I know that Dutch is useless outside The Netherlands except in Flanders and perhaps among Afrikaners in South Africa; like the citizens of many small countries, they must learn other languages or reconcile themselves to communicating by signs and grunts. Well, the Dutch, like the Scandinavians, have taken the more demanding path, and however necessary it has been for them, no one can withhold admiration for the extent of their success. And if anyone could, it would not be a citizen of this country; we are fortunate in having a language that is *lingua franca* all over the world, but that no more excuses our unwillingness or inability to learn other tongues than the

Hollanders' command of English is to be regarded as unremarkable because it was born of necessity.

It was after the programme was seen in The Netherlands that I was approached by the Dutch publishers with a proposal for a Dutch edition of *Enthusiasms*, and now I trust that I am soaring to the top of the Dutch best-seller list. At any rate, if I am not, it can only be because the Dutch understand English so well that they need no translation, and have all bought the original English edition. But I still think somebody should try making a joke in Dutch on the Wogan show.

*The Times* January 19th, 1985

# Confucius he say

WHAT IS THE DIFFERENCE between us and the Chinese? There are more of them, they are of a sallower hue, and they have, as we do not, a fold of skin in the eyelid, called the epicanthus, which has for centuries led them to be unjustly accused of having eyes which are set slantwise in their faces.

So much for the differences. Now: wherein are they like us?

The chief similarity, at any rate the one that concerns me today, is that they are no less keen than we are on a fat wallet and trousers a-jingle with coin. They resemble us also in their willingness to cut a corner or two in the pursuit of the spondulicks. I am unable to tell you what is the Chinese for 'Mind you, guv, I'd knock off a quarter for cash and no questions asked' or 'Well, I won't tell the tax inspector if you won't, so what are we worrying about?', but I am sure it exists.

That being so, I have some bad news for the present Chinese rulers. They have just published a series of stern decrees against foreign currency speculation, black market selling, unauthorized financial transactions, profiteering and raising prices without permission. Moreover, the new laws are accompanied by fearsome penalties for those who break them, akin to those with which Kai Lung was once threatened, at the instigation of the effete Ming-shu, which included 'hanging, slicing, pressing, boiling, roasting, grill-ing, freezing, vatting, racking, twisting, drawing, compressing, inflating, rending, spiking, gouging, limb-tying, piecemeal-pruning and a variety of less tersely describable discomforts'. But the bad news for Deng Ziaoping and his chums is that it is not going to work: foreigners in China will still be approached to sell, at a massive premium, the 'exchange certificates' which are the only species of currency usable in the 'friendship shops', which are in turn the only places where anything worth having is sold. The black market, too, will flourish unchecked, the practice of cornering the supply of consumer goods will go on, the brisk trade in purchase permits will not die out, and scarce items of value will continue to fall off the backs of lorries in ever-increasing quantities.

Why should this be so? It is so because economics, even more than nature, abhors a vacuum. In a society where there are not enough of the simplest and most necessary items to keep the whole population in a reasonable minimum supply, there will be citizens who undertake to remedy the deficiency. The more active and enterprising of these will engage to supply their fellow-citizens' wants directly, by making, importing or stealing the scarce items; the less constructive will do their bit by buying such goods at one price and selling them at another, higher price. And the solution to the problem of this illegal trafficking will never be found in the promulgation of decrees abolishing it or penalties punishing it: the only way to stop it is to increase the official and legal supply to the point at which the unofficial and illegal suppliers can no longer make a profit.

In countries such as Britain, where there are thousands upon thousands of shops selling blue-jeans and pop-music records, no black market in these goods exists, any more than it does for foreign currency. In the Soviet Union and China, where the jeans and the records are in short supply, and the foreign currency is the only kind that will buy anything, the black market flourishes (it is significant that the only kind of black market that exists in free countries is the one which trades in goods the supply of which cannot be increased by any means, such as tickets for over-subscribed sporting or artistic events).

It has often been pointed out, not least by me, that the countries which deny their subjects political freedom tend to be the countries which cannot supply their peoples' material wants either. What is less often noticed is that that is not a coincidence. In a sense, economic freedom is the most basic of political ones; only where the people are free to buy and sell, to lend and borrow, above all to own, will any substantial number of them enjoy either the liberty to speak their minds or the comfort of a reasonable standard of living.

Apologists for totalitarian regimes always evade this truth; try asking Professor Victor Allen why the people of the Soviet Union are much poorer than those of Western Europe. First, he will claim that they are not (no, second – *first* he will point out that Soviet democracy is of a far finer and purer kind than ours) and then he will adduce any number of reasons why they are, from the wickedness of the tsars to the unfortunate string of bad harvests caused solely by unreasonable weather: what he will never admit is that there is any connection between communist tyranny and communist poverty, and he still wouldn't admit the connection even if he were to admit the tyranny.

The Chinese rulers' campaign against illicit dealings follows hard upon their recent introduction of some suspiciously capitalist measures of economic reform; perhaps the threats are a way of indicating that the reforms must not put the wrong ideas into the citizens' heads. But unless the implications of the illicit dealings are understood, the reforms will fail in their purpose.

Amid the announcement of the measures to be taken against profiteering and the like, the Chinese leaders drew attention to the fact that government and other official institutions were also engaged in the illicit trafficking. Again that will surprise no one who has discovered that human beings are not yet perfect. We heard a great deal, Andropov-time, about the new broom's intention to sweep the Soviet Union clean of corruption, and we shall soon hear a great deal more about how Mr Gorbachov is going to carry even further the cleansing of Soviet public life. But not even Mr Gorbachov, let alone Professor Allen, is going to explain how the corruption got into Soviet life in the first place, and neither of them is going to admit that the worst and most blatant corruption is the kind that the Soviet Union's leaders themselves live by, the luxury in which they wallow while their subjects queue for hours in case there might be something worth buying at the front of the queue. (This way of life has been enthusiastically adopted by the rulers of the Soviet Union's imperial possessions; the thieving and racketeering of Ceausescu and his wife and their families is so gigantic, shameless and uncontrollable that there is, quite literally, nothing in the world to match it.)

However much more numerous, yellow and epicanthus-strewn than the rest of us the Chinese are, these are but the trappings and the suits; beneath them there beat a billion hearts to a rhythm much older than communism. Whatever form of government China has, there will never be any lack of Chinese anxious to turn an honest *renminbi* (it used to be a *tael* when Kai Lung and I were young), and a sufficient proportion of those will be quite willing to turn a dishonest *renminbi* if the other kind is too difficult to turn.

But why should that be matter for surprise? Our own home-grown Maoists used to claim that Chinese communism had created an entirely new kind of human being, just as their predecessors, the Soviet fellow-travellers, would claim that New Soviet Man had been born; the Chinese and the Russian varieties had in common the quality of not minding poverty, indeed of embracing it with cries of joy.

Some believed that; some still do. You will not, however, expect me to be among them. I believe that human beings the world over want to improve their lot, and that goes for black ones as well as white, yellow as well as brown. The ingenuity and assiduity with which some of them will pursue that desire has, throughout history, defeated every attempt, however comprehensive and brutal, to choke it off, and the latest attempt will fare no better than the earlier ones. No doubt Deng's political nearest and dearest will tell him that which he wishes to hear, viz., that speculation, profiteering, black markets and the rest have been utterly expunged at a stroke of his all-wise pen. But that is another, and even older, story.

*The Times* March 22nd, 1985

# Crime and punishment

THE REMARKABLE NUMBER of black South Africans who have entered police stations in robust good health, only to experience a sharp attack of death before emerging, reminds me yet again of the comforting truth (the reminder will not be of much comfort to the dead Africans or their families, of course) that an astonishingly high proportion of wicked men are also stupid.

You would have thought that after the murder of Steve Biko, which did South Africa almost immeasurable damage (though again, not as much damage as the two policemen did Biko), somebody would have passed down the word that since South Africa has enough laws, and enough reliable judges and magistrates, to convict any African of anything at all and put him away in silence for as long as might be desired, it is quite unnecessary, and even counter-productive, for the police to beat their prisoners' brains out with such depressing frequency.

From the murdered Imam in 1969, from the murdered Biko in 1977, from the murders by police continuing to the present day, South Africa garners nothing but harm; would it not serve her interests better for her leaders to take action sufficiently ruthless – say, hanging a couple of policemen with blood on their hands, *pour encourager les autres* – to stop it?

To the solution of this mystery there may be a clue in a recent South African court case. It concerned a group of five white youths, all aged fifteen or sixteen, who kicked and beat to death two black men, one of whom was sixty-eight years old; there appeared to be no motive for the killing other than the enjoyment of it.

The boys were arrested and charged with murder; they pleaded not guilty, though they later changed their plea, presumably on legal advice, to one of guilty of culpable homicide, which plea was accepted.

A clinical psychologist, a Dr Carnie, gave evidence for the defence. He claimed that tests proved that the boys 'were not violence oriented'; well, that's good to know, because if they *had* been violence oriented they might have really done somebody some harm. Dr Carnie also said that the killings (which he called 'the nasty incident', presumably to make sure that nobody would leave the courtroom under the impression that they constituted a *nice* incident) might never have happened if the boys had not been in a group.

I can understand that, of course. Although one of the men they killed was sixty-eight, the other was only thirty-six, and the individual members of the killer gang might well have hesitated to take on both men without the safety of numbers. At the end of the case, there was the regulation weeping mother, who said, 'All his life my fifteen-year-old son has been soft and gentle and would not harm a fly. I don't know what got into him.' (Neither do I, though I know what got into Mr William Nkosi and Mr Solomon Kuna – five pairs of boots and a number of blunt instruments.)

So far we have dealt with the 'culpable homicide' ('Oh why', sang Betjeman, 'do people waste their breath, devising dainty names for death?'); it now behoves us to consider the sentence. Mr Justice Curlewis, in passing it, saw the crucial point immediately: 'These are not the type of people that can be sent to a reformatory or to jail,' he said. I should think not; they might dislike it, for instance, or meet a socially inferior class of people inside, and after all, they had done nothing but bash the life out of two human beings. Mr Justice Curlewis also ruled out caning as a penalty; he did not, he said, think that would be 'suitable punishment' for the five culpably homicidal youths. Again, that seems to me reasonable; they might not have enjoyed the experience at all.

What, then, did he in the end decide was 'suitable' punishment for this 'type of people'? He sentenced them, the naughty old Judge Jeffreys, to spend their weekends for a whole year working in a hospital. The hideous cruelty of this sentence became apparent in his very next words, which must have caused gasps of horror in the court: 'the scholars, I understand, are all . . . keen sportsmen. For a year they can forget about any weekend activity.'

If we conclude that this is a case of an unscrupulous white judge letting off white youths in circumstances in which black men would have been hanged, we have missed the point. There is no reason at all to believe that Mr Justice Curlewis is anything but a fair and honest justicer, or that he did not believe every word he said. What is wrong with the judge is not that he is a wicked man, it is that he lacks the ability to see the facts of the case, the nature of the killers and the fate of their victims, in the way that would be natural to anyone who has lived his life outside South Africa.

When, after the Spanish conquest of Peru under Pizarro, the first reinforcements and supplies from home arrived by sea, the ships hove to just off shore. The Indians literally could not see the vessels, for their inability to comprehend sights so extravagantly unlike anything they had ever seen before led not to ordinary bewilderment but to hysterical blindness; communication between eye and brain was temporarily severed, and where the Spaniards saw a flotilla, the Indians saw nothing but an empty ocean.

So it is, I am sure, with Mr Justice Curlewis. A lifetime of accepting South African values, a lifetime of living within a set of unchanging assumptions, a lifetime of regarding black and white as two wholly different and eternally separate species, a lifetime of feeling part of a protective *laager*, one weakness or gap in which may destroy everyone – all this means that the judge's behaviour was not that of a wrong-doer, but the result of a withered imagination, made sterile by the South African osmosis.

That should not be surprising; what *should* be surprising is the number of South Africans who, though they breathe the same air as Mr Justice Curlewis, have managed to break free of the effect of it. I say that that should be surprising, but I must add that to me it is not. The same phenomenon, in a much more striking form, can be observed in the Soviet Union; men and women brought up amid lies have found the truth inside themselves, and lived by it, in yet another reproach both to the Manichee and to the fools who claim that environment is all. In every generation, in every unfree land, there are those who can see and understand the evil by which they are surrounded, and reject it.

Mr Justice Curlewis is not part of that evil; he is only unable to grasp it, and in that he is kin to most white South Africans (for the number who knowingly do evil cannot be much larger than those who see and defy it). One day, in South Africa, everyone will be able to see that for five young degenerates in search of an evening's amusement to kick to death two human beings is about as abominable a crime as it is possible to commit. I do not know when that day will dawn; but I am certain that dawn it will.

*The Times* July 30th, 1985

# Anyone for tennis?

JIRI JAVORSKY WAS for many years one of Czechoslovakia's leading tennis players; he was captain of the Czech Davis Cup team. He was regarded with suspicion by the Czech authorities, not because he took part in any dissident activities but because he would not, in his tennis-playing travels abroad, act as a spy, and also because he refused to join the Communist Party. He and his wife Vera have two sons, Jaroslav and George; pressure was put upon the father through the sons, who found obstacles in the way of their educational and employment progression.

When Mr Javorsky's days of competitive tennis ended, he worked as a coach, and in 1976 he was offered a trainer's job in West Germany. He was allowed to go, with his wife, but – as is customary in countries of the Soviet empire – they were forced to leave their sons behind as hostages; these were not allowed to visit their parents together. In 1977, George, the younger, was allowed to go on a visit to Heilbronn, where his father was working, when the Czech authorities made a mistake; the older son, Jaroslav, asked for permission to go abroad, and the official to whom he applied for an exit visa, failing to spot the fact that his parents and brother were all at the time outside the country, granted it. (What happened to the erring official is not known, but it is safe to assume that it was nothing pleasant.)

The moment all four members of the family were safely together in Germany, they asked for political asylum there, which was granted. But that left the fiancée of Jaroslav, together with her daughter from a previous marriage, still in Prague, and when she asked for an exit visa for herself and the child it was refused.

Jaroslav therefore decided, in 1977, to return to Czechoslovakia and rescue her. He travelled on a German passport, and incognito; he managed while in Prague to get papers for her which entitled her to travel, with her child, *within* the Soviet empire. The three of them then went to Bulgaria, and the last stretch of the escape was to be a train journey into Turkey. Before they got there, they were taken off the train; the fiancée and child were sent back to Czechoslovakia under escort, and Jaroslav was arrested and held in Bulgaria.

He was interrogated for a fortnight, with repeated beatings; finally, he admitted his identity. He was sent back to Czechoslovakia, where his fiancée was then arrested. She was held for four months, being continuously interrogated; Jaroslav insisted that he, and he alone, was responsible for the attempted escape and would accept all the guilt for it, and she was then given a two-year suspended sentence. Jaroslav himself was kept in prison for months before being 'tried' – and the quotation-marks are even more appropriate than is usual in such cases, for he was refused permission to have a defence lawyer of his choice, and assigned one who was simultaneously a member of the tribunal which was trying him, a most convenient and economical arrangement for the authorities.

Jaroslav Javorsky was sentenced to thirteen years' imprisonment on charges which included illegal departure from Czechoslovakia, assisting another person to escape and 'betrayal of the Republic'. He was sentenced in a category which normally applies to habitual offenders and those convicted of violent crimes. He was, and is, held in Valdice prison, where he has been repeatedly beaten (his foot was broken in one of these attacks but he received no treatment for it and the consequent deformity will now be permanent); two hunger strikes have had no effect except more beatings.

Jaroslav Javorsky was adopted as a prisoner of conscience by Amnesty in 1978. His case was raised at the Madrid Conference which followed Helsinki; the West German foreign minister has repeatedly raised it with the Czech authorities, and Bonn, in a very rare if not unique act, has made him a German citizen.

The reason for the peculiar viciousness of his treatment must be obvious to anyone who knows anything about the way these things go in the Soviet empire. Javorsky senior was a Czech sports champion; such people, together with prominent artistic personalities and similar internationally known figures, are treated far better than the average citizen (provided, of course, that they comply with all the demands of their rulers). If one of them defects, it is a double blow to the authorities; first because it must mean that for all their favoured material treatment, they still prefer freedom, and second because their flight, because of their fame, is known all over the world.

In Mr Javorsky's case, there was an added reason for the brutality visited upon his son. There had been a similar scandal when Jaroslav Drobny, another leading Czech tennis player, left his native country to settle in the West (he won the Wimbledon championship); following that episode, other Czech tennis players were banned from playing abroad, and the ban lasted for several years. Mr Javorsky had long since ceased to play in championship tennis, but his name was presumably known, from his former triumphs, to all those who follow tennis in Czechoslovakia and many who do so abroad (he twice reached the semi-finals at Wimbledon).

Jaroslav Javorsky is ill: he has skin and eye infections and kidney disease. It seems unlikely that he will survive to the end of his sentence, which expires in 1991. When he went on hunger strike for the second time, the news got out. What followed is described in a letter from his parents:

The news about our son is terrible. A few days before he ended his hunger strike, they pulled him out of hospital and he was beaten up terribly. Afterwards, he was thrown for twenty-four hours into an unheated hole – that was at the beginning of March. He got no water and they took away all the vitamins he had received in hospital, but that was still not enough. They asked for a statement against our son from his neighbour [in prison], who was also on hunger strike. He was an elderly man and they burnt his eyelids and started to burn off his eyebrows. Our son had to watch, and this was perhaps worse for him than if he had been going through it himself. One cannot call them animals, for this would be to insult animals. How could anyone do such a thing? They obviously wanted to know how it was possible that the news of our son's hunger strike had been made public and had even penetrated abroad. That was the reason for their rage.

The Javorsky parents conclude their letter with a plea, from their son, that I could hardly disregard; but it is worth remembering by us who live in freedom how much courage it took him to make it. 'In spite of everything', they write, 'it is our son's wish that his treatment should be made known as much as possible.'*

*The Times* April 11th, 1985

* In February 1986, Javorsky was released and allowed to leave Czechoslovakia for the West. He had thus been a little less than nine years in prison.

# From the house of the dead

THE GULAG LIVES, as Balys Gajauskas, a Lithuanian resident of it, could testify. And he should know.

Gajauskas was born in Kaunas, Lithuania, in 1926. After the Second World War, he joined the Lithuanian Resistance to the continued Soviet occupation of his country. In 1948, he was arrested and charged with treason; he was sentenced to twenty-five years in a concentration camp. He served the whole quarter of a century, and before I go any further I think it is worth quoting the testimony of a fellow-prisoner who spent seventeen years in the Gulag and who after his release was allowed to emigrate. Kestutis Jokubynas describes him thus:

> . . . It was always easy to find Balys Gajauskas' spot. A small cabinet and shelf, ingeniously fastened under the bunk bed, were always crowded with books . . . That is why a sudden transfer was a cause of so much worry – will there be time to collect and to pack everything? . . . Gajauskas, more than any other prisoner, was subjected to endless transfers from one camp . . . to another. This was a punishment for having too many friends, or for 'plotting' . . . Balys was fond of the popular saying in the camps: 'The government cannot punish us as much as we can bear.' And he did bear it all . . . The inhuman conditions failed to break him down, he . . . is a vivid example of a true partisan fighter . . . He returned full of confidence in humanity.

After his release in May 1973, Gajauskas returned to Kaunas to live with his ill and aged mother. A few days after he settled there, he was forbidden to live in the town. He refused to leave his mother; both were then persistently harassed and fined. In December 1974, their home was searched; religious books were taken (Gajauskas is a Roman Catholic), together with personal papers and part of a translation into Lithuanian of Solzhenitsyn's *The Gulag Archipelago*. Gajauskas was interrogated by the KGB, but released.

A little over two years later, there was another search of the Gajauskas home; this time a camera was taken, as well as letters and a diary. He was taken to KGB headquarters for interrogation. He never returned.

Five months later, in July 1977, Mrs Gajauskas was notified that her son was to be put on trial, under a law dealing with 'anti-Soviet propaganda'. She heard nothing more, and the authorities went to extraordinary lengths to keep secret the very holding of the trial, let alone the course of it; Mrs Gajauskas herself was only notified that it was about to start – in Vilnius, some fifty miles away – the day before it did so, and the Central Telegraph Office in Kaunas was given instructions not to deliver any telegrams to Irena Dumbryte, Balys's fiancée.

A Belgian lawyer, Vincent van den Bosch, had earlier informed the Soviet ambassador in Brussels that he wished to act for the defence, and asked to be informed of the charges; he also asked for a visa to enable him to attend the trial. None of his requests was met.

As is the custom with Soviet show trials, the courtroom was packed with KGB agents and carefully selected spectators; only Mrs Gajauskas and three or four other independent spectators were allowed in.

Balys Gajauskas was charged with planning to translate Solzhenitsyn's *Gulag*, compiling a list of Lithuanian political prisoners, collecting data on the postwar Lithuanian resistance, and owning a Polish book called *Bolshevism* (which was presumably critical of the subject).

Even the 'defence' lawyer, appointed by the KGB, insisted that the prosecution had failed to prove the charges, and pointed out that they were anyway brought under the wrong law; Balys should have been charged under a section in which the maximum penalty was three years' imprisonment. Naturally, this was ignored; the prosecution asked for seven years. The judge – we even have his name, Radsiunas – sentenced Balys to ten years in the most severe category of concentration camp, to be followed by five years of internal exile.

Immediately after Gajauskas was sentenced, the Lithuanian Communist Party newspaper published an account of the trial; it consisted mainly of abuse of the defendant: '. . . his bloody accomplices . . . a hardened maniac . . . bourgeois nationalist bands . . . this chameleon has revealed his true face . . . His efforts are in vain . . . received what he deserved . . . mock the most sacred feelings . . . spit upon the achievements of the Soviet Fatherland . . . one more warning to those who want to raise their dirty and often bloodstained hands against us . . .'

And so the survivor of Stalin's and Khrushchev's Gulag went off to Brezhnev's, Andropov's, Chernenko's and now Gorbachov's. Before doing so, however, he made a statement which subsequently reached the West. It reviewed in detail the farce of the legal proceedings, then concluded with these words:

The Soviet leaders speak of peace today. But the concentration camps represent a no lesser threat to mankind than war; peace will remain impossible as long as we continue living in fear and slavery. My trial in Vilnius is an example of how one purposely destroys a man who reads books. Such a trial belongs to the list of the trials of the Inquisition . . . My crime consists of having thought independently and having valued democracy more highly than Communist dogmas. I committed a crime, because I wanted to make use of all the fruits of the human mind, and not only those that are officially allowed. Now, as I and my friends proceed on the road of trials and tribulations, I still have the flame of hope and liberty before my eyes . . . separated as we are for long years from our near ones and relatives, condemned as we are to a humiliating death, even here we remain faithful to the ideas of democracy and liberty.

And then, like Sonia following Raskolnikov to Siberia (except that Raskolnikov *had* committed a crime, unlike Gajauskas), Irena Dumbryte found out where Balys was being held, travelled 1,000 miles to his concentration camp, and insisted at the gate that she had come to marry him.

Nonplussed, the camp authorities told her to come back later. She did, dressed in a wedding-gown, in which she waited outside the fence, while the guards mocked and taunted her. She was then told that she could not see Balys, because he had recently had one visit (from his mother), and would have to wait a year for another.

She persisted, and next day she was allowed to see Balys; he was already emaciated. A civil marriage ceremony followed; both of them being Catholics, they asked to be allowed a Catholic wedding. The request was refused with mockery. The ceremony lasted fifteen minutes. Irena was then made to leave, and told that she could not see Balys again for a year. She persisted again; in the end, she was allowed a two-hour meeting; at the end of it, her husband was not even allowed to touch her hand. That was seven years ago; Gajauskas is still in the camp.

I quoted earlier the testimony of one of Balys Gajauskas's fellow-prisoners of the Gulag. I conclude with his final words:

Balys Gajauskas is returning to the Gulag Archipelago by a well-known route for another ten-year stint. Following that, there will be five years of exile, again far from his homeland. It takes unimaginable strength to survive all that. We, who have known Balys, cannot help grieving about his fate. But at the same time we have no doubt that he will withstand this new trial with fortitude and honour, as has been his way until now.

*The Times* June 19th, 1985

# 'My useful idiots'

O F THE TWELVE EPISODES of the BBC's new television
series, *Comrades*, only two have so far been screened,
and of these I have seen only one. It is therefore difficult, and
would probably be unfair, to come to any general conclusion
yet on the nature and quality of the series. But the producer,
Richard Denton, has just described, in a long article in the
*Listener* (November 21), not only his attitude to the task of
making, with official permission, a series of films in the
Soviet Union, each of which consists of a portrait of a single
individual, but also his method of working, the conditions
under which the series was made, and his comparisons of life
in the Soviet Union with life in the West. And as it is, I think,
perfectly reasonable to deduce that the whole series will
reflect its producer's views (how, indeed, could it not?), it is
with his views that I shall today concern myself.

His principal contention is that the people of the Soviet
Union are much like people in other countries, particularly
Britain. In one sense, so obvious as to be practically a
tautology, he is of course right; I have no doubt that most
Soviet citizens love their children, want peace, obey the law
and prefer good weather to bad. But the system under which
they live does have a number of rather striking differences
with ours; of these differences Mr Denton is naturally aware,
which means that to maintain his thesis without denying that
truth (he is plainly not a communist sympathizer or fellow-
traveller), he has to make use of a curious form of
words.

When he makes or implies a comparison, 'we', 'the West' and 'the BBC' are the human beings contained in his reference, and he would have us believe that 'they', 'the Russians' and 'the State Committee for Television and Radio' are likewise the individuals thus collectively described. But they are not, and in a totalitarian society could not possibly be. A quotation from Mr Denton's article will help to make my point clear.

> I had noticed when filming in schools [Mr Denton made the BBC films about Radley and Kingswood] that teachers became increasingly suspicious, if not downright hostile, when they perceived that the production crew were making professional arrangements directly with the pupils rather than using the teacher-figure as an intermediary. Exactly the same response is observable in the USSR, and the authorities never felt happy with our insistence upon making our own phone calls to contributors, establishing our own contacts, making our own arrangements.

*Exactly* the same response? Does he mean that the teachers at Radley and Kingswood were conscious of the fact that if something displeasing to the British government had been said on his British programmes they might shortly find themselves in a prison, a madhouse or a concentration camp? And if he does not mean that, what *does* he mean?

What he means, of course, is that in Britain as well as the Soviet Union those in authority do not like unauthorized things being done. But that true statement leads only to a wholly false implication; that the *nature* of authority in Britain is similar to that in the Soviet Union. And it isn't, not even slightly.

Let us for a few more lines continue Mr Denton's paragraph where I left it:

> The Russians have little reason to trust the Western media, and in fact they trust us as much as we trust them: not at all.

Again, the quickness of the hand nearly deceives the eye. Western media distort the news; Soviet media distort the news; both true; therefore, give or take an emphasis or two, Western media and Soviet media are essentially the same. But there is no valid comparison between a system which, with all its faults and abuses, permits a wide variety of opinions, including those unremittingly critical of the authorities, and a system in which only one view is allowed, and those who challenge it are immediately visited with the full force of a savage law.

The key to Mr Denton's fundamental misconception of the nature of a totalitarian society can be found in another passage from the same article. He defends himself from the charge of meekly accepting Soviet restrictions by saying that he did not anyway want to make programmes critical of the Soviet Union, because 'The politics of the Soviet system had already been dealt with constantly and at length in the Western media'. But in a totalitarian system *everything* is politics; that is virtually a definition of totalitarianism.

There was an episode in last Sunday's programme which further illuminates Mr Denton's *Listener* article and offers little hope that the remainder of the series will be any more responsible. It showed a young man being called up for his two years of military service, and scenes from his induction and basic training. When he paraded before the board which reviews all Soviet conscripts, he was asked his attitude to military service; he replied, 'Service is an honourable profession and it makes a man of you.' This theme was repeated again and again by the recruit's mother and father, who said things like 'He must serve and do his duty to the Motherland' and 'Everyone has to serve, it's a Sacred Duty'. (The capitals were in the sub-titles.)

Now for anything I know, or Mr Denton knows, those were the very sentiments held by young Krylov and his parents. But if they weren't – if, say, he or his mother or father thought that their country was run by ruthless im-

perialists and that it would be a moral crime to serve in the
Red Army in Afghanistan or Czechoslovakia – they would
have had to be heroes of the stature of Solzhenitsyn to say so.
And they knew it. If Mr Denton did not know it, he ought to
be ashamed of himself. And if he *did* know it, he ought to be
considerably more ashamed of himself.

Does he seriously believe (I think he does) that when the
day's filming at young Krylov's barracks was finished, the
new soldier was not coached in what he was to say and do
when the filming resumed on the morrow? And the Krylov
parents at home, awaiting a letter as any Western parents of a
soldier son would; does Mr Denton suppose that there was
no prompter for Krylov senior's little speech about how
good it would be if all the nations agreed, so that no armies
would be needed?

What we have here is not, I insist, fellow-travelling; a very
different form of *trahison des clercs* is at work. It is a kind of
monstrous vanity. Mr Denton knows (and if he doesn't, let
him read Professor Paul Hollander's *Political Pilgrims*) how
many pitiful dupes have gone to totalitarian countries and
swallowed, in some cases with nothing but good intentions,
the lies they were provided with in ample measure. But Mr
Denton believes that *he*, unlike all his predecessors, is cleverer than the men who spend their entire lives deceiving men
like him, and who are trained in their job far more thoroughly than young Krylov was trained in the use of the Kalash-
nikov and the bayonet. He cannot be such a fool as to believe
that the Soviet authorities agreed to let him into the Soviet
Union, and to shoot miles of film there, without believing
that they would gain by what the British viewers saw. But he
can be, and is, such a fool as to believe that he could outwit
them. He condemns himself when, at the end of his article,
he sums up by saying that 'the preconceptions and prejudices
of the Russians about Westerners are *exactly* [my italics]
matched by our preoccupations and prejudices about them'.
There could be no better proof of his failure than that he has

been led, by those whose task it was to lead him there, to that conclusion.

*The Times* November 29th, 1985

# Weighing their words

EVERYBODY GRUMBLES ABOUT the *New York Times*, said Mark Twain (or possibly it was some other fellow who looked like him), but nobody does anything about it.

A few weeks ago, visiting New York, I did something about it; I brought back the Sunday edition. That, I may say, is an achievement more lightly claimed than carried out; indeed, it could scarcely be carried out at all. I weighed it when I got home; it turned the scale at 6lb 11oz. I then counted the pages; there were 402 in broadsheet (the size of a page from *The Times*) and 458 in tabloid. In addition, there were separate advertisement insertions totalling another 64 pages. (I did not, I discovered, have the complete edition; certain sections, of local suburban interest, are distributed only in the relevant places and not in the metropolitan circulation area. I am most *frightfully* obliged.)

The first thought that occurred to me in contemplating this experiment in acromegaly (actually, the *second* thought, the first being of murder) was to wonder how it ever gets delivered. I pictured the traditional scene of the paper-boy, style of Norman Rockwell, whistling cheerfully as he pedals on his round and tossing the paper, with well-practised aim, on to the doorsteps of his employers' customers, but apart from the obvious hazards, such as a boss-shot going through a window and killing the entire family at breakfast, together with the necessity for the paper-boy to be a trained shot-putter of more or less Olympics quality, there must be a problem of stock; no bicycle basket or saddle-bag ever invented could hold more than two of these monsters at a time, and the paper-boy would therefore be obliged to go back and forth for fresh supplies so often that he could hardly finish his round before Wednesday.

Possibly New Yorkers like to read the Sunday paper on Wednesday, but that brings me to the next point, the reading. Our Sunday papers are traditionally read in bed, and I have no reason to suppose that American habits in these matters differ from British. The difficulty of reading a newspaper which weighs as much as a combination of the *Oxford Dictionary of Quotations* and a very large haddock can be got round, of course, by separating the paper into its several (*very* several) sections, but that only solves one problem to pose another: on enquiring at the New York Missing Persons Bureau I learnt that at least twenty people a year are reported to have vanished from the city without trace, only to be found (in some cases years later) suffocated under a blanket consisting of 924 pages of the *New York Times*. (At the Welfare Department I discovered that there are constant complaints from tramps who have wrapped themselves in the Sunday paper before settling down for a winter's night on a park bench, only to find that it rendered them so hot that they were obliged to get up and roll in the snow in order to avoid spontaneous combustion.)

Now let us examine the evidence, taking it section by section. Section 1, itself divided into two parts, contains the main news. It has sixty-eight pages in all, starting with news of the president's legislative plans and ending with engagement and wedding announcements, one of the latter appearing under the memorable headline 'Sibyl Peyer has Nuptials' which sounds like a very unpleasant insinuation, of the kind that in our country is to be found not in respectable newspapers but chalked on the walls of school playgrounds. There was also 'Dentist affianced to Miss Copeland', and 'Susan L. Breshears Exchanges Vows With Birch Bayh 3rd, a Fellow Lawyer'. (Mr Geoffrey Wheatcroft has proposed that a new typographical symbol should be designed, which would be understood to mean 'I have not made this up'. Consider it used here.)

Section 2 is Arts and Leisure; there are thirty-eight pages of it. The main story on the front page is headed 'New Museums Harmonize with Art'; they do like their headlines exciting in New York, I must say. Still, since most of the advertisements in the theatre section seem to be for British plays and players, we shouldn't complain.

Section 3 is Business: sixty pages, of which the last thirty are advertisements for Business Opportunities and jobs, mainly managerial. Section 4 is 'The Week in Review', which has twenty-four pages, and for reasons not clear to me contains the leading articles, and on page 22 at that.

Section 5 is Sport; thirty-two pages; sample headline 'Hamill Assails Skating Trend'. (The cure for mixed metaphors, I have always found, is for the patient to be obliged to draw a picture of the result. I challenge the *New York Times* to draw a picture of somebody assailing a trend.)

Section 6 is the Magazine, equivalent to our Sunday colour supplements; in the week under discussion, it came in two parts, pp. 112 and 88 respectively. Section 7 is the Book Review, in forty-eight pages. Main headline on the front page is 'Writing for the Movies Is Harder Than It Looks'; writing headlines for the *New York Times* must be a hell of a lot easier.

Next comes, in Section 8, Real Estate. It is in two parts; of its eighty-eight pages, eighty are entirely filled by advertisements, and of the remaining eight, three are at least half given over to advertising; well, I never said the *New York Times* wasn't profitable.

Section 9 contains no editorial matter at all, its forty-eight pages being composed exclusively of employment advertising; the section goes by the traditional title of 'Help Wanted', and there must be several thousand jobs going, from Accountants to Word Processor Operators.

Section 10 is Travel; forty-two pages. Section 11 is the *Long Island Weekly*; twenty-six pages. (The last forty-nine pages of the Real Estate section are devoted entirely to Long Island.)

Section 11 comprises the Regional Weeklies, and was therefore, as I said, missing from my copy. Section 12 (eighty pages) is devoted to Education, which could hardly be said of those American universities which give degrees in journalism, or at any rate in headline-writing.

The remainder includes two sections which seem to be *hors série*, one, of forty-four pages, being an advertisement supplement on the theme of Home & Garden, the other, in twenty-four pages, containing details, for the week ahead, of television and radio programmes, theatres, concerts and exhibitions. And finally, there is a scatter of inserted advertisements and free offers, and a sixty-four page British advertising supplement, from which the reader can learn, among much other interesting information about Britain, that Manchester Airport is 'close to Scotland . . . and, of course, London'.

Analysis finished, I can now throw it away (though I shall need a demolition contractor rather than a dustman) before commenting. And the comment is obvious: who needs it? Who needs a newspaper, even a Sunday newspaper, which would ensure, if a purchaser were to drop it on his foot, that he would never walk unaided again?

In all, there must be upwards of a couple of million words in the thing. No doubt the readers are not expected to read all of them, and no doubt those uninterested in sport, say, or business, will throw out those sections without looking at them, as those not looking for work will ignore the 'Help Wanted'. Still, you do not have to be Leonardo to be interested in art and books, politics and economics, travel and interior decoration, schools and the property market; how are you to get through the acreage before you and still attend to the duties and pleasures of the day?

Newspapers expand editorially in direct proportion to the volume of advertising they can sell; since there seems to be no limit to the number of advertisers looking for space in the Sunday edition of the *New York Times*, many a forest has to be ravished weekly to provide the newsprint to accommodate them all, plus the editorial matter called forth by the newly-allotted pages. What is more, the *New York Times*, in common with all the 'quality' press in the United States, is so badly designed and laid out that even the keenest reader must miss dozens of articles and news reports that might well be of interest to him.

All newspapers live by advertising; in that respect British ones are no different from American. Presumably, if there were the same volume of advertising seeking space in this newspaper, it would expand accordingly. Does gigantism, however, make for better newspapers? On the whole, I suspect it does not. I wish the *New York Times* a long and prosperous future; I look forward to many a happy Sunday in New York, eventually enlivened by news of the first lawsuit leading to damages for loss sustained when a careless Sunday reader drops his copy out of the window and wrecks a passing truck; but I think this is one road down which I do not wish Britain to follow the United States.*

*The Times* May 15th, 1985

---

* Among the responses to this article there was a letter in which the correspondent informed me that just such litigation had already taken place; the plaintiff was a woman whose pet dog had been killed by a direct hit from a newspaper aimed at the porch on which the unfortunate beast had been sunning itself. My informant was unable to tell me how the case had been decided.

# These Germans and those Germans

THERE STANDS IN West Berlin (or did when I was last there, though some enthusiastic *Ostpolitiker* may have had it pulled down as too provocative) a memorial to those who died in the Berlin Airlift. I have an uneasy feeling that a substantial proportion of my younger readers may not know what that was, so I had better explain.

In 1949, Stalin wanted to incorporate West Berlin into his empire, but would not risk direct military aggression. He therefore ordered that all rail and road links between the Western zones of the city and West Germany should be cut, assuming that the free island would rapidly be starved and frozen into submission. He had, however, underestimated the West's determination to resist Soviet expansion. (By now, it has become practically impossible for a Soviet leader to underestimate the West's determination, but that is another and sadder story.) A gigantic effort was mounted to keep West Berlin supplied by air with everything it needed in the way of food, fuel and other essential supplies; some idea of the magnitude of the operation may be gathered from the fact that if a plane overshot the Berlin runway it could not go round and come in again, but had to return to base and start again next day, so tight was the schedule of landings. (I believe it was one plane every seven minutes, day and night.)

Older readers should resume here. The memorial is an elegant, towering column, consisting of three 'ribs'; these symbolize the three airports that kept West Berlin alive and free for the period (a year, beginning in May 1948) of the blockade. The airports were Tempelhof, Tegel and Gatow, and the memorial commemorates the seventy-six people – forty British, thirty-one American and five German – who were killed in the inevitable (but happily few) crashes or in related accidents.

Have faith; there is a point to all this reminiscence, and I shall come to it by and by, but first a little more information. The population of West Berlin at the time of the blockade was more than 2,000,000, which fact alone demonstrates the size of the task before the rescuers. The man responsible for the airlift was General Lucius Clay, the American military governor of the city; the technical side of the operation was devised and constructed by a team led by General W. H. Tunner. The Soviet authorities offered a ration-book to anyone in West Berlin (remember that this was more than a decade before the Wall went up) who would ask for one; of the two million West Berliners only 60,000, from first to last, took the Soviet bribe.

Ten years after the blockade and the airlift ended, there was a ceremony of commemoration in the city; General Clay made a speech, saying, 'No principle is more important to the free world than that Berlin should remain free.' In saying that, he echoed the words he had used more than ten years earlier, when the blockade began: 'When Berlin falls, West Germany will be next. If we mean to hold Europe against Communism we must not budge . . . I believe that the future of democracy requires us to stay.'

Hang on to those words; they will become relevant when I get to the point. So, even more, will the words used at the anniversary ceremony by Willy Brandt, then Burgomaster of West Berlin, addressing the western allies – America, Britain and France – who saved the city. 'We stand in your debt,' he said; 'you must know that we have not forgotten it and will never forget.'

The bells of history sounded for me recently, when I read Henry Stanhope's despatch from Berlin; the name of Gatow sprang from the page to set them ringing. Gatow, the smallest of the three airfields used in the salvation of West Berlin, is now an RAF firing-range; there is further irony in the fact that, as the report pointed out, it lies near the Berlin Wall. And it is in the news at the moment because – well, let Henry take up the story:

> Angry West Berliners who claim that their peace and prosperity are being shattered . . . are preparing to take their case to the European Court of Human Rights . . . About 800 people who live near the airfield in a leafy West Berlin suburb are objecting to the noise and other environmental pollution from the range . . . while politicians in West Germany have already begun to echo their plea . . . Herr Reiner Geulen, a Berlin lawyer . . . says that . . . the . . . dispute . . . has . . . badly affected the value of the £120,000 houses in an upper-middle class estate.

And now I think I have come to the point at last. There are several morals to this story (one of them is 'Never underestimate the greed, selfishness and treachery that the rich are capable of'), but the most important is also the most obvious. We have come a long way in the quarter of a century that has elapsed since General Clay said that 'No principle is more important to the free world than that Berlin should remain free', and Willy Brandt assured the West that Berlin would never forget. Clay died in 1978, but I do not suppose he abandoned his view of Berlin, even on his deathbed. Herr Brandt is still alive; how stands he, in relation to his words on the same occasion?

I imagine he, too, holds to his former view. If so, would he mind nipping over to the 'leafy West Berlin suburb' of Gatow and suggesting to the inhabitants that there are worse things than finding that the value of your house is depreciating because the RAF needs to practise saving you?

It is not very pleasant to live next to a firing-range, as, oddly enough, I am in a position to know. When I was a child, during the Second World War, I lived for a time in a

house on the edge of Primrose Hill. On that grassy knoll
there was an anti-aircraft battery, and on Blitz nights it fired
every few seconds, with a bang that each time not only
knocked a good deal off the value of the premises but very
nearly brought the premises to the ground. It was a long time
ago, and my memories are hazy, but I do have a distinct
recollection that neither I nor anybody else in the family felt
that the guns should be silenced, let alone that we should go
to court for an injunction to silence them. On the contrary, I
am sure that we were whole-heartedly on the side of the
gunners, and no less fervently opposed to those whom the
gunners were trying – heedless of what they might be doing
to property values or the environment – to shoot down.

What is the German for *nous avons changé tout cela*? I think it
is *Schweinerei*, at any rate in this matter. Do the inhabitants of
Gatow's leafy suburb ever pass by the Airlift Memorial? If
they do, do they have no idea of what the third of its ribs
refers to? Come to that, do they ever notice the Berlin Wall
itself? Would they prefer to live on the other side of it, and if
not why not? And do they suppose that if they *did* live in the
same state of helotry as their fellow-Germans from the dark
side of the moon they would be able to take their government to court to protect the value of their houses? Or that
they could induce a judge to order their government to give
up its military activities?

We can ask some even dafter questions. Do the Gatovians
think that, moving among the people on the other side of the
Wall, Henry Stanhope would be able to report that 'politicians . . . have already begun to echo their plea for human
rights'? Or that 'a Berlin lawyer who is representing the
protesters . . . dismisses any suggestion that the residents are
trying to bring a test case against the legality of the . . .
government . . .'?

One solution to this problem would be for the comman-
ding officer at RAF Gatow to make a frightful mistake one
morning and absent-mindedly order a massive prang ('Oh, I

say, I'm most *terribly* sorry') on the £120,000 houses of Gatow instead of the firing-range. Perhaps that is too extreme a method of making the point. If so, let him order a fatigue-squad to paint, on the western side of the Berlin Wall, Goethe's words: 'Possessions lost, something lost; Honour lost, much lost; Courage lost, everything lost'. Better still, let him have the words painted on the base of the Airlift Memorial.

★ ★ ★

I have had a good many letters about my recent column concerning the inhabitants of the 'leafy suburb' of Gatow, in West Berlin.

One of them came from Gatow itself. The writer was Oberleutnant G. von Lützow, and his letter read, in full and *sic*: 'This is our answer on you Mr Levin! The Gatower people! Are you Jewish? We think so!'

The 'this' referred to by the Herr Oberleutnant was a leaflet, which I shall discuss in a moment, but first I am obliged to confirm his worst fears; yes, I *am* Jewish. What is more, I am one of the dreaded Elders of Zion, engaged in taking over the world. As a first step, I have been instructed to gather a band of like-minded members of the Hebrew persuasion, and then to don impenetrable disguise, travel to Gatow, kidnap the Oberleutnant and forcibly circumcise him. What this will do to his standing in the shower room of the local rugger club I dare not imagine, but orders, as some people in his country used to say, are orders.

Now to the leaflet, which may henceforth be cited as Von Lützow's Reply. It is put out by an organization called the *Nationalistische Front*, and for those of my readers who know no German, I willingly translate: it means Nationalist Front, and the organizers helpfully abbreviate this to NF. The slogan of the German NF is *Nur der organisierte Wille bedeutet*

*Macht*; this is a little more difficult than the name itself, so I am again most willing to translate. It means 'Only the organized Will means power'.

I dare say. The rest of the NF's leaflet is couched in the kind of terms you would expect from that introduction. 'All foreigners out!' 'Protection of life instead of Capital!' 'Prevent usury and speculation!' The organizers declare that ('Germany for the Germans!') they have stood up and found their pride again – the pride to be German; they refer to their enemies and their enemies' German collaborators, and they put the adjective in inverted commas, to show that such people are not really German at all.

*Und so weiter*, which is the German for et cetera. There is much for comment here, and I shall duly provide some, but first there is a small but troubling matter to dispose of. Oberleutnant von Lützow gives no indication of his age; it is therefore not possible to tell whether he is a former member of the Wehrmacht or a serving officer of the Bundeswehr. If it is the latter, it might be a good idea for somebody with a higher rank than Oberleutnant to have a word with him; I don't know whether political campaigning is permitted in the German Armed Forces, but even if it is I imagine that an *Augenbraue*, or eyebrow, might be raised at the terms in which his favoured party couch their appeal to the German masses.*

There is more irony in this business than the Herr Oberleutnant may be aware of. I think I may claim to have been the most pro-German journalist in this country for the last three decades. I have repeatedly said that the nature and quality of the Federal Republic's rebirth is the most remarkable and heartening phenomenon of the postwar world, and has few parallels in any period of history. For the Germans to go, in hardly more than a decade, from the stinking ruins of

---

* The Oberleutnant proved to be on the retired list; not a moment too soon, if you ask me.

Nazism to a truly cleansed democratic republic is a tribute not only to them but to the human race and its powers of regeneration.

Look at the fate of totalitarian parties, Communist and neo-Nazi, in the Federal Republic. Originally they were banned, and the constitutional provision against them is still in force, but for some years now those which have not been too blatant about their nature and aims (there is no reference to Jews as such anywhere in Oberleutnant von Lützow's NF leaflet) have been tolerated. And they have been tolerated for two excellent reasons.

First, it has come to be thought better, in a soundly-based democratic state, for anti-democratic organizations to be allowed to do their work in daylight rather than in the dark, where they may prove to be ultimately more dangerous. (In Britain, neither the National Front nor the Socialist Workers Party is banned, and I hope that neither ever will be.)

The second reason for the toleration of anti-democratic *groupuscules* in Federal Germany is provided by the strictness of the Constitutional Court which is charged with ruling on applications for an order of prohibition made by the government of the day. The court has shown itself to be very firm in its interpretation of the provisions under which a party may be banned; the upshot has been that even some of the vilest organizations have been left alone, provided they stay within the law and also, even though only barely, within decency.

It is not, therefore, a love of paradox that prompts me to welcome Oberleutnant von Lützow's letter and leaflet rather than shuddering at them. For they remind me of how insignificant in Germany his kind are, how little progress they have made in their forlorn desire to turn the clock back to half-past hell, how firm are the foundations of modern German democracy, how weird would be the thought that free Germany should ever again fight on the opposite side to Britain or France.

There will always be the occasional Oberleutnant von

Lützow, as there will always be an NF in Germany and also in Britain. But they do not matter. What does matter is that in neither country will they ever play any significant part in the political process, just as their mirror-images on the left (at least when they sail under their own colours) will ever do so. We in Britain may well feel proud of the immense antiquity of our parliamentary institutions and freedoms. I rather think that the Germans have at least as much right to feel proud of the extraordinary youth of theirs. Meanwhile, it is legitimate to ask the other protestors of Gatow whether *they* are proud of the company they are keeping.

*The Times* September 24th, 1985 and October 4th, 1985

# Bad dogs and Englishmen

SELL YOUR AUSTRALIAN shares *now*; revolution is about to break out there, and the End of Civilization As We Know It will almost certainly follow. For the Australian government has just announced that at least 1,300,000 kangaroos are going to be killed in a drive to control their numbers – which, when last counted, totalled some 17 million, or almost exactly one and a bit kangaroos for every man, woman and child in the country.

Let us consider this uproar calmly. Those who think that 17 million kangaroos are a bit too much of a good thing argue that if they are not culled many more will die, and in worse ways, owing to a lack of suitable foods; this argument is put forward first, though if those putting it forward weren't afraid that the ecologico-conservationists would start culling *them*, they would admit that it should really come second to the claim that kangaroos are in any case a pest and ought to be stamped out.

The uproar that will ensue, even without that last point, is of the anthropomorphic kind familiar in Britain. Anyone who has never been kicked by a kangaroo is quite likely to think of them as merry creatures with their young sticking their heads out of the familiar pouches to make terribly amusing remarks; if A. A. Milne had never existed, it would not be in the least necessary, much less advisable, to invent him. I have no reason to suppose that Australians, though presumably not brought up on Winnie-the-Pooh, will be any less given to going ooh-ah when they see the kangaroos on television just before the machine-guns open up.

Now the more suspicious of you will already have guessed that I have introduced today's subject with an illustration from the Antipodes in order to trap you into thinking yourselves superior to those silly Australians, with their fuss about a lot of kangaroos being killed, so that I can triumphantly demonstrate, with evidence concealed till the last moment, that we are every bit as silly. Not so; I propose to demonstrate that we are very much sillier, and perhaps, by the time I have finished, that we are something rather worse than silly.

Down in Devon, which is a lot nearer than Australia, at any rate from where I am sitting, a boy of thirteen was recently savaged by an alsatian. He had, it seems, appeared on a doorstep, curiously garbed, and cried, as the door was opened, 'Trick or Treat'. (This suggests that the incident must have happened at Hallowe'en, and that the pleasant American custom of children making such visits, to be given bars of chocolate and the like by those who prefer to treat rather than be tricked, has crossed the Atlantic.) The dog leaped upon him and bit him frightfully; the child had wounds to the groin which required twenty stitches.

Later, there were court proceedings, and the dog's owner was ordered to have it destroyed; in making the order, the magistrate said that he did so 'in view of the savagery of the attack and the dreadful injuries sustained'. No; not even the most suspicious among you can have guessed what I am leading up to. For miles around, sympathy is being expressed, money raised, protests lodged, *on behalf of the dog*.

Moreover, the dog's owner has been giving tongue. It appears that she is sure that Danko, for such is the beast's name, acted as it did only 'because he was frightened'. It further appears that the hound is 'gentle and placid'. Nay, 'he is wonderful with children' – so much so, apparently, that 'I never worry about him when strangers visit'.

Well, you should, dearie, and you should start the worrying as soon as possible. You should also notice the striking discrepancy between your *claim* that the animal is 'gentle and placid' and the *fact* that it caused 'dreadful injuries'. You should also decide whether it is absolutely correct to describe as wonderful with children a creature which has just done its level best to eat a thirteen-year-old, and succeeded to a remarkable extent. While you are about it, you should explain why, when a child accidentally frightens a dog, it ought not to occasion surprise when the dog tears bits out of him. And to end this catalogue of shoulds, *you should stop referring to your horrible thing as 'he'.*

Danko, as I say, was – is – an alsatian; these loathsome animals are literally untamable, and their ownership should be controlled as closely as is that of firearms. But that is not the most important aspect of this matter. The owner of a dog which has horribly savaged a human being, and a child at that, might be expected to announce immediately, without waiting for the law, that it is to be destroyed, and to add to the announcement – or indeed to precede it with – an unqualified public apology to the victim.

That is to say, such actions might be expected by those who were not sunk in the odious sentimentality which in this country passes for an attitude to animals. But as far as I can see, most of this country's population is not only sunk in such an attitude, but drowned full fathom five in it.

Those who persuade themselves that animals are human beings will sooner or later come to believe that human beings are animals. Why is it so difficult to get into the heads of people like this dog-owner the simple fact, which needs no emotion attached to it (though I cannot see why it should not have plenty), that a dog which has all but dismembered a child ought not, in any circumstances, to have the opportunity to do it again?

It is, I think, yet another outbreak of the greatest plague of our time, that failure of imagination which leads to the drying-up of the healing salve of empathy. From that atrophy of fellow-feeling have in this century sprung things far more terrible than a failure to distinguish carefully enough between the rights of a boy and of a dog; I do not, after all, suppose the dog-owner wasn't sorry for the child.

But she was very much too sorry for the dog. There is a variant of the Pathetic Fallacy at work here, attributing human feelings and qualities to animals, and the result is a dangerous skewing of the perspective, so that the dog's rights become equal to the boy's, if not greater, and in no time graffiti will have appeared on every wall in the area: 'Danko is innocent OK'; 'No capital punishment for dogs'; 'We demand second bites for all'.

Two legs good, four legs better. Not all those who have contributed to the dog's defence fund are curs, but they should ask themselves why they identify with an animal rather than a person, and what this says about their own limitations, their own shrinking from becoming fully human, with all that that implies of pain and fear and effort and hope and joy. When they have finished, they might also cast an eye over Dante:

> You were not born to live the lives of brutes,
> But virtue to pursue, and knowledge high.

*The Times* January 29th, 1986

# With Noddy in the sky

A FEW WEEKS AGO I flew from Zürich to London by British Airways, and I have a complaint to make. It is not, however, one of the more familiar complaints; the flight was only a few minutes late, I was not obliged to wait for the next one because of overbooking, my luggage was delivered as safely as I was, and the aisle seat I asked for turned out to be on the aisle. What I am complaining about – and the complaint is not so trivial as it will at first appear – was that I was told nine times (I counted them) in an hour and a half that everybody involved wished I would have, or was having, or had had, an enjoyable flight. The captain told us that he hoped we would enjoy the flight, the flight officer urged us to relax and enjoy the flight, the chief steward promised faithfully to do everything in his power to make the flight enjoyable. They all did it several times, in various tenses and occasionally in the subjunctive, and they did not fail, when we landed, to enquire most solicitously as to whether we had enjoyed the flight.

Acting as spokesman for the entire complement of passengers in a full Boeing 757, I now state plainly that we did *not* enjoy the flight. But the reason had nothing to do with any deficiencies in the service or the driving, for there were no such deficiencies. The reason is that enjoyment is entirely irrelevant to flying; it makes no more sense for the crew to ask whether we enjoyed the flight than for them to ask whether we enjoy our shoelaces, or four o'clock, or teaspoons.

This is not the same as saying that flying is unpleasant, though as a matter of fact it is. As aircraft have become bigger and faster and more numerous, and the number of passengers has multiplied, flying has become more and more exhausting and disagreeable. The discomfort is greater, the noise worse, the inefficiency of airports beyond all bearing; and the food is invariably filth. (It is widely believed that the food on British Airways is worse than that on the aeroplanes of other nations, but the belief is a myth. British planes serve British filth, but French ones serve French filth, and American ones American filth; I have no doubt at all that Air Bulgaria serves Bulgarian filth, and the only time I flew by El Al they served kosher filth. What is more, there is no fundamental difference between classes, except that in first class they serve first-class filth, in economy they serve economy filth, and in business or club class they serve business or club filth.)

My objection to the incessant harping on 'enjoyment', however, is based on something quite different from the actual drawbacks of flying. It is yet another manifestation of what I have termed the Nanny State. For nobody on a train or a bus talks about enjoying the trip, and the passengers would think any official demented if he started to do so. Only in aeroplanes (and I think that the phenomenon is confined very largely to the flights of the English-speaking world) is the question raised.

In the early days of regular civil flights – up to the mid-1950s say – flying was so unusual an experience for most travellers that the airlines felt obliged to reassure their passengers that it was perfectly safe for them to be several miles up with no visible means of support, and by constantly telling them that they were enjoying themselves, or could be doing so, it was felt that the necessary reassurance was supplied.

That, however, was a long time ago, and by now flying is a perfectly ordinary and familiar activity for hundreds of millions of people. Yet the airlines seem unable to remove the swaddling-clothes, unwilling to admit that we have grown up. They regard their function of carrying us swiftly through the skies – an entirely prosaic and businesslike proceeding – as *giving us all a treat*, and we all know to whom treats are given: to children. The truth is that airlines think of their planes as hospices for cases of terminal arrested development. (If you want a symbol of the attitude, look at the hysteria invariably generated by a change in the flight attendants' uniforms; Nanny has changed her blue apron for a white one. But Nanny still knows best.)

I have mentioned before the American airline on which the safety demonstration is preceded by an announcement to the effect that it is being given 'so you should know what to do in an unusual situation'. That is only taking imbecility a step or two further than the average airline patter; how many times have you heard an aircraft's captain announce that if it were not for the impenetrable cloud beneath the plane, stretching to the horizon all round, Clermont-Ferrand or Kansas City or Dover would be clearly visible to the passengers sitting on the left-hand side? I am sure that children can be thrilled by the news that they are flying over invisible cities, as they can be thrilled by the fact that a Christmas tree with presents on it is coming down the aisle, called 'Duty-Free Shopping', but it seems impossible to persuade those in charge of the airlines that the grown-ups are less easy to please and, more to the point, that it is unnecessary to feel obliged to please them every five minutes, or indeed at all. (As for the 'In-flight entertainment', I shall say nothing about it, burning with a hard, gemlike flame as I do so.)

In all the years I have been flying – I suppose I have used two or three score airlines for a good many hundreds of flights to a couple of dozen countries – I have only once been on an aeroplane on which the passengers were invited to complete a questionnaire; it was an American airline, and the questions were all directed to the quality of the aircraft and the service; there was no space for general comments, let alone questions designed to enable the passenger to say what he thought of the airline's entire approach to the business of flying. I am occasionally stopped by a damsel in the baggage-claim area at Heathrow who wants me to answer some questions, doubtless to while away the hours, but her interrogation seems designed to find out only such mundane things as what proportion of the arriving passengers are natives and what proportion visitors, and to discover how the categories break down between travel for business and for pleasure; useful, I dare say, but no help to the regular patron of airlines who wants to tell those in charge that they are getting it wrong, and have been doing so for upwards of a quarter of a century.

In which, of course, they are not alone; whence my belief that the airlines exhibit only an extreme form of the growing tendency, on the part of large national or commercial orga-nizations, to treat their applicants or customers as children, and children, moreover, who need protecting *from themselves*. In the case of airlines, I wonder more of them don't reintroduce the old custom (dating from a time when aircraft were less well pressurized than they are today) of giving us all a sweet to suck. Then, it stopped our ears from popping; now, it would be to remind us of our infant status – be a good boy and you will get a sweetie.

But I don't want a sweetie. I want to be treated as a responsible adult, who is perfectly willing to fasten his seat-belt, put his hand luggage under the seat in front of him and refrain from smoking in the non-smoking areas, but who doesn't much want to be offered a rattle, a teddy-bear or a plastic spaceman, and doesn't at all want to be told every ten minutes that he should be enjoying himself at the lovely party, and that if he isn't it's his own fault.

*The Times* August 3rd, 1985

# Catalogue aria

A CATALOGUE COMES UNBIDDEN through the letter-box; I examine it idly at the breakfast-table. It offers useful or necessary things like luggage, toolkits, domestic electrical apparatus, kitchen equipment, furniture, stationery and office sundries, toys, clothes. It also contains – well, let it speak for itself:

> Ready in a couple of minutes. That's how long it takes for your nails to dry with this battery operated nail drier. Having painted your nails, place them under the drier, press the panel switch, wait a couple of minutes and your nails will be ready for action. Batteries not supplied. £14.95.

There is a photograph of this indispensable device; it is made of red plastic, shaped rather like a hamburger in its bun, and measures perhaps four or five inches across. A hand, with painted nails, is seen making use of it.

On the next page, there is an Earring Caddy. The anonymous author of the prose continues:

> Keeping earrings together. Earrings often get lost around the bedroom or left around the house. Gather them together with this beautiful little brass Earring Caddy. The lid is covered in burgundy leather and it features an in-built mirror. There are six compartments for your earrings and your initials are gold blocked on the exterior.

The Earring Caddy will set you back only £3.95; a snip, I should say. The Shower Caddy costs a little more – £7.95 –

but then, 'Taking a shower can be made so much easier with this clever little Shower Caddy'. It is, we learn, 'Made from durable plastic; there are two shelves to take shampoo, face flannel, conditioner, etc. and a soap dish'. We are assured that, 'You'll wonder how you got by without it'.

The same is true, only more so, of the 'dual-purpose meter that inspects your plant's health'; the two purposes are respectively a moisture-tester and a light-measure. Readings 'are displayed instantly', and presumably if they show a deficiency you no less instantly provide your plant with more moisture or more light. (Now at last I know what Goethe's last words were: 'More moisture'.)

Finally, there is 'Wet Tunes', a waterproof radio that is fixed on the shower wall with Velcro, so that, 'When you are singing in the shower, you can now be accompanied by the music of your choice, be it Frank Sinatra or Frankie Goes to Hollywood'. (I know what you're going to say, you old cynic of a reader – what if you don't like either kind of music? The answer will wipe the sneer off your face – presumably with the face-flannel in the Shower Caddy: 'Alternatively you could simply listen to the news'.) It costs £24.95; never mind the width, feel the *quality*.

One thing I must make clear immediately. I do not believe that the manufacture and sale (for £14.95) of a battery-operated fingernail-drier should be prohibited, restricted or even specially taxed; no doubt Mr Michael Meacher, when he is Minister of the Siege Economy in Mr Wedgwood Benn's government, will lay before the House of Commons an Order, under the Discouragement of Bourgeois Frivolity at the Expense of the Proletariat Act, requiring the manufacturers to cease producing it and re-tool their factory to turn out ration-book holders instead, but since he will have by then closed down the Tate Gallery under the same statute we probably shan't notice.

For my part, I have always found charming the sight of an elegantly dressed lady fluttering her hands through the air to dry her just-painted fingernails, and Lavish Jack Levin is hardly going to worry about the taxi clock ticking up outside the door while she does so. Besides, the battery-operated nail-drier ('batteries not supplied', though) guarantees dry nails 'in a couple of minutes', and although I have never held a stopwatch while waiting for the manually-operated version to be completed (she might think I *was* worried about the taxi), I don't think it ever takes more than a couple of minutes anyway. But tastes differ; those who want battery-operated fingernail-driers, brass earring caddies with six compartments and their initials on the burgundy leather, and/or moisture-testers for the garden and shower caddies for the bathroom, are entitled to have them, and those who have realized that there is a market for them are entitled to make and sell them.

Only I do sometimes wonder whether it is really the harlot's cry from street to street that shall weave old England's winding-sheet, or whether it will be a different cry altogether: 'Come buy! Come buy!' A few years ago, there was a Christmas catalogue that advertised a gift 'for the man who has everything', which consisted of a solid gold finger with which the everything-owner was to dial telephone numbers. But that, I assumed, was a jest, as was (at least I hope it was) the Neiman-Marcus catalogue that one year offered His-and-Hers Underground H-Bomb Shelters. The manufacturers of earring caddies, waterproof radios and machines for telling you whether the soil you are standing on is wet or dry are presumably serious.

If nobody wants their goods, they will go out of business; that is known as the operation of the market. (Of course, the Labour Party and points left will argue that people are persuaded by the advertising to think they want what they do not really want, but I will take the argument seriously only when it is applied to the advertising for football-pools and indeed for the Labour Party.) The problem, of course, is: how do we teach people not to want such goods?

Certainly not by lecturing them, despising them or putting obstacles in their way. It is not at all clear to me that *tout lasse, tout casse, tout passe*; has the design of mass-produced clothes, shoes, furniture, saucepans, lighting fixtures, carpets, pens, suitcases, towels, watches, bicycles and motor-cars gone up or down since the Second World War? Up, far up, every one of them, and hundreds more familiar items too. Why? Because of that indefinable thing, the very mention of its name likely to cause riots, which has also been steadily rising these past few decades: public taste. If you will look closely at the next leather-jacketed youth you see reeling, stoned to the eyebrows, along the pavement you will notice, just before he hits you, that the jacket is of a quite stylish cut.

On the surface of the sea that is a free economy (and there is no such thing as political freedom without the economic kind) all sorts of odd, even sinister, things will be found bobbing. Leave them alone; they will, in time, become waterlogged and sink. But the study of them before they do so can be instructive.

Nobody invents, patents, makes and sells a battery-operated fingernail-drier unless he thinks that people will want to buy it – and enough people, moreover, to give him a profit. Let us suppose he is right; even if he is not, there have been objects far more absurd and even disgusting which have had a great vogue, even if only for a short time. What is it that makes people send off £14.95 (plus £2.50 for postage) for such nonsense?

It cannot be satiety; there are plenty of wants unfulfilled that must have a higher priority than an earring caddy. Obviously, it is not need, either; nobody needs a machine to tell him when to water the garden. It cannot even be acquisitiveness; nobody is going to think himself ahead of his neighbours if he has a marble rolling-pin (£6.95) or a pill-box with a built-in alarm to tell him when to take his medicine (£14.95), nor are the said neighbours going to be impressed by a key-ring which bleeps when you lose it (£12.95) or a luggage-strap with your name (up to eighteen letters) on it (£3.95).

It is, I think, the search for novelty; the very word has acquired an entirely new meaning, not the original, neutral 'newness' but an object sold to lie about the house collecting dust until it is tired of and thrown away. There is a restlessness in our air that makes people dissatisfied with what they have got, and makes them want not *more* things but *other* things. Such people are not greedy; they are simply trying to fill an unrecognized non-material want with a safely intelligible material one. Looking round the possessions they already have, they find something missing, and persuade themselves that it is a device for telling them what the time is in Tokyo as well as where they are (£14.95). Soon after they get it (allow twenty-eight days for receipt) they return to the feeling that there is something missing, and decide, perhaps, that it is The Hot Rod, 'a mini immersion heater that you plug in, place in the cup of liquid, turn on and within a matter of minutes you have a piping hot drink' (£7.95). But soon after it arrives the same odd feeling of disappointment will be felt again.

There is nothing wrong with owning a mechanical fingernail-drier. The mistake is to believe that the emptiness which cries out to be filled can be filled with such novelties. What we need is an advertising campaign to sell, instead of novelties, oldities – by which I mean not second-hand earring caddies but self-understanding, contentment grounded in feeling, the ancient conviction that the universe is the right way up and knows what it is about. These things cannot be illustrated in a glossy catalogue; on the other hand, they are free for the taking, or at least the seeking, and there is no charge at all, let alone £2.50, for postage and packing.

*The Times* August 20th, 1985

# Don Alfonso

*Lorenzo da Ponte* by Sheila Hodges[*]

I THINK I HAVE to delare an interest; this is not only a book I wish I had written, but one which for many years I had been determined to write, as soon as I could bring myself to face the prodigious quantity of research needed to do it properly. My criticisms therefore can be attributed to envy, spite and disappointment; on the other hand, my praise must be regarded as so objective that it counts as magnanimity.

It needed doing; Mozart's librettist (he invariably spelt the composer's name with a double z) has had remarkably few biographies, and none for a very long time. This is partly because he wrote his own memoirs, and partly because it has proved very difficult to unravel the real facts of his life; even Miss Hodges, who has dug deep and returned to the surface with many a find, has to admit defeat again and again.

I say the 'real' facts, because Da Ponte's own account is about as reliable as Baron Munchausen's. Miss Hodges is at pains to rehabilitate him from the charge, often levelled, that he was a monstrous liar, but although she has unearthed confirmation of several of his more extravagant claims, there remains a mass of material in his book that has the very ring of inauthenticity.

Yet it is not only the lies that make Munchausen the right comparison; it is the gaiety and good-heartedness with which he told them. Da Ponte was *splendide mendax*; every encounter with a great man, whether genius or monarch, ends with

[*] Grafton 1985.

his being showered with extravagant compliments and admiration, while every failure is entirely the fault of his implacably-scheming enemies. And whether it is triumph or disaster that he is recounting, the reader is to know that he invariably found the perfect witticism with which to round off the episode. (He wrote his memoirs in his old age; his *esprit de l'escalier* was composed on a staircase thirty-five years long.)

Da Ponte was a rake, a hack, a speculator, a cadger, an intriguer; Miss Hodges tries to rescue him from at least the worst of his sins, but happily fails. He was also, even though only intermittently, a genius, and her presentation and analysis of his very real talents is the best and most valuable part of her book.

Da Ponte started as a penniless Jew from the ghetto of Ceneda, near Venice; baptised, he became a priest, though a somewhat unorthodox one – after a string of mistresses, he ended up with a kind of wife, though how he squared that with the Church neither he nor the author can quite explain. His adventures throughout his life, even discounted for fantasy, were astounding and hilarious; he started dozens of mad business ventures which all collapsed in ruin and bankruptcy, he picked reckless quarrels with those who could do him harm and wrote savage denunciations of them when they had done it, he fled or was expelled from half a dozen cities, and he ended his days (after trying his hand at being a grocer) with the most unlikely apotheosis imaginable: as Professor of Italian at Columbia University, New York. (And even that produced more ruin, for the post was unpaid, and indeed he eventually had no pupils at all, pay or no pay.)

The chief fault of this book is that its author is plainly too respectable to love Da Ponte enough; she writes like a woman who has never been drunk, let alone bankrupt, while as for adultery, she wouldn't dream of it. (For all that, she hints that our hero had an affair with his stepmother.) But she can be forgiven her virtues, and her somewhat less than sparkling prose, for her recognition and exact delineation of the unique fusion of genius that took place when Da Ponte wrote the librettos of *Figaro, Don Giovanni* and *Così fan tutte*.

Neither Strauss and von Hofmannsthal, nor Verdi and Boito, nor Wagner the composer and Wagner the poet, got anywhere near those combinations of music and words.*
And Miss Hodges makes clear that although Da Ponte often talked and wrote as though Mozart was some kind of apprentice needing his librettist's genius to eke out his own weaknesses, there is no doubt that the writer fully realized that he had been collaborating with a musician who was one of the rarest and most precious spirits the human race has yet produced, and that his librettos for Mozart, though the finest he ever wrote (the finest *anybody* ever wrote), were still only the servant to an eternal master. And of course, it was that realization which enabled Da Ponte to summon up resources he did not know he had; he had written many fine librettos before – for Salieri, among many other composers – but even the best of these lacked the final inch of genius that genius drew out of him.

For all his quarrelling and character-assassination, Da Ponte made many friends whom he kept to the death, and he was much loved as well as much hated. (Much of the hate came from envy, or from fear of rivalry from a superior talent.) And he had many of the last laughs; he outlived most of his enemies (he was eighty-nine when he died), and saw many of them variously ruined, imprisoned, banished, gone mad and in one case hanged. He was – in character to the end – reconciled to the Church on his deathbed.

Almost none of the operas, other than Mozart's, for which Da Ponte wrote the words has survived; he did a revised version of Cimarosa's *Il matrimonio segreto*, an opera which is still performed, but the rest lie gathering dust. One, how-

---

* On reflection, I think this claim is too sweeping.

ever, has suffered a stranger fate than any; Martin y Soler's *Una cosa rara*. Mozart said of it that in many ways it was very pretty, 'but in ten years nobody will take any notice of it'. Mozart was wrong; Soler's opera has survived to this day, and will survive for ever, for it is both alluded to by name, and quoted musically, in the supper scene in *Don Giovanni*.

*Observer* October 13th, 1985

# And what rough beast

I FIND THAT THROUGHOUT the whole of Orwell's Year, I
have made no mention of 1984 and its dread associations.
No doubt my readers are as relieved as I am surprised, but on
the very last day of this ill-omened span, they will surely
pardon me if, in developing a theme that has been ringing in
my head for some time, I touch once or twice upon matters
which would not have been quite so symbolically apposite in
1983. Let us ring up the curtain on my subject with Chesterton's *The Horrible History of Jones*:

> Jones had a dog; it had a chain;
> Not often worn, not causing pain;
> But, as the IKL had passed
> Their 'Unleashed Cousins Act' at last,
> Inspectors took the chain away;
> Whereat the canine barked 'hurray!' . . .

And we might as well begin with animals. When, a month
or two ago, a group, claiming, not very plausibly, to be
concerned for the welfare of animals announced that they had
put poison in Mars Bars on the shelves of supermarkets, one
of the television news bulletins carried an interview with a
man who claimed to be a spokesman for such a group; he
denied having anything to do with the Mars Bars affair (the
gang which did it announced later that they had not in fact
poisoned the sweets, and for the moment at any rate wanted
only to give a warning of what they might do next time if
Messrs Mars continued to displease them), but made clear

that he and his colleagues thought that virtually any action, let alone threat, was justified in the struggle they imagined they were waging.

He was, it has to be said, a pathetic-looking creature; the very dogs he thought he cared so much about would have snarled at him as he passed by. He gave the impression that he had been computer-programmed with every expression and phrase in Roget (particularly the clichés) referring to animals and their treatment by mankind, and as soon as the interviewer pressed the appropriate key, they all came pouring out.

It was obvious that his animal campaigning was the only thing of any interest or meaning in his life; indeed, it plainly *was* his life, and since everything else around him was dissolved in his one testing-acid, it followed that the interests and opinions, and even safety, of those who disagreed with him were of no more account than those worldly concerns he had long since renounced, and could be no less easily disposed of.

I have written more than once about those whose love of animals is in truth a hatred of human beings, and I do not intend to go over that same ground today. But presumably even the most hate-crazed animal liberationalist, as he smashes up laboratory equipment or chases dangerous beasts out of their pens, occasionally stops to think how he started and what the reason was; surely somewhere in his muddled brain there was originally a feeling that it is wrong to ill-treat animals.

> . . . At which, of course, the SPU
> (Whose Nervous Motorists' Bill was through)
> Were forced to give the dog in charge
> For being Audibly at Large . . .

Let us now turn – the connection between the instances I relate will become clear in time, I assure you – to Mrs Victoria Gillick, who a few days ago won, in the Court of

Appeal, her case against the medical dispensation of con-
traceptive pills to girls under sixteen years of age without
their parents' knowledge.* Now on the rights and wrongs of
such action by doctors I have expressed no public view, and I
shall express none now; what interests me is not Mrs Gillick's
legal action, but what has happened to her and her family
since she began it. She has revealed that they have suffered
physical and verbal attacks, that some of her children have
been kicked and punched in the street, that gangs have tried
to kick down their front door nearly every night, that she has
had to take two of her children away from their school
because of the bullying they were being subjected to, and that
she has received obscene telephone calls and hate mail.

Presumably, too, those who wish girls under the age of
consent to be provided confidentially with contraceptives
must think, or at least must once have thought, that such
action is wise and right, and for all I know it may be; but as
Madame du Deffand said in a rather different context, it is
only the first step that is difficult, for if you begin by thinking
that very young girls should be protected by contraception
given in secret against becoming pregnant, and end by trying
to kick down the door of someone who holds a contrary
view, something decidedly odd must have happened to you
on the journey in between. And what has happened seems to
me very similar to what afflicts the animal liberators; both
groups have allowed one dominant belief to grow so large in
their minds that not only do other, lesser, beliefs vanish
beneath its shadow, but the most rudimentary standards of
civilized behaviour are swept away. Whatever view may be
taken of cruelty to animals or infant contraception, and
however passionately the view may be held, is it not passing
strange for some to threaten, abuse and ultimately assault
those who do not share it?

* The House of Lords later reversed the judgment of the Appeal Court.

> . . . None, you will say, were now annoyed,
> Save haply Jones – the yard was void.
> But something being in the lease
> About 'alarms to aid police',
> The USU annexed the yard
> For having no sufficient guard . . .

Now let us travel – by night will be best, with our coat-collars turned up and our hat-brims down – to the Bold Colliery in Lancashire. In a suburb of the nearby town there lives – lived, rather, for he has now deemed it best to go elsewhere – a miner who went on working when others around him would have preferred that he did not. The better to emphasize this preference, they first beat him up and then plastered posters on his house and elsewhere in the vicinity, with his picture on them. Above his photograph was a headline reading, 'This is a scab', and beneath it the designation 'Strike-breaker and traitor'. There followed further matter, including such passages as, 'A scab is a two-legged animal with a waterlogged brain and a backbone of jelly and glue . . . Where others have a heart, he carries a tumour of rotten principles . . . Judas Iscariot was a gentleman compared to a scab – Judas Iscariot had character enough to hang himself, a scab has not.'

Without doubt, feelings have run high in the miners' strike. It would, however, be a nonpareil altimeter that could measure the height of the feelings required to engage in behaviour such as that. Again, something real and important has become the *only* real and important thing, and then even reality and importance have vanished and it has become the only thing of any kind.

What I am talking about is a phenomenon that has existed for centuries, but of late has monstrously grown; in 1984, it seemed to me that it made its most significant advances yet. It is the phenomenon of the Single Issue Fanatic. Until very recently, he (or she – oh, my *word*, or she) was usually to be found turning the fanaticism inward; he believed that the earth was flat, or that crime and banditry, distress and perplexity, would increase until the bishops opened Joanna Southcott's Box of Sealed Writings, or that he had been cheated out of his inheritance by the Pope and the Queen Mother. But today, he not only multiplies daily and hourly, his concerns are with matters that impinge upon us all, or if they do not, he makes it his implacable business to see that they soon will.

> . . . Now if there's one condition
> The CCP are strong upon
> It is that every house one buys
> Must have a yard for exercise;
> So Jones, as tenant, was unfit,
> His state of health was proof of it . . .

What is more, and worse, the typical Single Issue Fanatic of today is not content, say, to make us use the metric system instead of our familiar inches and pints and hundredweights, or to shout and yell at us until we agree that Britain should disarm unilaterally, or even to force us, whether we would or no, into a closed shop. There has been a significant, and sinister, change of emphasis; instead of restricting himself to a claim that he is pursuing the public weal with such nostrums, he now insists on regulating the private sector as well; the typical Single Issue Fanatic now concentrates on doing us good, by *his* definition of *our* good.

The most intense variety of this new breed is undoubtedly the anti-smoking zealot, but on him, too, I have said enough for the time being. But hot on his heels come now the diet police. Today's fashionable theory (it will be the opposite one next Friday fortnight) is that fat and salt are lethal; one sniff of either and you roll over, stiff as a board. Of course it is a capitalist conspiracy (there will now be a short break while I sing 'Oh, I am the man, the very fat man, who waters the workers' beer'), and the only way to defeat it is to pass legislation making it a criminal offence to stand a friend a glass of milk, let alone a bacon butty.

But *l'appetit vient en mangeant*; as soon as it was law to fasten seat-belts in the front of cars, an agitation arose to make them compulsory also in the back, though hardly a word had been said about any extension while the campaign was going on.

The next stop will be alcohol, mark my words. (That's a capitalist conspiracy, too – did you ever see the BBC programme on vodka?) Again, there is an instructive difference between the old pussyfoot and the new; the old preached against the evils of drink and insisted on the enforcement of the licensing laws, but today's looks forward to the day when ferociously enforced legal regulations oblige us to take our ration-book to the state-run drinkshops where two and a half drachms will be measured into a plastic container by an assistant looking as though he could do with a drink, and consumed at once on the premises.

> . . . Two doctors of the TTU's
> Told him his legs, from long disuse,
> Were atrophied; and saying 'So
> From step to higher step we go
> Till everything is New and True'
> They cut his legs off and withdrew . . .

There is another, and equally depressing (and dangerous), difference between the earlier version of the Single Issue Fanatic and ours; it is the terms in which he couches his arguments. Just as in the extreme form of the new fanaticism everything, including violence done to opponents, is regarded as legitimate, so among those who would not go so far there is a feeling that, provided the cause is good enough (and for the Single Issue Fanatic it always is), anything may be said. There is one of these people in Michael Frayn's most recent play, *Benefactors*; he has been engaged on a campaign concerning a local authority and planning permission, and when it is over he looks back over his side's methods:

> But the sheer pleasure of it! We sprayed the walls two storeys
> high – 'Vandals Out!' We shouted Council meetings down –
> 'Democracy now!' We didn't have to worry about being fair or
> truthful or tidy. That was the great liberation. Fairness and
> tidiness and truth are for people who've got what they want
> already. We had nothing; we could do anything.

Note particularly the first words and the last: *the sheer
pleasure of it . . . we could do anything.* The Single Issue
Fanatic, whether he knows it or not, is after power, and he
seeks it because of the horrible joy he will have when he gets
it – the joy of making other people do as he tells them.

> . . . You know the ETST's views
> Are stronger than the TTU's;
> And soon (as one may say) took wing
> The Arms, though not the Man, I sing . . .

Is my claim an exaggeration? If you think so, look back to
the examples I gave a couple of thousand words ago. Would
anyone not convinced, in his monomaniac Fanaticism, that
he can indeed 'do anything' tell the world that he has put
poison in sweets and then threaten that he would actually do
so next time? Would anyone not blinded by a belief held to
the edge of madness, and possibly over, abuse and assault
Mrs Gillick and her children? Would anyone whose Single
Issue Fanaticism had not, in a very real sense, dehumanized
him, do what was done to the miner who went to work?

I do not think so. And yet, so far from understanding why
others would see people who could do such things as evil, the
perpetrators would be amazed and genuinely resentful at the
thought. Surely it is good to stand up for ill-treated animals?
Surely it is right to seek to help troubled adolescents? Surely
it is admirable to stand beside your workmates rather than
against them?

Yes, but if that is the only cause you are interested in, if it fills your life, waking and sleeping, if you are absolutely determined that nothing matters except making others see it the way you see it – why, then, you are a Single Issue Fanatic, and as sure as twice two make five, you will end up believing that you may properly do *anything* to bring about what you desire.

> . . . To see him sitting limbless there
> Was more than the KK could bear.
> 'In mercy silence with all speed
> That mouth there are no hands to feed;
> What cruel sentimentalist,
> O Jones, would doom thee to exist –
> Clinging to selfish Selfhood yet?
> Weak one! Such reasoning might upset
> The Pump Act, and the accumulation
> Of all constructive legislation;
> Let us construct you up a bit –'
> The head fell off when it was hit;
> Then words did rise and honest doubt,
> And four Commissioners sat about
> Whether the slash that left him dead
> Cut off his body or his head . . .

These were not, it is true, the dangers that Orwell foresaw. But I cannot help feeling that he would recognize them, and think them as deadly as those he depicted, and perhaps more so. The Single Issue Fanatic is the terror that walketh by night, and is far more difficult to see and to combat. Yet he must be combated, and beaten, or we shall all, in one way or another, suffer the same fate as Jones.

> . . . An author in the Isle of Wight
> Observed with unconcealed delight
> A land of old and just renown
> Where Freedom slowly broadened down
> From Precedent to Precedent –
> And this, I think, was what he meant.

The Chinese have long had the custom of designating their calendar with the Year of the Dragon, or of the Dog, or the Pig. I think we need another sort of year, a year in which the Single Issue Fanatic is faced and fought – by all of us, everywhere, at whatever point he may attack. Come; let us make 1985 Cakes and Ale Year.

Ring out the new, ring in the old! Enough of condoning wickedness and excusing criminality! Enough of these harbingers of the Nanny State! Enough of those who would tie our hands lest we scratch ourselves, and our feet lest we trip, and our tongues lest we say something that is not on the List of Things it is Proper to be Said! 1984 has come, and in a few hours will be gone. We did not fall into the tyrannous and terrible net of Big Brother in the course of it, but we did fall, by stealth not conquest, a little further into the hands of the Single Issue Fanatics. In Cakes and Ale Year, we shall start the process of breaking their grip, of taking back our right to decide what is good for us, of resisting the thieves who would steal from us more of our liberties, of declaring that a cause which is promoted by violence instead of reason is a bad cause, of saying no quietly though others are screaming yes, and of eating many cakes and drinking much ale.

We shall march to the beat of *Liberty Bell*, our banners shall bear the emblem of a cocked snook, and our prayers will be offered to St Peter of Alcantara, because he is the patron saint of watchmen, which is what we are. And our New Year's Resolution – all together now – shall be to ensure that when 1985 comes to an end, this country will be recognizably more free than when it began. Now who will stand on either hand, and keep the bridge with me?

*The Times* December 31st, 1984

# Golden means

THE TRUSTEES OF the Natural History Museum in South
Kensington (that amazing building which looks as
though it was designed by the Emperor Domitian in the last
throes of the DTs) have announced that they are to impose a
modest admission charge, starting at the beginning of April
next year; possibly they thought that by giving thirteen
months' notice of their intention they would escape criticism
of the proposal, inevitable if the shocking news were to be
released only on the eve of Black Tuesday.

In this reasonable hope they were, as I could have told
them, reckoning without the Army of the Righteous, who
have dedicated their lives to ensuring that nothing they
approve of shall ever be changed. In command of the
vanguard on this occasion was Lord Jenkins of Putney, never
reluctant to set his tonsils aquiver in a bad cause. Before you
could say turnstile, he was accusing the museum's trustees of
wanting to send small boys up chimneys, and insisting that if
the plan were to be carried through it would inevitably lead
to a vast increase in the incidence of kwashiorkor, rickets,
bilharzia and phossy jaw.

This could be the end of civilization as we know it. Or not,
as the case may be; I have never been able to see why Britain,
almost alone among the civilized nations of the earth, refuses
to charge for admission to the national art and scientific
collections. Nobody thinks it strange that although the
National Theatre and Covent Garden are heavily subsidized
their patrons still have to pay for their seats, or that, despite

public ownership of the Post Office, stamps are not free, or that those who were responsible for the nationalization of the mines failed to include a provision for coal to be given away at the pit-head to anyone bringing a wheelbarrow.

Visitors to Florence must pay to enter the Uffizi; in Munich a charge is made for inspection of the treasures of the Alte Pinakothek; the same is true of the Rijksmuseum in Amsterdam, the Prado in Madrid, the Kunsthistorisches-museum in Vienna, the Museum of Fine Arts in Brussels, the Museum of Modern Art in New York and the Louvre in Paris. Indeed, of some forty public galleries and museums in Paris, all but three charge for admission, though almost all of these have at least one day a week when the fee is waived, as do almost all the places on my list. And it is not self-evident that the citizens of Italy and West Germany, of The Nether-lands and Spain, of Austria, Belgium, America and France, have less artistic sensibility than we do, and even if it were, that might not necessarily be the direct consequence of the fact that they charge for admission and we do not.

As it happens, the Natural History Museum is instituting charges because the alternative would be to sack eighty members of the staff, which I should have thought Lord Jenkins would deplore even more strongly. But given the fact that even Maecenas and Lorenzo de' Medici had to draw the line somewhere, there will never be enough money for museums and galleries to put on as many exhibitions as they would like, or to improve their buildings to the extent that they would like, or to acquire as many additions to their collections as they would like; what is the objection to their charging reasonable sums (with concessions to the truly unmonied and a free day a week) to those who wish to enter, and whatever the objection is, why does it not apply to the rest of the world?

I do not see why we should stop at art galleries. Apart from the apparently implacable resolve on the part of the librarians to extirpate the practice of reading, what was the real reason that authors were paid for library loans of their books not by a charge of a penny a book a withdrawal, but by the weird, cumbersome and inadequate system that was finally adopted, Public Lending Right? It was, surely, our national determination to go on pretending, in the teeth of the evidence, that there *is* a free lunch, that resources are infinite, that Christmas comes far more often than once a year, that it is profoundly immoral to charge anybody for anything except in a shop, if there.

I will go further. Try to put out of your mind your knowledge that I wish to send women down the mines and restore the Combination Acts, the Elizabethan Poor Law and the Slave Trade; can you tell me, coherently, why those who can afford to pay for some or even all of their medical treatment under the National Health Service should not do so? I do not use the NHS; but I have an unrestricted right to, and if I did, I would not think it odd, let alone outrageous, for a man with my income to make up at least some of the expense incurred by the taxpayers (despite the fact that I am one of them) whenever any of my numerous, distressing and astonishingly varied diseases has to be attended to. What is more, I would not think it wrong for a man with considerably less than my income to be obliged to stump up *something* towards his medical treatment, be it no more than £1 for a visit to the doctor and a fiver for an operation. Such rates would still be far below what the facilities cost, and there is already a precedent in the charges for NHS prescriptions.

You see what I am getting at? If you do, but are so appalled by it that you find it too painful to dwell upon, let me do the dwelling. What is wrong with a means test? Not what *was* wrong; the old one, before the Second World War, earned its odium by the crude and offensive way in which it was drawn up and applied. But for the life of me, I cannot see why a reasonable and humanely administered form of it is in itself a sin that cries aloud to heaven.

It takes not more than seven seconds' thought to realize

that we already have a gigantic means test, enforced throughout the land and applying to all classes and conditions. It is
the progressive income tax, under the terms of which, when
a government wishes to spend or waste a few billion pounds,
it raises the wind by confiscating, without apology or thanks,
much of the income earned by the citizens, with those who
earn more obliged (very properly) to pay more. And, most
curiously, this means test is not denounced, indeed is applauded, by those who scream themselves hoarse at the
suggestion of graded payments for medical treatment, let
alone graded reductions in welfare benefits.

Or charges for admission to museums and art galleries
maintained at public expense, even if there are no such
charges on Sundays; which is where I started. The denoun-
cers and hoarse-screamers point to the terrible example of the
Victoria and Albert Museum, which has recently begun to
solicit a *voluntary* entrance fee of £2, and has seen its
attendance figures fall sharply. My view of the V & A's
scheme is that £2 is too high and the voluntary nature of the
charge absurd, but that the principle is valid. Let Sir Roy
Strong reduce the charge to 50p and make it compulsory, and
then keep his nerve; within a year, everyone will have
forgotten that it was ever free, and will be handing over the
money without demur or even thought. It will be easier, of
course, if other public museums and galleries were to do the
same, and I hope they will. And if they won't, perhaps the
government, when it has finished re-enacting the legislation
for whipping sturdy beggars through the streets at the cart's
tail, might take a deep breath and compel them to.

*The Times* March 6th, 1986

# Come the day

*Emma Goldman* by Alice Wexler[*]

WHEN I WAS learning to read, the comics I devoured still used a stereotyped anarchist to represent violent villainy; he was invariably portrayed wearing a fringe beard, dark glasses and a cloak, and carrying a spherical bomb, gently smoking and labelled BOMB, which he would throw at people in the next frame (BANG!).

He wouldn't seem so funny today, for obvious reasons, and he wouldn't have seemed so funny a few decades earlier either, for reasons made clear in this excellent biography, warmly sympathetic but sufficiently detached, of a woman who is now quite forgotten but in her day excited as much terror and loathing among her enemies as she aroused affection and admiration among those whose cause she upheld; for Emma Goldman was an anarchist very much in the tradition which lingered on into my childhood, by no means averse to a bit of bomb-throwing if it was likely to lead to the collapse and destruction of all existing institutions and the inevitably consequent ushering in of the Anarchist nirvana.

Born in what is now Soviet-occupied Lithuania, she emigrated to the United States in 1885, when she was sixteen; she was already thinking dangerous thoughts, and within a few years had thrown herself into the work of bringing revolution to America, an aim from which she would not be moved until, some thirty years later, she was

[*] Virago, 1985.

deported (she had never been naturalized) during the 'Red scare' witch-hunts after the First World War of that Ur-McCarthy, A. Mitchell Palmer.

Her ideas (too definite a word really) were an *olla podrida* of Marx, Bakunin, Freud, Ibsen, Chernyshevsky, Emerson, Kropotkin, and Nietzsche, but it was her championing of those who were without champions that made her a kind of bloodthirsty saint, for while she was 'attacking patriotism before soldiers, mocking religion to clergymen, deriding the ballot to suffragists, publicly declaring her sympathy for terrorists . . . and . . . practising free love and smoking up to forty cigarettes a day', she also inspired the devotion of the downtrodden and of those who worked alongside her to raise them:

> She held before our eyes the ideal of freedom, taunting us with our cowardice for having acquiesced so tamely in the brutal artifice of present-day society . . . There were thousands of men and women all over the country who loved her. She performed a distinct service – that of removing despair from those who would otherwise be hopeless.

She was obviously a magnetic orator, rousing audiences to fervour, rage or tears (and sometimes all three) with the passion of her beliefs, though she had more than a touch of Mrs Jellyby; when her half-sister's beloved son was killed on the Western Front in October 1918, Emma said to another relative: 'If I can muster up spirit I will write to her – when one lives in the universe, it is most difficult to speak the language of one limited part . . .'

She could never fully make up her mind about violence as a political means; often she questioned its efficacy, and occasionally its morality, yet her repudiation of anarchist support for Czolgosz (the assassin of President McKinley) was brief, and she soon began to idealize him, then to glorify him, and finally to make of him an icon which she worshipped for the rest of her life. Miss Wexler says neatly (perhaps too neatly) that Emma 'defended the absolute freedom of the individual, including the right of the individual to commit terrorist attacks'.

Inevitably, there were constant quarrels and anathematizings among the faithful; her Messianism was strong, and she rarely brooked disagreement, let alone defiance. The most powerful strand in her personality and her ideology alike was her Impossibilism; she rejected as a corruption of the faith any attempt to use the parliamentary road to Utopia, denouncing those who voted in elections as 'scurrilous and immoral', and she scorned no less intensely those who contracted a conventional marriage, which she equated with prostitution. One of her associates and rivals, the magnificently-named Voltairine de Cleyre (she sounds like something out of Amanda Ros, but it was perfectly genuine), went further, and insisted that *any* enduring relationship between two people was to be condemned.

Emma's Achilles' heel turned out to be in a most surprising place. She told an implausible story about being raped as a young girl in Russia; certainly for most of her life she seems to have regarded sexual relations with more guilt and revulsion than pleasure, though she had several affairs and a couple of marriages. But in her fortieth year, she experienced a *coup de foudre* for a strange figure – a hobo-doctor, bisexual and mother-fixated – with whom she fell so completely and uncontrollably in love that she was consumed with a kind of erotomania; the language she uses in her letters to him would be considered extreme even in these more unbuttoned days, and they are made the more weird by being signed – after pages of almost pornographic ravings – 'Mommy'.

Whether she ever really achieved anything is doubtful; the Impossibilists rarely do (her mantra was 'I do not judge an act by its results, but by its cause'), and her refusal to have any truck even with proposals for nationalization or indeed State welfare will remind a modern reader of some of today's left-wing *groupuscules*. But she was consistent (as Impossibilists often are); she opposed votes for women because she also opposed votes for men, thinking it outrageous that individuals should delegate their political rights to political representatives, and even more outrageous that the will of the majority should prevail.

The book leaves off at the moment of her deportation, though she lived for another twenty years; I hope a sequel is in hand. Emma Goldman was a violent termagant and probably did more harm than good; still, she gave succour to those who needed it most (in prison her thoughts and care were lavished on her suffering fellow-prisoners, not on herself), and she cannot be denied a grandeur of soul. But there is one more modern parallel in her life:

> Disgusted with many of her former associates, disillusioned by the spectacle of hatred unleashed by 'the masses' toward Leon Czolgosz, and faced with the shattered morale of a severely diminished movement, she began to seek new contacts and connections, particularly among the American-born middle-class liberals and radicals who showed an increasing interest in her work.

She found them, too; and Radical Chic was born.

*Observer* March 10th, 1985

# They also served

As we approach the fortieth anniversary of VE-day, there is increased discussion of whom Britain should invite to the celebrations. There is some feeling that there should be no such celebrations; there is controversy over the question of Soviet participation; there is embarrassment looming over the Poles, who were, after all, the first victims of the war. (The embarrassment concerns not *whether* the Poles should go there, but *which* Poles. Do we invite traitors like Jaruzelski, or heroes like Stanislaw Losinski, who has wartime medals for valour from Poland, Britain, France and Yugoslavia, but who is exiled from his homeland, like so many of his kind and generation, because he believes in freedom?)

Amid all this, there is one group of whom I have heard no official mention at all, yet who seem to me to deserve not only a place, but an honoured one. Surely it cannot be right to forget, when we are commemorating a victory over German Nazism, those Germans who fought Nazism in their own country, and who mostly paid for doing so with a hideous death by torture and slow strangulation.

Too little attention has been paid to the German Resistance over the years since the war ended, yet although its practical effect on Hitler's Germany was negligible, it must never be forgotten that the heroic band who actively fought against the evil that had engulfed their country preserved a precious fragment of German honour which might otherwise have disappeared for ever.

Weak if we were and foolish, not thus we failed, not thus;
When that black Baal blocked the heavens he had no
  hymns from us.
Children we were – our forts of sand were even as weak as
  we,
High as they went we piled them up to break that bitter
  sea.

It is popularly believed that the German struggle against
Hitler was confined to the single episode of the July 20 bomb
plot. The view is erroneous. From the earliest days of Nazi
rule, brave German men and women had conspired to thwart
it; there were many like Carl Goerdeler and Fabian von
Schlabrendorff (the latter being one of the few direct partici-
pants in the bomb plot who lived to tell the tale), who were
active anti-Nazis from the beginning, rallying the fainthearts,
seeking help from abroad, tending the embers against the day
when they could burst into flame, never losing their courage
and determination through all the years of frustration and
lost hopes as Hitler went from success to success. Throughout the war, there were members of the German Resistance
who used their official positions to get vital information to
the Allies, or who did what they could to jam the bureau-
cratic machinery of the Final Solution or help its intended
victims to escape from Germany (or even – and in some ways
these were perhaps the bravest of the brave – who hid Jews in
their homes).

One of the July 20 conspirators, when he was sentenced to
death before the infamous 'People's Court' of Roland Freis-
ler, spoke his own epitaph, and in doing so defined the whole
history of those Germans who tried so hard to wrest back
their country from the evil men who had stolen it: 'A ship
may sink', he said, 'but it does not have to strike the flag.'

When the bomb plot failed, von Schlabrendorff broke the
news to one of his fellow-conspirators, General Henning von
Tresckow, who declared that he would commit suicide, since

'they are bound to find out about me during the investigation, and then they will try to extract the names of others from me'. His last words, before he drove off to his death, were recorded by von Schlabrendorff, and are worth quoting in full:

> Now they will all fall upon us and cover us with abuse. But I am convinced, now as much as ever, that we have done the right thing. I believe Hitler to be the arch-enemy, not only of Germany, but indeed of the entire world. In a few hours' time, I shall stand before God and answer for both my actions and the things I neglected to do. I think I can with a clear conscience stand by all I have done in the battle against Hitler. Just as God once promised Abraham that He would spare Sodom if only ten just men could be found in the city, I also have reason to hope that, for our sake, He will not destroy Germany. No one among us can complain about his death, for whoever joined our ranks put on the poisoned shirt of Nessus. A man's moral worth is established only at the point where he is prepared to give his life for his convictions.

Those who were in the German Resistance and survived are now mostly dead; well, 1944 was a long time ago. (One of the survivors is Otto John who, whatever the solution to the mystery of his subsequent career, was an active anti-Nazi from beginning to end.) But there is a generation of the resisters' children, now part of the democratic Germany their parents never lived to see, who could and should carry to Britain on May 8 the faith their fathers died for.

The son of Claus von Stauffenberg, the man who put the bomb under Hitler's table, is now a colonel in the Bundeswehr; Manfred, the son of Field-Marshal Rommel, is the mayor of Stuttgart, and not long ago said bluntly 'Thank God we lost the war'; the son of Count von Moltke, leader of the purest of all the resistance groups (the 'Kreisau Circle'), still bears one of the noblest names and titles in German history; there are other sons and daughters, and widows;

they should all be conducted to their seats in Westminster Abbey to give thanks, for Victory in Europe, alongside those who fought against the same evil as did their honoured dead.

For surely the VE-day ceremonies will not be limited to retrospective rejoicing. Such an occasion would be shockingly incomplete if it did not also stress the theme of reconciliation. The friendship that has grown up since the war among Britain, France and Federal Germany has provided the cornerstone of European peace and security; such a historical triumph should be proclaimed, and the descendants of the Germans who gave their lives to bring that dawn nearer should be there to hear the proclamation.

I believe that the Prime Minister is a woman of sufficient imagination to see the importance of such an invitation; it is certainly the kind of gesture that would have come naturally to Churchill. Perhaps I can leave the theme for the moment by conjuring up a picture that should appeal not only to her but to anyone with enough historical understanding to take in its full significance. Not long ago there was a meeting between Manfred Rommel and Monty's son, the present Viscount Montgomery (of El Alamein, remember); it was, of course, a friendly encounter. Now would not the sight of those two sitting side by side in friendship say more than volumes about the peace that has followed the war, and about the ultimate unity of purpose that bound the victors of VE-day to those, among the defeated, who worked for the same victory?*

*The Times* March 14th, 1985

---

\* In the end the problem of Soviet participation and of the choice among Poles proved too embarrassing for the Foreign Office, and no contingents from anywhere overseas were invited other than Ambassadors to Britain.

# Vons and rebels

The Berlin diaries 1940–1945 of Marie 'Missie' Vassiltchikov
Edited by George Vassiltchikov*

IT IS RARE FOR a book to sum itself up as early as the
Acknowledgments, but the editor of this extraordinary and
touching document, who is the diarist's brother, maps his
sister's world with great exactitude when he thanks, among
others,

> Count Andreas von Bismarck-Schönhausen, Baron and Baro-
> ness Axel von dem Bussche-Streithorst, Count Johannes
> ('Dicki') and Countess Sybilla von und zu Eltz, Baroness
> Ermina von Essen, Princess Petronella Farman-Fermayan,
> Countess Rosemarie von Fugger-Babenhausen, Mrs Sigrid
> ('Siggi') Kurrer, born Countess Schlitz von Gortz, Mrs Caroline
> de Lacerna, born Princess Schönburg-Hartenstein, Mr C.-C.
> von Pfuel, Baron Anton ('Toni') Saurma von der Jeltsch,
> Countess Dorothea von Schönborn-Wiesentheid, born Coun-
> tess von Pappenheim, Princess Carmen ('Sita') von Solms-
> Braunfels (born Princess von Wrete), and Baron Philippe de
> Vendeuve.

This, then, is life among the upper crust in Nazi Germany,
from the high tide of Hitler's triumphs to the smouldering
ruins of the thousand-year Reich. And the diary kept, in
almost perfect English, by Missie (as everyone called her),
eked out with letters and notes, paints a triply extraordinary
portrait – unique in my own reading in first-hand accounts of
the Nazi State – of what life beneath that terrible harrow was

* Chatto and Windus, 1985

like for people who were not at all accustomed to life *beneath* anything.

The first layer consists of the exploits of her circle of Bright Young Things, a little late for the Thirties but *toujours gai* nevertheless, even when the war has reached such a pitch of frightfulness that they have to open their own oysters. Missie herself is seen contributing to the merriment while working in the German overseas radio, by making up ('I had nothing better to do') a news item about riots in London, with the King hanged at the gates of Buckingham Palace; she then watched, fascinated, as it made its way towards a news broadcast to South Africa.

When the reader has got the cast firmly fixed (in aspic, presumably), another, darker, theme appears: the effect of the war, particularly as the tide turns and the saturation bombing begins and gathers pace. There is a giant set-piece (though it is important to remember that it was not written as such, but jotted down day by day) which describes the destruction of Berlin in the second half of 1943, and is written with a vividness, detail, understanding and humanity that ranks it beside Pepys on the Great Fire. From then to the *Götterdämmerung* in the Bunker, her chronicle of destruction and defeat will hold any reader enthralled.

But while they are dancing amid the ruins, Missie is dropping hints in her diary, and it is the subject at which she is hinting that gives the book its third strain, the one that makes it unique. For as July 20 1944 approaches, we learn that she and her circle, staggering under the weight of their vons and their hyphens ('Rüdge Essen is back from Sweden, bringing lobsters, American *Vogue*, etc.'), and dodging bombs no less skilfully than their *gleichgeschaltet* neighbours, were almost without exception fervently anti-Nazi from the beginning, many of them active in the Resistance, and many of those destined to pay with their lives for their convictions.

Through her pages and her life pass many of the bravest names of Nazi Germany: Gottfried von Bismarck, Peter

Bielenberg, Hasso von Etzdorff, Ulrich von Hassell, Hans von Haeften, and above all that heroic, tragic figure Adam von Trott. Missie was clearly very close to him, and after his arrest in the wake of the unsuccessful bomb-plot she and her friends are seen moving mountains to discover news of his whereabouts, and thinking of ways to rescue him: even then, some of these innocents did not realize what kind of evil they were fighting with their peashooters.

It is here that Missie and her diary reach remarkable heights. The set-piece of the bombing has the power of the finest descriptive reporting, but her account, day by day and sometimes hour by hour, of what followed Stauffenberg's attempt to kill Hitler is more than that: shot through with pain, hope and selflessness, it leads us to the very gates of hell, where we can hear the screams of the tortured and the choking of the hanged.

When it is all over, and the survivors can breathe again, she marshals all her powers of observation for the final months, as Germany disintegrates. As the reader by now will expect, the Bright Young Things, tempered in the furnace, rise to the occasion. Typical of them is a Hungarian madman, Geza Pejacsewich (strictly speaking Count Geza Pejacsewich von Verocze) who is, of course, Sisi Wilczek's brother-in-law; Missie runs into him in the ruins of Vienna, where they are all trying to escape before the Russians arrive, and 'at the sight a load fell off my chest, for nobody here has more guts and initiative or is more of a daredevil'.

True enough, for after he fails in his heroic attempts to obtain a car in which they can all get out, Missie scrambles aboard the very last train, with Geza left behind, never to be seen again. But when they get to Gmunden,

> Suddenly we heard the hooting of a horn. It was Geza Pejacse-wich! He was with his brother-in-law, Capestan Adamovic. They were safe and sound and had even brought along all our luggage, coats, etc. But that's not all. Somewhere Geza had

discovered a trailer which he had hitched to the back of his car and into which he had piled the abandoned belongings of many other friends. It is amazing how much one determined and gutsy man can achieve even in times such as these! Only my mauve accordion and one of Sisi's suitcases had to be left behind.

*Observer* December 8th 1985

# *God* save *the Queen!*

*Lilibet* by a loyal subject of Her Majesty*

THE PUBLISHERS OF this account, in verse, of the Queen's life from birth to accession stoutly declare that they will respect the author's wish to remain anonymous. In the copies sent for review, however, they have inserted an item from the gossip-column of this very newspaper which claims to identify the poet as Mr A. N. Wilson, the novelist and literary critic, which seems a curious way of carrying out a promise.

Some rather more likely choices must be ruled out. The Great McGonagall is dead; Beerbohm's Savonarola Brown is fictitious; the leading contemporary candidate, Mr Clive James, could well have written it, but is not much given to hiding his thingummy under a whatsit.

Fortunately, my job is not to unmask the shy versifier but to review the book. It is written in 125 eight-line stanzas of one shape – a sestet, rhyming A–B, A–B, A–B, with a final couplet rhyming C–C. This suggests a shot at *ottava rima*, but if so it is something of a boss-shot.

The story opens with the arrival of the then Home Secretary at 17 Bruton Street, to preside (though not, I take it, at the actual *accouchement*) over the royal birth; it ends in Kenya, with Prince Philip about to break the news of King George's death to our heroine. It is abundantly illustrated with photographs of the Queen and other members of her family, including four-legged ones.

* Blond & Briggs, 1985.

So much for the width; now let us feel the quality.

As it happens, the quality can be judged from the first two lines:

> Midnight in Mayfair. Hush'd are the dark bricks
> In Bruton Street of Number Seventeen.

Here is a poet who starts as he means to (and does) go on. It is already evident that he knows naught of scansion ('Mid*night* in Mayfair, hushed are *the* dark bricks'), and that he finds it easier to twist into gibberish the normal shape of an intelligible sentence ('In Bruton Street of Number Seventeen') than to find a way of conveying the thought in normal English.

Immediately afterwards he demonstrates that his attitude to rhyme is much the same as his grasp of scansion – that is, it lacks a certain something: we shall find 'piano' rhymed with 'manner', 'large' with 'George', 'her' with 'Battenberg', 'sins are' with 'Windsor', 'novelty' with 'of duty', 'raids' with 'spade' and 'hat on' with 'Mountbatten'. Prince Philip's surname is rhymed properly elsewhere, but exceptionally severe readers might well wish it hadn't been:

> Delay and disappointment could not flatten
> The ardour of Lieutenant P. Mountbatten.

There is some evidence that the poet was bitten by a definite article in youth; the infant Princess spends her pocket-money without recognition 'from shopkeeper', the Minister at Bruton Street is 'Home Secretary', Glamis is 'dark with Royal curse', and 'chance of holiday could not be missed'.

Oddest of all these habits, however, is one which clearly stems from the fact that he has noticed, in the works of many ancient and well-regarded writers, that an apostrophe sometimes takes the place of an 'e'. So he gives us, among scores and scores of examples, smil'd, ask'd and frown'd, together with danc'd, chanc'd and enhanc'd (these last three all in one stanza, which also includes cruis'd), and goes further than the famous poets he has consulted by also substituting an apostrophe for an 'a', an 'i', a 'u' or even a diphthong, giving him dow'ger, caref'lly, fav'rite and on one occasion Lil'bet herself. So idiotic is his use of this device that he even *un*scans with it a line that would otherwise fit:

> In Lilibet, the latent quality
> Of roy'l courage and deep charity.

There is, it is true, an apparently limitless public demand for slop and gossip about the monarchy, and consequently an apparently no less copious supply of it. Mass-circulation newspapers and magazines can hardly let a week go by without a picture or feature or report concerning the action and words of the Royal Family; dozens of books on the subject are published every year, the 'serious' ones being, if anything, worse in their triviality and pointlessness than the unashamed rubbish; royal tours, events, speeches are prominent in television and radio bulletins.

I doubt very much if the members of the Royal Family enjoy such stuff – very few of them, after all, are fools – but they no doubt put up with it as they put up with many another inconvenience (listening to bores politely for hours on end being probably the worst) as part of the job. At the same time, there is a very small amount of satire on, or criticism of, the monarchy or particular members of it, most of it more feeble and silly than the adulation.

But where in that spectrum is our anonymous poetaster supposed to fit? Where does he *want* to fit? His ghastly lines will not appeal to the multitude; if they are supposed to be satire they are so blunted with incompetence that they altogether fail of effect; and if they are designed to please the Queen it must be obvious that unless she has recently taken leave of her senses she is very likely, on dipping into her presentation copy, to be sick all over her breakfast.

If the author would care to reveal his intentions along with his name, he may make a small contribution to sociology;

certainly he has made none to biography, history, royalty or poetry. Anyone inclined to dispute that judgment should be prepared to say which of those exacting disciplines is enhanced by the following typical verse, concerning the visits of the Prime Minister to Buckingham Palace as World War II approaches:

> To Crawfie, he's a prissy little man.
> But Mummie says you should not speak like that.
> It's not much, but he's doing all he can,
> And Hitler is a loathsome little rat.
> Papa prays God to send them all a plan
> To keep the peace and not bomb London flat.
> Chamberlain's uncle's fact'ry made tin tacks.
> How much they all prefer Lord Halifax.

*Observer* April 29th, 1985

# Calling the tune

A T THE END OF the Second World War – it may even have been before VE-day – John Barbirolli conducted a concert in a little Dutch town near the German border. I cannot now remember whether it was with his own orchestra, the Hallé, or whether he was conducting one of the Armed Forces' orchestras, but I remember vividly the speech he made before the music started (it was recorded, and broadcast later). He announced that one of the works to be performed, the Mendelssohn Violin Concerto, had not been played anywhere in Germany for twelve years. This absence from German concert platforms, he explained, had had nothing to do with the work's musical quality; it had been banned because Nazi ideology had imposed an arbitrary political test upon it, which it had failed. The Mendelssohn Concerto was written by a Jew, and that was enough, amid the mad evil that was Nazism, to bar it from every concert-hall in Germany.

Barbirolli's speech has remained in my memory for forty years, which is not, I think, surprising, for it was a tiny but hugely symbolic illustration of why Nazism had to be destroyed, a definition, if you like, of what the Allied cause ultimately meant.

For forty years I have kept that memory bright, not only because I was one of those who, if the war had been lost, would have perished in the gas-chambers for the same illogical reason that banned performances of Mendelssohn's music, but much more because it marked out in everlasting fire the boundary between freedom and tyranny, tolerance and persecution, art and power, integrity and corruption, right and wrong.

In all those forty years, it has never occurred to me that such tests might one day be applied to the performance of music in this country, because I could conceive of no circumstances, other than the invasion and subjugation of Britain by a totalitarian enemy, in which the question could even be raised. But I had reckoned without what is now familiarly and justly known as the Fascist Left, and in particular, that movement's capture of the government of London.

Since at least the middle of July, the GLC has been imposing upon all promoters of concerts and other events at the South Bank concert-halls (Royal Festival Hall, Queen Elizabeth Hall, Purcell Room, Waterloo Room and Hungerford Room) a *political* requirement which they are obliged to fulfil on pain of having their bookings refused or cancelled – similar to, but worse than, the GLC's attempt to blackmail Miss Zola Budd into making public statements against South Africa, with the threat of refusing her the use of stadiums if she would not co-operate. In the GLC General Conditions affixed to every contract for a performance in the South Bank Halls, there is now a stipulation (Section 4, Clause 34) that:

The Licensee [i.e., the promoter] (i) shall not engage for appearance at the performance or performances to which these conditions are applicable any entertainer actor musician or other artist or any group of such persons named in advance publicity who refuse/s to signify in writing his/her/their intention not to appear as a performer in any of the following territories (a) in any part of the Republic of South Africa or (b) in the Homeland territories of Bophuthatswana Transkei Ciskei Venda and Kwazulu or (c) in Namibia unless and until the system of apartheid shall no longer prevail in that territory, any dispute as to whether the system of apartheid prevails in any territory to be referred for determination to the Director of the United Nations Centre against Apartheid and (ii) shall not contract with any entertainer actor musician or other artist or any group of such persons to appear at such performances unless the contract expressly includes the following terms . . .

There then follows a declaration, which must be obtained *by* the promoter *from* the artist, the terms of which match, but in the first person, the wording above ('I/we declare that I/we have no intention of performing in any of the following territories . . .'), with the addition of a sub-clause which reads as follows:

It is agreed that if before the time of performance of this Contract, I/we do so perform or contract so to perform [the promoter] may without notice terminate this Contract in which event no fee shall be payable thereunder to me/us and any fees paid in advance shall be refunded by me/us to [the promoter].

By an irony which I relish, I think I must be the very first person to be excluded from the South Bank Halls by the Fascist Left's political test; if so, I am very happy to stand alongside Felix Mendelssohn, also banned for non-artistic reasons by an earlier generation of totalitarians. I was not, it behoves me to add at once, proposing to play the piano at the Festival Hall, let alone sing Wagner, so before conclusions are jumped to, let me explain what I *was* engaged to do. There is an admirable group called Arts Liaison, which has raised substantial sums of money for artistic and benevolent causes. One of their regular items is the staging (normally in the Waterloo Room at the RFH) of a public interview with a celebrated musician, and I have conducted several of these. To mark Elisabeth Schwarzkopf's forthcoming seventieth birthday, Arts Liaison proposed that I should do such an interview with her; Madame Schwarzkopf agreed, and all was settled – until I learned that I would be expected to pass a test of ideological purity.

Naturally, I refused to pay the GLC's blackmail demand, and since the organizer of the event had no intention of insisting that I should, the occasion was abandoned. Happily, the Cinema at the Barbican Centre turned out to be available for the date fixed – Monday, December 2 – and the interview will now take place there.)*

It is no use saying that we only have to wait until next April, when the GLC is abolished and this evil business is swept away. The Royal Festival Hall was indelibly stained by the propaganda exhibition held there in February 1983, when the GLC handed over the whole of the ballroom area (and at a peppercorn rent) to the Soviet Union to stage a parade of lies; but the stain represented by this latest outrage is far worse, and far more difficult to expunge. Moreover, if there is one thing we should all have learnt about totalitarianism it is that its appetite doth grow by what it feeds on. It is not at all impossible that a Labour government may be in office after the next election; if so, it may well restore the metropolitan councils. We can then look forward to a further set of political tests for musicians who wish to perform on the South Bank.

First, without doubt, Israel will join South Africa in the category of GLC pariahs. (I am not indulging in fantasy; indeed, I may be understating the case. When the *Labour Herald* printed a foully anti-semitic cartoon Mr Kenneth Livingstone, boss of the GLC, not only defended its publication, but said that the only thing he regretted about it was that it did not go far enough.) After that, I would expect a requirement for artists to promise that they will not criticize the Soviet Union, possibly extended later to a ban on performances by Soviet-born artists such as Rostropovich and Ashkenazy who have defected from the democratic socialist fatherland. After

---

* It did, most successfully. (When I explained to Madame Schwarzkopf the reason for the change of venue, she said that it reminded her of certain events, not all that long ago, in her native country.)

that . . . but those of sufficiently macabre tastes can project their own continuations.

Meanwhile, we remain in the present. In the capital of the United Kingdom, principal concert-halls are now closed to any artist who refuses to sign a document that has nothing whatever to do with his or her qualifications to perform, but is a political instrument designed to further a party cause.

★   ★   ★

In practice, the policy of requiring musicians and impresarios to salute Mr Livingstone's grubby flag on pain of being turned out of the halls has had little effect; most concerts are arranged so far in advance that the bookings were pretty well complete up to and beyond the last date (March 31) on which the GLC's writ will run.

One man, however, decided that this thing must be challenged. (Remember that if this week it is barring the platform to those who refuse to sign a pledge not to play under apartheid, next week it could well be barring the auditorium to concert-goers who will not sign a petition for the removal of American bases.) Jasper Parrott is one of the partners in a very enterprising firm of concert-promoters, Harrison/Parrott, and one concert they were planning, though it was to take place after the GLC disappeared, had to be contracted before that date. (By an irony which would certainly escape Mr Livingstone, both the artists concerned, Gidon Kremer and Andras Schiff, are refugees from the Soviet empire.) Mr Parrott, with the full support of his partner, decided on legal action.

Now it has been clear all along that the political test devised by Livingstone would not stand up in court. Though the GLC are the 'owners' of the South Bank halls, they are not the owners in the sense of a man who owns his house, to which he may refuse entry on any grounds he chooses; such a public institution must be run properly, and the courts will be quick to see that it is. And imposing political demands on musical performances (and conspicuously one-sided political demands at that) would certainly be knocked on the head by a court. Unfortunately, our law precludes a court from acting in such matters except on an application made to it. Mr Parrott therefore armed himself for the battle.

Mr Parrott armed himself not only with legal advice, but with his cheque-book, for since Livingstone would be using not his own money but that of other people (viz., the ratepayers of London), he would not need to count the cost.

In these matters, it is deemed best to first ask politely for what you want, and issue the writ only when it is refused. Mr Parrott therefore asked the GLC to allow him to put on his concert without obliging his artists to pass Livingstone's political purity test; he pointed out that they both loathed apartheid, as he did himself, and that neither intended to play in South Africa.

Mr Livingstone promptly beat a tactical retreat; using as the excuse the artists' and promoters' opposition to apartheid, he most graciously agreed that the concert could go ahead as planned, without a promise of ideological obedience; by this means, he has avoided a defeat in the courts, and retains the imaginary but untested right to compel musicians to agree with his politics if they wish to perform on the South Bank.

That, it will surely be agreed, is an unsatisfactory outcome. While there is no legal ruling, and in the absence of legislation, not only will Livingstone be able to pursue his policy of censorship (which, for the reason I have given, will have little practical effect), but he and others will be encouraged to deploy the same or similar techniques in the future and elsewhere. Indeed, Sheffield council have already started to do so: without declaring that a pledge never to perform in South Africa is required if artists are to use the public Sheffield concert-hall, there is pressure on artists not only to give such a pledge but to make a public statement about it.

There is one further matter. After my first article on the subject, I was interviewed on the radio, and Mr Livingstone was invited to reply. In the course of his remarks, he said that certain people supported the South African regime because they made money out of it, e.g., by trading. Then he went on as follows:

> There are other people whose fear is that if you bring down South Africa there will be a communist regime takeover – and that is a risk I'm prepared to see. I would much rather see South Africa under a communist regime than under the present one if that's the choice I am faced with.

Note first that our hero is quite cheerful about other people's future: '. . . that is a risk I'm prepared to see . . .' '. . . if that's the choice I'm faced with . . .' The fact that it will not be he who runs the risk, nor he who faces the choice, is apparently of no moment. But that is not the most important aspect of his remarks.

South Africa is a vile tyranny. But resistance to that tyranny is legally possible, and is pursued. The Soviet Union is another; but no lawful resistance is possible. Even after decades of National Party rule, a substantial number of South African judges are truly independent of the state, and political cases have been decided against the rulers (Mr Donald Woods, then editor of the East London *Daily Dispatch*, actually won a libel action against J. B. Vorster). No Soviet judge, at any level, decides on any political case; he simply gives judgment, and imposes sentence, as instructed by his political masters.

The South African press is hedged about with more than a score of restrictive laws; but within those restrictions, South African journalists can and do denounce the evils of the regime. In the Soviet Union no journalist anywhere can or may criticize the regime. In South Africa lawyers like Mr Sydney Kentridge defend the oppressed and accuse the oppressors, and remain at liberty; the Soviet psychiatrist Dr

Koriagin is in a concentration camp for revealing that a dissident who was certified mad by the authorities was in fact sane. In South Africa, trades unions work under great difficulties; in the Soviet Union there are no unions, and anybody trying to start one will be behind barbed wire within the week.

South African Nationalism is riddled with anti-semitism, but Jews are entirely free to practise their religion and study their sacred books; in the Soviet Union anti-semitism is directed and encouraged by the state, and Jews can be, and are, imprisoned for teaching Hebrew scripture.

I could extend that catalogue for a score of pages, but my point, I trust, is made. Given a choice between a vile regime that can be ameliorated, and one which cannot, Livingstone chooses the latter. Given the choice between a total tyranny and a partial one, he supports the former. Given the choice between a country in which some are free and a country in which none is free, he plumps for unfreedom. Given the choice between great wickedness and much greater wickedness, he decides that big is beautiful.

So be it. But before he and his kind manage to turn *this* country, never mind South Africa, into a political replica of Bulgaria, there is still the matter of the South Bank concert-halls to be considered. At present the GLC is imposing, unhindered, a political test on artistic performance. Is there no interested party who will, without giving Livingstone a second opportunity to slip out of the legal net, seek a declaration that although countries like the Soviet Union and South Africa may demand political or racial conformity as the price of admission to the Artists' Entrance, this country does not intend, at the behest of the Fascist Left or anybody else, to emulate them?*

*The Times* September 12th and December 11th, 1985

* No one took up the challenge. But with the abolition of the GLC at the end of March 1986, the new authority entrusted with the management of the South Bank halls immediately brought this policy to an end.

# Mind your own business

NOT FAR FROM where I live, there is a branch of one of the chains of shops that do photocopying and printing, as well as selling stationery. The other day I went in to get a refill for a pen. I paused on the threshold and nearly turned back; I nearly turned back again when I reached the counter. The reason I recoiled was a notice stuck on the door, an identical copy of which stood prominently on the counter inside. It read, 'We do NOT give facilities for change, telephone books or anything not directly pertaining to this business'.

When I was a boy, there was a sign that hung behind the counter in a local shop, reading 'Please do not ask for credit, as a refusal often offends'; I have described that elsewhere* as 'perhaps the most powerful monument ever erected to meanness of spirit', but I think the modern one is actually worse. The old one, after all, was to be seen in a very poor neighbourhood during the Depression; I have no doubt that the shopkeeper was frequently being pressed to give credit, and it was unlikely that he was himself finding it easy to keep his head above water (it was the traditional 'corner-shop', not a branch of one of the multiples). What was wrong with the wording was not its indication that credit would be refused, but the horrible, sickly dishonesty of the excuse.

The latter-day version is worse because there is nothing to excuse. The shop did not expect to be asked for money

* In my book *Enthusiasms* (Cape 1983).

gratis, nor for copies of the telephone directory to take away; what was being refused was something that would cost the shop nothing but a tiny kindness, a miniature helping hand, a microscopic gesture in the direction of friendliness and fellow-feeling:

> For a' that and a' that
> It's coming yet for a' that,
> That man to man the warld o'er
> Shall brothers be for a' that.

Such, at any rate, were the sentiments of Robert Burns, and I dare say that if he had happened upon so notable a denial of his prediction he would have marched into the shop and been sick all over the counter, even if he hadn't been drinking.

There was no point in remonstrating with the people in the shop. Presumably this sort of thing was company policy, and all they were doing was carrying it out; certainly, the assistant who served me with my trifling purchase was as courteous and helpful as could be wished. (I may say, incidentally, that the proclaimed refusal of a glance at the telephone directory is particularly ironic, since the shop has two public telephones on the premises. I would not be surprised to learn that it is a breach of contract to provide a public phone but refuse the use of directories, and if I am right a request to me by British Telecom for the name and address of the offending firm will be instantly met.)

Now I am not complaining that I was refused change or a sight of the S-Z, and even if I had been I would have done no more than turn on my heel with a muffled oath – or more likely an unmuffled one – and left, raising no public fuss later. What I object to is the attitude behind the notice, which I think is becoming more prevalent today than ever before.

In Arthur Koestler's *The Scum of the Earth* he recounts the details of the flight from Paris as France was collapsing in the face of the *Blitzkrieg*. One phrase from it has stuck in my mind for well over twenty years; describing the columns of refugees, he describes also the farmers standing by the road in the summer heat, 'selling them water at one franc the glass'. I have always thought of that scene as a potent symbol of our time, a sign as vivid, chilling and immediately intelligible as a twist of barbed wire. More important, I have always thought of it as defining a kind of behaviour that *could not* take place in Britain.

*Autres temps, autres moeurs.* A meanness has crept into our life, of a kind that we never used to know. Those water-sellers in France in 1940 were practising the ancient peasant miserliness that had been bred in their bones for hundreds of years; a glimpse into the heart of that strange, dark tradition was made possible at the time of the Drummond murders, when a curtain was briefly twitched aside to reveal a closed, ruthless world with the Dominici family seeming as alien to us as would a band of Martians, for the very word 'peasant' has not been used in this country, except as a joke, for centuries. I remain of the opinion that such a scene would still not be possible along the country lanes of Britain amid such a catastrophe. But I am by no means as sure about the towns, and still less about the motorways.

In the Alec Guinness version of *A Christmas Carol* there was a strictly uncanonical scene in which Scrooge and Marley meet and decide to go into business together. Scrooge is attracted to his equally grasping partner by the skinflint attitude he displays, and says admiringly, 'You're a hard man, Mr Marley'; Marley's reply is 'It's a hard world, Mr Scrooge'.

So it is, so it is; but so it always has been, and once upon a time the fact was taken to mean that it behoves us all to do what we can to make it less so, not more. It is not only in *Lark Rise to Candleford* that we can see how economic necessity brings out the best rather than the worst in people, for I can remember it from my own childhood, and I am sure that the 'Please do not ask for credit' sign has remained in my mind because it so contrasted with the rest of life around me.

But now a terrible ugliness is born. Who can doubt that we are more bad-tempered in public, less considerate, more indifferent, less helpful? How many times in the past few years have we read of screams in the night that were ignored until a body was found the next morning? How few times did we read of such things in earlier days? How much more is there now of refusal to do anything but go by the book, a refusal signalled by that no less typical cry of our time, 'It's more than my job's worth'?

In Alan Bennett's early play *Forty Years On* there is what I called at the time an Antiphon for a vanished England:

**Headmaster:** In our crass-builded, glass-bloated, green-belted world Sunday is for washing the car, tinned peaches and Carnation milk.

**Franklin:** A sergeant's world it is now, the world of the lay-by and the civic improvement scheme.

**Headmaster:** Country is park and shore is marina, spare time is leisure . . . We have become a battery people . . . fed on pap in darkness, bred out of all taste and season . . .

**Tempest:** Were we closer to the ground as children or is the grass emptier now?

**Miss Nisbit:** Tidy the old into the tall flats. Desolation at fourteen storeys becomes a view.

**Matron:** Who now dies at home? Who sees death? We sicken and fade in a hospital ward and dying is for doctors, with a phone call to the family.

A gloomy view: but is it not recognizable, instantly, as the world we have made and now live in? And can you not hear a knell for that world when you see a sign, on the door and the counter of a bright, smart, modern shop, which tells you that nothing will be given over that counter – no, not so much as a peep into a telephone directory or the splitting of a 50-pence piece – unless it is 'directly pertaining to this business' and thus can be charged for?

'If you want to know the time', the jingle used to run, 'ask a policeman.' Mark my words, before any of us are much older, somebody is going to make the policeman charge sixpence for the information.

*The Times* August 16th, 1984

# To be continued

*Lord Alfred Douglas* by H. Montgomery Hyde[*]

WHAT! WILL THE LINE stretch out to the crack of doom? Are we fated to go on reading about Wilde and Douglas, pro and contra, to the end of the world and beyond? Will the rival armies never make peace or even get tired and shut up? Will no man rid me of this turbulent beast?

There is, it has to be said, fertilizer for this monstrous beanstalk. No one can have the last word, because all the leading figures – Oscar, Bosie, Queensberry, Ross, Harris, Turner, Sherard and the rest – were not only liars but liars who changed their lies as often as other men their shirts, and the truth about who was to blame, and for what, is now eternally undiscoverable, if indeed it wasn't at the time.

Mr Montgomery Hyde has a fair claim to be the Dr Kissinger of the struggle; he has written several accounts of Wilde, characterized by their fairness, he knew Bosie, and now this full and painstaking study of the other half of the tragic duet sums up (quietly, thank God) for the defence.

Insanity did not just *run* in the Queensberrys; it galloped apace – the third Marquess even turned his hand to cannibalism (he cooked a member of the kitchen staff and was discovered tucking in). To define true madness, as Polonius found, is not easy, but from this book alone it is surely clear that Bosie was deranged; the trouble is that for all Mr Hyde's scrupulous championship, his hero also shows as so horrible –

[*] Methuen, 1984.

the 'screaming, scarlet Marquess' was hardly more screaming or scarlet than his son – that we cannot even bring in a merciful verdict of guilty but insane, for the defendant was mad, bad *and* dangerous to know.

The twin drives of Bosie's life were hatred and self-pity; the first flame burned down eventually (he lived to be seventy-five, remember), but the second never even flickered – when Wilde was behind the bars of Reading jail, his lover, who was living in Capri, wrote, 'I am not in prison, but I think I suffer as much as Oscar, in fact more', and fifty years later he was still at it, writing to Hesketh Pearson (who had sent him some of the typescript of his biography of Wilde):

> I can't write at length. I am far too ill . . . the last few pages about the *De Profundis* letter are less than fair to me. You do not sufficiently make clear how monstrous and ridiculous O.W.'s charges against me were . . . I gave him far more money than he gave me . . .

As for the hate, well, here he is writing a mild billet-doux to Freddie Manners-Sutton:

> I beg to inform you that neither I nor Olive will ever speak to you again, and that I forbid you to come to this house. Furthermore, I will tell you quite plainly that I consider you to be a low, huckstering, Jew-minded pimp.

And here he is replying to Wilfrid Scawen Blunt, who had reproached him for unforgivable behaviour towards his friends and declared that he would not give Bosie 'any further countenance':

> Of what value has your countenance ever been to any man? To be known as your friend or associate has always been something in the nature of a social handicap. What are you but a contemptible cad, whom most people consider a half crazy old gentleman . . .?

And here is a perfumed note to Robert Ross:

> Ransome . . . is a filthy rotten sort of person . . . But *you* are
> and have been all your life a filthy bugger and unspeakable
> skunk.

And here he is in uxorious mood, writing to the wife of his
bosom:

> I got your curious letter . . . to the husband whom you treated
> so basely and whose forgiveness you were so anxious to obtain a
> month or two ago. I confess that I now take very little interest
> one way or the other in your moods. It is quite evident that
> money and self-interest are the only motives that sway
> them . . .

And finally (though it was by no means finally for Bosie),
here he is dropping a friendly line to the lawyer who had
cross-examined him in one of his countless law-suits:

> In the course of the ridiculous and disgusting exhibition of
> impotent rancour and malice which you provided in your
> opening speech . . . you made a reference to the 'place where the
> plaintiff so properly belongs' by which you were understood to
> mean prison. You ought to know all about it considering that
> your father did five years penal servitude for heartless frauds, the
> victims of which you have never compensated to the extent of a
> penny out of the enormous income which you get from the silly
> people who are foolish enough to employ your fifth-rate abilities
> as counsel.

Mr Hyde's two chief arguments in Bosie's favour are that he
was a poet of consequence and that he became a devout
Catholic and thereafter truly reformed his life. Unfortunately, the evidence he produces – extensive quotation –
shows only that Bosie's poetry was mostly forced and
lifeless, with no more than a handful of good lines, and that
his religion had all the profound spirituality of a Gordon
Fraser Christmas-card; and although Mr Hyde is certainly

entitled to an acquittal for his client on the charge of having betrayed Wilde, he cannot get round the fact that Bosie egged on Oscar to launch the fatal action against Queensberry.

The best of the book is the vivid picture it paints of the social and cultural climate of the Nineties and after, in particular the frenzied terror of homosexuality that was so widespread (and which now lingers only in the prurient swineries of *Private Eye*); the worst is the astonishing profusion of illiteracies (I take it that Methuen have now joined the growing list of publishers who have dispensed with editing and proof-reading): 'failed to satisfy the author even less . . .' '[because of the lack of evidence] the ability to prove immoral tendencies could indeed be formidable . . .', 'Bosie gave Tennant a bill for £500 which he had no intention of meeting and in fact did not do so', 'Hoping to supplement his dwindling income and increasing debts due to poor health . . .', 'in which Butterworth joined in . . .' All the same, Mr Hyde has said the best that can be said for Bosie; it is too much to hope that he has also said the last.

*Observer* November 12th, 1984

# A view from the laager

I T WAS EURIPIDES who first suggested that when the gods wish to destroy a man they first drive him mad, though I have always thought this technique unnecessarily complicated; what is the point of being a god if you cannot go direct to your objective? But even supposing that the gods accept a self-denying ordinance, and invariably employ the two-stage approach, they would surely be baffled if, when they embarked upon the first, ground-clearing operation, they found that their intended victim was already unglued to an extent which rendered the operation superfluous, and they would be even more astonished to learn that the loosening of the screws had been embarked upon by the mooncalf himself.

In just such a position the South African government finds itself this morning, as cuckoos, heedless of the season, are to be heard singing from every bush. Here is an official statement, put out at the highest official level in Pretoria, designed to make clear South Africa's position and policy:

If by 'apartheid' is meant,

1. Political domination by any one community of any other;

2. The exclusion of any community from the decision-making process;

3. Injustice or inequality in the opportunities available for any community;

4. Racial discrimination and impairment of human dignity; the South African government shares in the rejection of the concept.

I have repeatedly asked, without ever getting a serious, let alone a satisfactory, reply, why the Soviet Union regularly holds what are called 'elections', in which there is only one candidate in each constituency, who is invariably voted for by never less than 99.9 per cent of the electorate, and frequently by many more. The burden of my question is that nobody within the country, nor anybody outside either – nay, not so much as Mr Mick McGahey or even Mr Tony Chater – believes that these performances have anything to do with elections; one of my correspondents suggested that an appointment to the Supreme Soviet was the equivalent of our Honours List, and although I can see much force in the analogy, it still does not explain why the Soviet leaders go to such trouble and expense to make a claim that *everyone* knows is false.

The Soviet parallel with South Africa (it is not, alas, the only one, and most of the others are considerably more serious, as many a black corpse would testify if it could only sit up and sing) is obvious. The four-part catalogue set out in the South African government's statement (which could not possibly have been promulgated without President Botha's direct approval) is an exact definition of the system of apartheid as practised in South Africa for some decades now; but that is not my point. My point is that nobody, however well disposed to South Africa and its policies, believes that 'the South African government shares in the rejection of the concept' as there defined.

Why, then, are such words composed and published? The correspondent who drew my attention to the statement, and who is himself one of the most honourable and courageous of all those who resist apartheid from within South Africa, offered an explanation no less ingenious than the theory of the Soviet honours list and much more persuasive. Here it is.

It is no doubt difficult for a government to say in so many words: 'We have been wrong all along; our policies have been wicked and disastrous and we are going to change them.' It is easier to say, however unconvincingly, 'Those wicked policies are not our policies at all; we believe in something quite different.' Such a statement, even if no one believes it, signals to the world and, above all, to the government's own constituency at home, that its traditional and fundamental policies, however much in its heart it still cherishes them, are no longer publicly defensible. And it gives notice that if international pressures on South Africa continue, apartheid itself may have to go.

My friend supports his case by pointing out that the lunatic claim was followed by an assurance that a programme of reform would shortly be embarked upon, though even from the sketchy details given it is clear that no attempt will be made to demolish even one of the four pillars of apartheid, let alone all of them. And I have to say that, for all its logic, this explanation of the impossible seems to me ultimately unconvincing.

The metaphor of madness may not be entirely metaphorical. If a man lives entirely in a world of unreality, surely it is not surprising if he ceases in time to know what reality is. For years we have all talked about 'the laager mentality'; but the cliché, though ground to fine dust by over-use, did once mean something, particularly if we recall what a laager actually is. It is the circle of ox-wagons, drawn up for defensive purposes, in which the Voortrekkers camped for the night when on the march. Stop for a moment and conjure up the scene as night came on, with the limitless veld all round, the watchmen posted at the points of the compass, and everyone within the mysterious pentacle, outside which no safety was to be found. With so powerful an oriflamme from their past, is it really surprising that those in power in South Africa have come to believe, to the point of obsession and beyond, that they, and they alone, are defending something precious and vital, while outside the magic circle there are only enemies, fearsomely equipped with wondrous powers and implacably resolved on the destruction of the precious ring and all within it?

Remember that the American pioneers, as they pushed westward across the opening continent, slept in just such a formation. They were not, of course, defending themselves against the black man, but the metaphor holds good; remember how long and how tenaciously racial segregation was defended in the United States (the Supreme Court decision in Brown v Board of Education, which made the first real breach in the circle of wagons, was only thirty-one years ago). Americans today tend to rub their eyes as though waking from a dream when they are reminded that their own system of apartheid endured until the middle of the 1960s, when Lyndon Johnson and Hubert Humphrey armed themselves to break it; much more significant is the amazement of Americans when they remember with what arguments the evil thing was seriously defended. It is not at all unusual to hear Americans, reflecting on that so recent past, express themselves in such terms as 'We must have been crazy'.

Perhaps, if we do not use the word too literally, they were. Certainly many of the Southern *jusqu'auboutistes* believed they were doing God's work, and their opponents the Devil's. For that matter, the gentleman who approached me in a public place last week and assured me that scientists had perfected a device for photographing people's memories, and another which shot thoughts, by means of laser-beams, into people's brains, and that both techniques, together with others no less remarkable, had been used on him, undoubtedly believed what he told me. But he was wrong, for all that, and so were the defenders of American apartheid, and so are those who defend the same system, far more monstrous in its completeness, in South Africa.

Is it any wonder, do you think, that if you defend the indefensible long enough, with arguments in which there is no substance at all, you will end up unable to believe that the world is round? (And *that* is not as much of a metaphor as you might think, either; Oom Paul Kruger, to the day of his death, believed it was flat.) It is not at all impossible that President Botha, scoundrel though he is, saw, as he initialled the statement I have quoted, nothing strange, let alone hypocritical, in such words, but believed them to be no more than the plain and literal truth. How he may be disabused of so fatally eccentric a notion is another matter. But let us not be too surprised that he holds it.

*The Times* December 4th, 1985

# The empty Grail

IN 1967, THE ROYAL ACADEMY put on a very large exhibition of the work of Sir John Millais, PRA, the first such show to be mounted for a good many decades; I felt I ought to go, as I had never seen any substantial number of the works of the Pre-Raphaelite Brotherhood at one time, let alone nearly 400 by a single member of the group.

After about three-quarters of an hour touring the Academy's Millais-laden walls, I began to feel very ill, and after a further half-hour, I began to suffer from hallucinations; half an hour after that, I rushed screaming into the street, and I knew no more until I came to in a darkened room which, I noted with some surprise, had bars on the windows.

Very careful nursing, and the love of a good woman (several, actually), enabled me to leave the institution in a matter of months. Time went by; I felt gradually stronger; when I learned, a few weeks ago, that there was a huge exhibition of the Pre-Raphaelites at the Tate, I reasoned that a period of seventeen years' convalescence was surely sufficient, and paid it a visit. I went right round it very carefully; I went right round it again; I looked at every picture at least twice; then darkness descended. I was found several days later wandering about the Quantocks insisting to the sheep (my only audience) that my relatives were trying to murder me for my money.

Never, in all my life, not even at the exclusively Millais exhibition in 1967, have I seen so much sickening rubbish in one place at one time. There are 250 exhibits; there are not a dozen among them – this is not a number plucked from the air to make my point, but the result of *counting* as I went round – which can be looked at without revulsion, let alone which can be thought of as works of art.

My feelings are not simply, or even mainly, a reaction to the sentimentality, horrible, false and dehumanizing though it is. Nor did I find the exhibition so repellent solely because of the suffocating ugliness and vulgarity of the draperies, the hideous colours and even more hideous combinations of colours, the putrescent flesh-tones, the brutal 'butch' women favoured as models, the doll-like children, the perfumed animals, the drawing-room trees, the salt-free sea. All these charges are true, far more deeply and poisonously true than my few adjectives can convey, but they are not the worst. The worst goes to the heart of the exhibition and of the Brotherhood itself. From the first room to the last, these pictures are a pack of lies.

I must explain what I mean. Among the Pre-Raphaelites' preferred themes, there are three which are worth taking particular note of. There are religious pictures – of Christ, of Apostles, of saints; there are Shakespearean scenes; and there are historical episodes, recording actual or imagined events, these in particular often being equipped with titles like the triple-decker captions to old *Punch* cartoons, such as *Berengaria's Alarm for the Safety of her Husband, Richard Coeur de Lion, Awakened by the Sight of his Girdle Offered for Sale at Rome,* or *A Huguenot, on St. Bartholomew's Day, Refusing to Shield Himself from Danger by Wearing the Roman Catholic Badge,* or *A Converted British Family Sheltering a Christian Missionary from the Persecution of the Druids.* (These are not parodies by me, but the actual titles, capitalization and all.)

Now if you look closely at the faces and the disposition of the bodies in the pictures of all three of these groups, you will be struck by the emptiness and inauthenticity of them; vapidity and lifelessness are the dominant characteristics.

Ford Madox Brown's *Christ washing the feet of St. Peter* looks like a respectable assistant at Lilley & Skinner showing a customer the latest line in patent leather; Millais's *Ferdinand Lured by Ariel* looks like a man asking directions near Heathrow and obliged to cup both ears to hear the answer; it is not surprising that Henry Wallis's *Chatterton* is dead, for the waxwork he has made of the poet has plainly never been alive.

The more elaborate the detail, the more direct the allegory, the more familiar the scene depicted, the more banal, unimaginative and superficial (I have never seen, not even in a Jackson Pollock, paint spread so thick to make a picture so thin) is the result; if you listen carefully before Holman Hunt's *Rienzi Vowing to Obtain Justice for the Death of his Young Brother, Slain in a Skirmish between the Colonna and Orsini Factions* (another title I have not invented) you can hear the model whining that he is getting pins and needles in his right leg and please can he have a cup of tea, and if you look no less thoroughly at Millais's *Ophelia* (perhaps the most famous picture the Brotherhood ever produced) you could draw the outline of the zinc bath she was lying in. But it is not the ghastly unreality of everybody and everything in these pictures that leads me to charge them with artistic falsehood: there is evidence more damning.

Imagine yourself cutting out (I was tempted to do it in more than my imagination) the faces of the central figures in three representative pictures – Holman Hunt's *The Shadow of Death*, Millais's *The Black Brunswicker* and Ford Madox Brown's *Geoffrey Chaucer Reading the 'Legend of Custance' to Edward III*. Five minutes later you will have no idea of which is which; the labels on the pictures in this exhibition could be taken off and re-affixed at random without anybody being any the wiser. Christ and King Lear; the Virgin and Mrs Thomas Fairbairn; Aurora Leigh or Lucrezia Borgia; Jerusalem or Putney; on these walls it's all one.

That, however, is not because the Pre-Raphaelites were

incompetent draughtsmen (though if you look too closely at those sweeping folds, those tumbling tresses, they begin to disintegrate); it is because the highflown hocus-pocus with which they deceived themselves and with which they are still deceiving multitudes (the Tate was crammed at 10 a.m.) was a false front behind which there was a group of knowing journeymen posing as artists. From Exhibit No. 1 to Exhibit No. 250, there is no feeling, only calculation, no heart, only thought, no passion, only assiduity, no vigour, only force, no fire, only smoke, no humility, only discretion, no love, only desire, no God, only religion, no nature, only scenery, no art, only technique, no understanding, only knowledge, and above all no genius *and no regrets for the lack of it.*

There is a Max Beerbohm cartoon in which Queen Victoria is earnestly asking one of the Brotherhood, 'But what were they going to do with the Grail when they found it, Mr Rossetti?' Max did not provide the answer, but I can; they were going to drink cocoa out of it.

*The Times* May 7th, 1984

# Black and Blue

A FEW YEARS AGO, the then Home Secretary said to me, in precisely these words, 'The Met's in a mess'. With the remarkable intuition that has carried me to the very pinnacle of my profession, I instantly deduced that he was not talking about the well-known opera house in New York. But if the Home Secretary held that opinion then, he would be a bold man who claimed that the condition of the Metropolitan Police has strikingly improved since. Or so it seems to me, and I imagine that few of my regular readers will believe that I am so extravagant an admirer of Arthur Scargill, Bernie Grant, Ted Knight and the Militant Tendency that I would endorse without hesitation their courteously expressed claims that the police force is an evil instrument of class oppression, staffed by brutal thugs only too eager to do the dirty work of their capitalist masters.

When Stephen Waldorf was reduced by police marksmen to the condition of a colander, I held my peace; people who think they are dealing with a dangerous gunman are apt to behave as though they are, and it is too easy for others, afterwards, to insist that they should have got themselves shot dead making certain.

When Mrs Cherry Groce was shot and seriously wounded by a police bullet after police had made a forcible entry into her home in search of her son, who did not live there, because he was wanted for questioning (he has since been tried and acquitted), I raised an eyebrow or two, and began to think it possible that some policemen had been watching

more American television programmes than was quite healthy for them. And when Mrs Cynthia Jarrett died in a similar
incursion, I was content to wait for the inquest, and did not
much care for some of the things that emerged therefrom.

Still have I borne it with a patient shrug; all three incidents
could reasonably be ascribed to advanced cases of the jitters
among the boys in blue; small consolation for the victims
(Mrs Groce may be paralysed for life), and in a trained and
disciplined force strictly inexcusable, but there are some very
nasty characters behind closed front doors these days, and
that which may not be excused can be, by anyone with a little
imagination, easily understood.

Now, however, there has been a case in which the
behaviour of the police officers concerned was not only
inexcusable in any circumstances but raised questions about
the condition of the Met and its leadership that go very far
beyond the incident itself; indeed, I may as well say plainly
what I thought when I read the details, which is that if the
Commissioner is not willing to take rapid, ruthless and
well-publicized action to root out the kind of behaviour there
displayed, which is of a kind that is very unlikely indeed to be
a single, self-contained incident, it would be better for all of
us if he were to be succeeded as soon as possible by someone
who is.

Here are the details. Patrick Wilson, a black man in a
wheelchair, was stopped by police who claimed that they
suspected him of having illegal drugs concealed about him.
Mr Wilson said that in the course of their action they made
racially offensive and abusive remarks to him; he therefore
went in his car (he cannot walk, but is able to drive) to the
office where his girlfriend, Miss Susan Farbridge, worked
(and to which he had just taken her when the incident
occurred), so that he should not be without witnesses.

When Mr Wilson and Miss Farbridge and the police were
all together at her office, she explained about his disability;
*both* of them were then arrested and taken to a police station,

where they were both strip-searched. In the course of the journey to the police station, PC Roderick Paterson and PC Neil Rossiter assaulted Mr Wilson by dropping him on the floor of the van; he had already been assaulted in his car. In the course of Miss Farbridge's examination, she was 'assaulted by search'; she was also forced, when naked, to jump up and down.

Sergeant Raymond Gull and WPC Karen Connell falsely claimed that they believed Miss Farbridge had drugs about her. No drugs were found on either Mr Wilson or Miss Farbridge, but they were falsely charged with other offences: Mr Wilson with careless driving and assaulting a police officer, Miss Farbridge with obstructing a police officer. Both were subsequently acquitted of all charges. They then brought an action for damages against the Metropolitan Police.

By the time the civil case was to be heard, the Met were running scared; they offered Mr Wilson £2,505 to settle out of court. The odd sum is easily explained; if damages are offered and refused, and a court awards less than the offer, the plaintiff is obliged to pay all the costs for both sides from the date of the offer. Lawyers estimate what a plaintiff might get, and advise their clients to offer slightly more; here, the Met plainly guessed that Mr Wilson might be awarded £2,500, and the extra fiver, if he did, would ensure that the costs would fall on him.

As it happened, Mr Wilson was awarded a total of £1,750, while Miss Farbridge was awarded £2,000 altogether, and Mr Wilson was ordered to pay the costs, but the judge, in a reconvened hearing, changed his decision; he said that he had not fully taken into account what he called 'the disgraceful conduct' of the police, and awarded Mr Wilson his costs after all.

Out of the corner of my eye I can see *The Times* lawyers beginning to bleed from the ears, so I had better pause to explain my confident ascription of wrongdoing to the offic-

ers in the case. It was the jury in the civil action (and, by
inevitable implication, the magistrate in the prosecutions of
Mr Wilson and Miss Farbridge) who concluded that, as the
plaintiffs contended, Mr Wilson had been unlawfully
arrested, maliciously prosecuted, falsely imprisoned and for
good measure assaulted, and that Miss Farbridge had been
unlawfully arrested, falsely imprisoned and likewise (and
humiliatingly) assaulted.

And it was the judge who declared that the conduct of the
police had been 'disgraceful' and that they had behaved
'oppressively and in abuse of their powers'. The names of the
officers in question were attached as specified above to the
offences described.

And just in case anyone wants to believe that the jury
was packed by defence challenges so as to be entirely
composed of drug-maddened voodoo-followers with an
average of forty convictions for grievous bodily harm, I must
draw attention to the fact that they refused Mr Wilson a
verdict on one of the most important of his indictments: they
decided that although Mr Wilson had no drugs about him,
the police were not lying when they said they thought he
had, so that it was proper for them to search him.

I am unable to accept, in a case as scandalous as this, the
'rotten apples' theory. Of course there are dishonest policemen and policewomen, as there are dishonest butchers,
bakers and candlestick-makers; why, I have even heard of
journalists who occasionally say the thing that is not. But
what can be the climate in which these officers were trained
and assigned, and what must be the tenor of the force of
which they are members, if such a catalogue of dishonesty
and wickedness is seen when the carpet is rolled back?

Mr Wilson said, after the case, that he had often been
stopped by the police 'just for being a black Rastaman'. I
would normally discount a good deal of such a claim; after
this case, I do not, particularly in the wake of the Groce and
Jarrett affairs.

If there is in the Met a tendency to believe that the doors of black people's houses can be broken down with more readiness and less excuse than those of white people's, and if *five* officers conspire to commit unlawful arrest, malicious prosecution, false imprisonment and assault on a black man and his white companion, and then lie themselves even deeper into the mire while their superiors, who can see a barn door by daylight, are striving to prevent the case coming to court, then it seems to me that there is something very much deeper and rottener at the heart of the Met than the inevitable incidence of a few bad and dishonest members of it.

These things have been said before. But they have not been said by me. The fact that I am saying them now is important only in one particular: if those whose instinctive as well as logical sympathies have always been engaged on the side of the police are now finding that that is ceasing to be true, it must mean that we feel that there is good reason for our shift. There have been too many incidents, and too many plainly genuine complaints and grievances, for the Met or anyone else to go on repeating that there is nothing more to it than a few officers who have let the force down. It now seems to me more likely that a subterranean stream of poison is running through the force, and that the Wilson-Farbridge scandal may be far less exceptional than it should be.

When Sir Robert Mark became commissioner, he caused surprise by making clear that his greatest priority would be to root out corruption in the force he led. What, asked some, more important than catching burglars, making the streets safer, stopping the heroin-peddlers? Yes, much more important, for a house that is built upon sand cannot stand. It is perhaps time for the present commissioner, or his successor, to undertake, with no less energy, implacability and urgency, to sweep his force clean of a very different, yet perhaps even more pernicious, plague. That Home Secretary was right.

*The Times* December 17th, 1985

# Stranger than fiction

*Marthe* Translated by Donald M. Frame[*]

Is THIS BOOK what it purports to be, or an epistolary novel written in an immensely plausible pastiche of Zola? We are told that the letters of which it consists were discovered 'a decade or so ago' in a French château. How they came to light, in what château they were found, who authenticated them (I do hope it wasn't Lord Dacre), where the originals now are, whether the hand-coloured photograph on the jacket is supposed to be of Marthe herself – on all these matters we are given no information at all. Moreover, the story is too pat for comfort: everyone who needs to be dead for the tale to be rounded off smoothly does indeed die on cue, and there are no loose ends left to puzzle the reader.

On the other hand, the translation and notes are by Professor Donald Frame, and I cannot believe that the translator and biographer of Montaigne would be party to the staging of such a drama, however engrossing the result. Perhaps the original French edition (it is praised on the jacket by *Le Monde*, but Lady Bracknell would certainly have said that nowadays that is no guarantee of respectability) explained everything, and the fault lies with Viking for not providing the book with a provenance; after all, they have not provided it with an index, they have set it in ugly Souvenir, and they have had it bound so badly that when I opened it flat the pages began to fall out.

For the rest of this review I shall assume that the book is

[*] Viking, 1985.

authentic. If so, it is an astounding and invaluable portrait of petit-bourgeois France in the last decade of the nineteenth century. Marthe is the twenty-year-old daughter, pregnant by a family servant, of the implacably genteel Émilie de Montbourg, née de Cerilley; her mother is desperate to find a respectable husband for her. Only gradually do we discover that Marthe has been promiscuous since she was fourteen, that she is an incurable liar, and that she is mentally disturbed.

More gradually we learn that she suffers from hysteria, fainting fits, colic, neuralgia, pimples ('eat more grapes,' says mother), 'morbid ardour' (nymphomania, I take it), urine-retention, phlebitis, 'white, yellow and even pink discharges' and earache. Abruptly, it is revealed that the seat of all her disorders is hereditary syphilis; her father, now dead, got it from a dancer in Caen and passed it on to his wife to transmit to Marthe. (Marthe's sister is another chronic invalid, as indeed is her mother, and her brother has died young just before the tale begins.)

The husband-hunting is horrible and comic at the same time. Plagued by false testimonials ('the curate lied'), mama clutches at straw after straw. The station-master at Tourette is qualified, but socially impossible; a tax-collector seems more promising, but there must be a guarantee that he does not hold 'advanced republican opinions', and the severity of his expression in the photograph he sends is alarming, even with his assurances ('. . . my character is among the gentlest and merriest . . . my manner is cheery'). What is more, his parents are in the retail wine-business, which would never do. But stay: it seems that that is a mistake, they are wholesalers, which makes all the difference. Besides: 'By the way, M. Granjean already has a nice set of furniture for a bachelor. His cleaning woman is sixty. That's a good point of decorum.'

The next candidate is a post-office clerk ('The baker brother-in-law is a great drawback, although they don't have

the same name'), and after him a pharmacist, who is 'good to
the poor and to animals'. On the other hand, 'pharmacy is
not what it used to be'. But then again, 'A wife doesn't get
involved in a pharmacy'. But the fool ruins everything by
putting up an enormous sign *with his name on it*. Exit the
pharmacist, enter another station–master ('I must pick up this
new trail'), who also comes to nothing.

At last, they land a man with the cherished 'de' in his
name; after prolonged negotiations Marthe becomes Mme
Robert Caron d'Aillot. Then the trouble really starts, but it is
impossible to see whom to blame. Is Marthe unfaithful, does
Robert beat and threaten her, was he only after her money,
is she writing at his dictation or are her expressions of
happiness genuine?

Probably the answer to all these questions is yes, but for
Marthe's mother, herself violently unstable, her daughter is
perfect and Robert an unqualified villain. Mother thinks he is
plotting to murder her daughter, but he and his family ('liars,
vulgarians and swindlers') suggest that mother actually *did*
murder the illegitimate child. Among the factions, only one
man resists hysteria: Charles de Cerilley, Marthe's uncle and
head of the family. Constantly trying to restrain his sister, to
make Robert behave better, to persuade everybody to take
into account Marthe's congenital weaknesses, he is cynic and
sage at once, though consumed like everybody else with
avarice and the horror of scandal.

As for the greed, Zola would hardly have dared to invent
it. 'The moral situation is very sad,' writes mother, 'but
think of the pecuniary one.' They think of nothing else; the
merest sniff of a legacy or a marriage portion and half the
countryside is up and laying claim. The match-making is full
of accounts, estimates, debts, bankruptcies, interest and
promissory notes, and the tone is consistent to the end; after
the divorce, 'they'll give back the furniture and the pawn-
tickets'.

To keep up a front for the neighbours is all; as Marthe

approaches her shaming childbirth, mama's sister turns very practical: 'If misfortune were to strike the mother, we must be in agreement as to the illness she died of . . . Meningitis . . . would be logical. Diphtheria? Or peritonitis?' Even Marthe's mother can calm down and talk sense when she wants to: 'If all young people confessed to the families of their intended, how many marriages would take place?'

The world of public affairs obtrudes rarely, but when it does, the cast responds in character: at the assassination of President Sadi Carnot, 'the most urgent thing is to muzzle the press and oppose all dubious opinions', and the explosion of a naval powder magazine is linked to 'the great upheaval the Dreyfusards have threatened'.

If 'Marthe' is a novel, it is a very clever one; if it is history, it is an infinitely revealing document, showing, down to the very last mean, narrow, selfish detail, a world more like that of Thérèse Raquin than Zola ever dreamed of.

*Observer* 7th July, 1985

# Easy as a, b, d

JOURNALISTS OF MY KIND frequently find themselves enlisted in a cause which is not their own, and to which, indeed, they are indifferent. They feel obliged to join in any row going, however, because the common element in so many campaigns is the injustice being practised against the group who solicit a public voice for their complaint. Thus, in recent years I have found myself championing the rights of homosexuals though I am not a homosexual, of smokers though I do not smoke, and of Freemasons though I have never rolled up my trousers for any reason more sinister than to go paddling.

It is therefore with a sense of relief as well as pleasure that today I find myself speaking up on behalf of a body which I not only admire and value very highly, but of which I am actually a member, albeit in an honorary capacity. Arms and the Indexer I sing.

Of my seven books I compiled the index to only one, the first, and swore a mighty oath, when I had finished the task, that I would rather die, and in a particularly unpleasant manner, than do it again. My excuse was that I wanted to see how it was done: I had always been fascinated by indexes (you must *not* call them 'indices', lest you bring down upon your head the wrath of the Society of Indexers, who have a special, and very awful, curse for those who use that forbidden word), and always, when reviewing a book, taken care to commend good ones and castigate bad, reserving my sharpest darts for those non-fiction books which have no index at all. I have, incidentally, never seen why even a novel should not have an index.

In stumbling through my do-it-yourself index, I discovered two things very quickly; one was that it is an appalling and prolonged labour (no wonder Hercules published his autobiography without one), and the other was that it demands a very high level of technical skill, which can come only from training and experience, neither of which, of course, I had. In my presumptuous ignorance, I thought that anyone who could recite the alphabet could compile an index, but I found as soon as I started that almost half of the entries (and it eventually ran to fifteen two-column pages in very small type) posed a problem, from whether Charles de Gaulle was *Gaulle, Charles de* or *de Gaulle, Charles* (it is the latter), to substantial and recurring problems like how much to cross-reference and in what circumstances; I believe there are more *qvs* in that index than in any other book ever published. (Mind you, I managed to slip in a very rude joke about poor Mervyn Griffith-Jones, though only Ned Sherrin spotted it.)

When to the sobering realization that I was devoid of the gifts required to be a real indexer was added the discovery that it took me an immense length of time to do it at all, I concluded that from now on I would seek expert hands, and not only on Belloc's principle:

> Lord Finchley tried to mend the electric light
> Himself – it struck him dead, and serve him right.
> It is the business of the wealthy man
> To give employment to the artisan.

I discovered that there is a professional body, the Society of Indexers, and that it gives an official qualification, attained by a rigorous expert assessment of an indexer's work, which alone entitles him or her to be included on the Society's register. I also, however, discovered the lady (I was introduced to her by my publishers) who has indexed all my subsequent books, and who is not only The Greatest Indexer in the World but the Very Nicest Too. (Authors and others who want an index made should get in touch with the Society's Registrar, who is Mrs Elizabeth Wallis: her address is 25 Leybourne Park, Kew Gardens, Surrey. She will advise on which registered Indexer would be suitable for the work contemplated – some specialize in particular sub-jects – and give other essential information. But those who would like the services of My Very Own Indexer should write to me; if they seem sufficiently respectable I shall give them her name and address.)

But there is, difficult though you may find it to believe, a particular point to this column. It is the truly shocking level of payment that this very remarkable and responsible work commands. Publishers sometimes pay indexers the same hourly rate as proof-readers; I salute the craft of proof-reading (in which I do have some skill of my own), but the comparison is invalid, for indexers need far more hard-won knowledge and understanding than a proof-reader, and it is not too much to say that they not only enhance and make more useful the books they index, but that their art at its best can be a genuinely creative part of a published book.

Yet the minimum rate proposed by the Society of Indexers (it is not enforced, and hardly could be) is at present no more than £5.25 an hour, and publishers have been known to complain to indexers that they are 'pricing themselves out of the market'. Apart from the lamentably low level of reward for so high a level of professionalism, the hourly rate is an absurdity in itself, for it takes no cognizance of the widely different varieties of index, some of which are far more complex and demanding than others.

A few publishers absorb the cost of an index, and one who does so has expressed himself uneasy at the majority who charge the author for it instead; 'I do not', he said, 'charge the author for having an artist design a book jacket, nor for the skilled work of my in-house editor.' My own publisher is

among the majority; I do not begrudge a penny of what my
beloved indexer charges, but then her fee is only a tiny
fraction of what my books earn me, and I know that there are
writers to whom the indexer's charges represent a substantial
proportion of a small advance that is unlikely to be increased
by subsequent royalties. No doubt that would be true also in
the case of very small or specialized publishers, but it is high
time general publishers took the view that the work of the
indexer is as essential as that of the jacket-designer or for that
matter the printer and the supplier of paper, and carried the
cost.

This is by no means so esoteric a subject as you may
imagine. Hardly a week goes by without a book reviewer
complaining at the low quality (or absence) of the index to a
book he is dealing with; the Society's quarterly magazine has
a regular feature consisting of excerpts from reviews, and the
number of adverse comments is considerably greater than
that of indexes praised. And quite right too, for I have read
many books of outstanding quality, interest and value which
have been seriously and irretrievably damaged by an inadequate index; one that comes to mind is the *Diaries of
Cosima Wagner*, which came in two volumes, though my
public explosion of rage at the useless index to the first
volume had no effect on the quality of the second, which
was just as bad. Even my own publishers have recently
sinned inexcusably, and I know of very few who never do
so.

This, then, is a plea for an admirable profession, equipped
with real skills, to be accorded both the respect and the
reward that it deserves. I have no interest to declare; though I
was honoured to be invited to join the Society of Indexers I
am not available to do other people's indexes, and a lousy fist
I would make of them if I were. But in their obviously lesser
and unspectacular way, indexers suffer from misprision and
injustice, just as homosexuals, smokers and Freemasons do,
and I felt that, having repeatedly done my duty by the last

three, I could do no less than bang a drum for the first.

*The Times* December 23rd, 1985

*My affection for indexes, and my admiration for indexers, goes back a long way; invited by the Editor of* The Indexer *to contribute to a symposium of authors' attitudes to indexing, I supplied this.*

I indexed my first book (very badly) because I wanted to know what this strange but to me intriguing job required. Fortunately, I then happened upon Mrs Oula Jones, of the Society of Indexers, 'since when I have used no other'. But although I will never again do it, I like to see how it is done.

Indexes have always fascinated me; when I am Prime Minister I shall bring in a law making them compulsory in all books, including novels. I can and do read indexes for pleasure (the index to the definitive Pepys is one of my favourite bedside books), and some well repay the attempt, but even in the drier ones there is much to instruct the reader and even delight him. To look through a really well-planned, ample and understanding index is like doing *The Times* crossword with the solution at one's elbow; all the fun of seeing into the compiler's mind without the labour of working out how his mind operates. When the book is my own, the same fun is obtained, but an additional element enters into it.

Names, places, books, operas – these are the bones of an index, of course, and many an index passes muster with nothing more, provided it is thorough enough at that level. But I want more for myself, and I have been fascinated to see how my indexer has worked herself into my mind so that she can see the book through my eyes and give me the extra element, which consists of themes, concepts, principles, attitudes; my books tend to have more of these than of facts, but they do inevitably pose a problem for an indexer. To start with, should the index limit itself to the themes discussed? Surely not; it should also encompass the themes in the author's mind, from which his writing springs. To give an obvious example; I write a great deal about freedom, but the *word* may well not occur in a passage devoted to the *subject*. The indexer sees this, and under the heading 'freedom' will direct the reader to discussions of it in its various contexts. But it is not something that is automatically obvious.

There are more nebulous problems; what does my indexer do about irony, to which I am much given? There is plenty of opportunity to take the irony literally and index it at face value; the reader will then find the reference easily enough, but will have a shock when he discovers that it is by no means what it seems – another problem that to the uninstructed would not spring to mind. (There are accidents, too. In one of my books I mentioned Clive James; it was only the slightest passing reference, in a list of half a dozen names, but it so chanced that the 'Clive' was the last word on one page and the 'James' the first word on the next. I am sure that Mrs Jones, who is very nearly as wicked as I am, relished the effect as much as I did, for the effect was that Mr James, who would never pick up any book without at once turning to the index to see if he was mentioned in it, must have leaped to the conclusion that I had written a two-page essay on him, with concomitant disappointment when he found I had not.)

The ultimate test of an index, at any rate of an index to a book that is composed of the author's feelings rather than of an objective dispassionate account of a subject that does not require feeling, is: could the reader construct the author's outlook, *ex pede Herculem*, from the index alone? I think, in the case of my books and my indexer, the answer is yes. Indeed, I read her indexes with that principle foremost in my mind, because I know that if the principle has been adhered to, the index will have done its job properly; I take it that the proper job of an index is not only to inform, but in a real sense to explain also.

Sometimes, it is not too much to say that I learn something about my book from the index, in which there is a connection that I have not consciously spotted. (Sometimes, indeed, I do not spot it even when I read the entry, and have to turn rather irritably to the page indicated, while Mrs Jones no doubt chortles quietly to herself.) But this curious filleting of a book which, when filleted, is lovingly reconstructed on the plate, never ceases to fascinate me, and never ceases to remind me of what a skilled and demanding labour it is, not to be embarked upon by amateurs who imagine that just because they can write a book they can also index it. I think I should be made Prime Minister very soon.

*The Indexer* October 2nd, 1984

# Big person is watching you

UNIVERSITIES, FOR ALL their pretensions, generally have a lamentable record of giving in, particularly where free speech is concerned, to governments, pressure groups, rioting students and assorted wowsers, and American universities in this respect are usually worse than most. So when I learned from the *New York Times* that one of them – and Berkeley, at that – was under attack on a matter of principle, I felt that I would not have long to wait before I got the news that the authorities had surrendered.

It may yet happen; but I have to report that so far Berkeley is not only standing firm on its battlements, with the drawbridge raised, but is energetically pouring boiling oil on to the heads of the besiegers, accompanied by cries of derision.

It began when the vice-chancellor received a complaint from an official (a lawyer, of course) in the Office of Civil Rights, which comes under the Education Department of the state government of California. The complaint was levelled against the directory of courses offered by Berkeley, at first blush an unlikely candidate for offences against civil rights. Had Berkeley, I asked myself, been offering tuition in lynching, in the daubing of anti-semitic slogans, in the framing of those with unacceptable political opinions?

Nothing so trivial; the complaint was directed at references, in the course calendar, to 'mankind', 'manpower' and 'man-made'. The official (hereinafter known as The Pest) demanded the removal of such words and their replacement by words of indeterminate gender, such as 'staff development' for 'manpower' (The Pest seems to be illiterate as well as impudent), 'human-produced' for 'man-made', and 'the human species' or 'human populations' for 'mankind' (which would do wonders for Goldsmith's epitaph on Burke – 'Who, born for the Universe, narrow'd his mind, And to party gave up what was meant for the human species' – and even more for Donne's 'Any man's death diminishes me, because I am involved in human populations').

The Pest proposed that he should discuss his proposals with officials at the university; he and his colleagues would join the men of academe to 'draw up a common list of questionable phrases'. Since he had complaints about Berkeley's course descriptions in, among others, the departments of Business Administration, Science and Mineral Engineering, Anthropology, Palaeontology, Philosophy, Natural Resources, Public Health and Military Affairs, it seems unlikely that the university would be in a position to get on with its normal work for a year or two, while the discussions continued.

The Pest's demands were made known to Berkeley teachers. One of these, a Professor of Journalism ('Now God, stand up for bastards') by the name of David Littlejohn, came out of his corner swinging:

> Pretending, or asserting, that the syllable 'man' signifies males exclusively can lead one into such barbarisms as 'ombudsperson' or 'freshperson' . . . 'Man' and 'Mankind' are universally understood to include both men and women . . . Except to avoid obvious terms of derision or words commonly regarded as insulting, it is regarded as culturally sound to let languages evolve according to normal daily usage, and as culturally unsound to try to legislate them artificially according to the mandates [The Pest would probably insist that that should be persondates] of political pressure groups . . . In no case should good English words, which are a part of our common history

and heritage, simply be legislated in and out of usage according to the whims of persons or groups who suddenly declare themselves 'offended' . . . In no case should the university accept the idea that the Office of Civil Rights is a better judge of appropriate language in its publications, or descriptions of its courses, than the university itself.

That, you might say, is telling 'em. But Professor Little-john made one serious mistake, which may yet cost him and Berkeley dear. He said that he, and other members of the faculty, were 'astonished that the Office of Civil Rights was able and willing to waste its time and our money on matters of this sort'.

If the good prof is really 'astonished' that The Pest and friends would waste their own time and other people's money on such monkeyshines, he had better stop being astonished pretty sharply, because I can tell him now that The Pest is not going to accept this rebuff and go and boil his head for a turnip. He is going to burrow into the woodwork, find sympathetic, or intimidatable, state legislators to follow him into it, and eventually emerge with powers to enforce his demands. The truth in these matters may be stated as a scientific law: 'The persistence of public officials varies inversely with the importance of the matter on which they are persisting.' Since the matter between The Pest and Berkeley is almost infinitely unimportant, it follows that he will be almost infinitely persisting; Berkeley may be in for a long siege.

This rubbish is by no means confined to America; it has steadily oozed across the Atlantic. (As long ago as 1972, I reported from the Democratic presidential convention the ominous news that a speaker on the platform had represented himself as being 'one of the co-chairpeople' of his state delegation, and the appalling Gloria Steinem had introduced a talk at a 'fringe' meeting by describing the star turn as 'a spokesperson' for the subject under discussion. I added the much more ominous news that on both occasions I was the only person in the hall who laughed. If only Britain had listened to me.)

*Vive la différence!* For what is behind this wearisome nonsense has nothing to do with discrimination against women. It is part of one of the worst of all the plagues of our world, the desire to pretend that all human beings are, or if they are not should be obliged to become, identical. Since inequality is built permanently into the human gene structure – so that most of us, for instance, could never run a mile in four minutes or play the violin like Sir Yehudi Menuhin (however long and hard we trained and practised) – and since the people who direct the movement I have described cannot (for reasons still obscure) bear to face that elementary truth, those who wish to push their mad and odious view forward must with one hand pretend that our inability to rival Sebastian Coe or Sir Yehudi is due only to our environment, and with the other find instances in which the names of things can be made equal even if the things themselves cannot.

It is this tide that has swept over a word like 'élite' and changed its meaning from something admirable to something hateful; the same noisome sea has drowned vital educational principles; driftwood from our taxation system bobs in the same flood. And because men and women are different, it follows that those who want to turn us all into helots of a totalitarian and illusory equality must do what they can to deny the existence, let alone the nature, of that difference. And since they cannot do so in reality, they try to do it in words.

Whence The Pest and his approach to Berkeley, and whence, also, my fear that the brave stand made by Professor Littlejohn may not be enough to defeat the enemy except temporarily. I wish him and his more robust colleagues well, and warn them to be on the watch not only for the enemy outside the walls, but for fainthearts and traitors within.

The name of The Pest, incidentally, is Paul Grossman. Shouldn't he change his name to Grossperson? Or would that be so apposite that even his fellow-Pests might laugh, and see the point?

*The Times* July 19th, 1985

# Shaw embattled

*Bernard Shaw: Collected Letters Vol. III 1911-1925* Edited by Dan H. Laurence[*]

THE FIRST VOLUME of this truly monumental work appeared in 1965 (at, incidentally, a price of three guineas). Volume II was published in 1972. The thirteen-year gap that followed was caused by certain unhappy circumstances that need not be discussed now that all is well again.

I have every hope that the next instalment will be hard on the heels of this, but the original intention, which was to complete the selection in four volumes, must have been abandoned; the last quarter-century of Shaw's life certainly produced enough to fill two more cullings, if not three.

For my part, I would welcome forty, and Shaw would be equal to the challenge. In all history, only Voltaire and Erasmus can stand comparison as correspondents; Professor Laurence speaks of 'tens of thousands' of extant letters, and the total Shaw wrote cannot be far short, if short at all, of six figures.[†]

The quantitative aspect is not a mere curiosity; it is further testimony to Shaw's almost unimaginable energy. The variety of his activities dealt with in the correspondence – theatre, politics, business, friendship, advice, argument, motoring, family, Ireland, journalism, love, condolence, music, debating, autobiography and dozens more – itself beggars belief, yet the letters reveal an extraordinary depth and breadth to his involvement in them.

[*] Max Reinhardt, 1985.
[†] It seems that this was an understatement; the true figure is around 250,000.

Take the plays alone. He cast them (not only the British productions but the American, and to a considerable extent the foreign-language versions as well), directed them, and dealt with every aspect of both the *mise-en-scène* and the financial considerations. There are letters here, many of them long and meticulously detailed, to his impresarios, managers, directors, players and designers, together with replies, equally thorough, to his friends' letters of congratulation or criticism.

The same complete absorption in the subject can be seen in his political activities, and an even greater intensity is displayed in the immense letters (one of them is thirty pages long) to his biographers, in which he virtually wrote their books for them. As for the advice, with which he was constantly free, two qualities are apparent throughout; first, it was offered without stint to acquaintances and even strangers as well as friends, colleagues and business connections, and second, it was almost invariably wise, practical and perfectly matched to the character of the recipient.

The hinge of these years is the First World War. That must be true, of course, of any public man and most private ones who lived through it, but for Shaw, who could not be content to sit and watch, there was another, darker, dimension. 'Common Sense about the War', his notorious pamphlet (absurd term for a work that runs to 35,000 words, for all that it was published as a supplement to the *New Statesman* and in the magazine's format), in which he denounced the Junkers of Britain as well as of Germany, brought on the greatest public crisis of his life.

Denunciations rained thick and savage upon him; he was ostracised by friends and colleagues, forced out of the Dramatists' Club, abused as a traitor. I had never before read the work that caused him such trouble, and did so only now, and with a mounting sense of stupefaction, for what he wrote – most of it is indeed common sense, though there are also some very silly flights – is of the mildest and least offensive character imaginable, and anyway he is at pains to stress throughout that, however the war started, Germany must be beaten.

The episode came closer to knocking Shaw off balance than anything else in his life; what he writes about the controversy is full of his usual insouciance (and there is a wonderful letter, full of charity and clarity, to his old friend Henry Arthur Jones, who never spoke to him again), but it clearly marked him. It can hardly be a coincidence that his creative spring dried up alarmingly at the time, only to gush forth later with enhanced vigour in *Heartbreak House* and *St Joan*; both of these were planned and written in the years covered by this volume, and Professor Laurence's selection of relevant letters enables us to see their conception, growth and completion.

As with the earlier volumes, and everything we know of his life, the lack of rancour, grudge or bitterness is astounding, and at its most noticeable in the 'Common Sense' uproar. He says of himself: 'I am only a writing machine: my soul exists only in my books', and although in the deepest sense that is true, this book shows us a man of warmth, kindliness and generosity of spirit.

And wit. There is hardly a letter in the book, even on the grimmest of subjects, that does not dance and sparkle with the brilliant, effortless gaiety of his prose; he could not write five lines on the most ordinary business without infusing them with laughter. Here he is, for instance, concluding a letter (full of real compassion) to Ellen Terry on the subject of caged animals:

Captive lions and tigers are worse than prisoners of the Bastille in old romances; but there is one maneless lion . . . in the Zoo (born there) who likes to have an audience . . . and will let you pet him. Except for the softness of his chest fur it is rather like trying to shove Primrose Hill over on its side . . . but he makes Androcles credible. The maned lion, Dick, is a furious brute. I pitied his poor cruelly bullied wife (judging by appearances) until she yawned, walked under his chin, and hit it up – perhaps trying to make him bite his tongue – with a toss of her head that would have lifted the dome off St Paul's. After that I understood what had spoiled his temper, and pitied *him*.

As in the earlier volumes, Professor Laurence's editing is a model of illuminating and unobtrusive scholarship, so much so, indeed, that I am delighted to have found two entire mistakes in a book of a mere 1,000 pages; Beecham was not knighted in 1916, but inherited his baronetcy then, and Lord Beaverbrook's family name was Aitken, not Beaverbrook. The excellent index is properly credited (M.G. and T.F. Evans), and Max Reinhardt, our leading Shavian publisher, deserves the warmest praise for his perseverance with this notable series, as also for the high standard of production these handsome volumes maintain.

*Observer* 2nd June, 1985

# Ars brevis, vita longa

ANOTHER POP SINGER has gone bankrupt, £30,000 in the
hole. He once, it seems, had a record which was first in
the charts, but he then fell out of favour; now he is in debt to
his bank, credit-card companies and the Inland Revenue. His
assets come to £51.

There is nothing particularly special about this case, not
even the sum of money he owes, which is almost trivial by
the usual standards of entertainers' bankruptcies. But there is
a moral in it, and the path to the moral is signposted by one
word in the *Daily Mail*'s report of the case. His brief success
was gained with a song called *Out of Time*, or, as the *Mail* put
it, 'the classic *Out of Time*'.

It was Andy Warhol (and look who's talking) who said
that in the future 'everyone will be famous for ten minutes'.
The bankrupt pop singer had his ten minutes in the 1960s,
where all this nonsense started, but for that fleeting moment
he, or at any rate the song he sang, was a 'classic'.

I do not want to be grimly logical, but history's sieve, to
the workings of which I have so often drawn attention,
operates in art even more inexorably than in politics, and
whoever is shaking it starts from the presumption that an
awful lot of shaking has to go on before it becomes clear that
the last bit is not going to fall through. When it *is* clear, the
intractable lump can be safely called a classic; but not before.

Of course, we don't have to sit about waiting for history to
come back into court and give its verdict, though one of the
worst failings of criticism today is its unwillingness to call

rubbish rubbish, a reluctance most marked in painting and sculpture but prevalent in all the other arts as well. I believe, moreover, that this reluctance is rooted not only in simple cowardice but in the pestilent argument (it has been running through our culture for more than two decades) that it is politically impermissible to believe that anybody is better than anybody else in any way.

The bankrupt pop singer was not the first to find the laurels withering on his brow. Whatever became of Terry Dene, and where now is 'Larry Page, the teenage rage'? Where are all those who capered and yodelled to so little permanent effect that their very names awake no echo? But it is not only the failure of criticism to which I refer that has brought about this state of affairs; there is a failure on the part of the consumer to remember that there is one sure guide to the nature of art that does not need to wait upon the findings of the sieve.

How do we know whether a picture, a symphony, a novel is a work of art? This is as much as to ask what do all works of art have in common with all other works of art, and at first sight it would appear to be a question with no possible answer, or indeed meaning. But if you think hard enough about your experience of art you will realize that it does have a meaning, and an answer, and moreover a meaning and an answer of the most practical and easily tested kind. How many times have I heard the Thirty-eighth Symphony of Mozart? I have no idea, though it must be well over a hundred; well, I am going to hear it again when the Vienna Philharmonic play it in London shortly, and the only thing I know for certain about the performance is that I shall hear in the music qualities, depths and meanings that I have never experienced before.

There is the clue: a work of art is inexhaustible. Who stays away from *Hamlet* because, having seen it once, he now knows that Claudius killed Hamlet's father? And who but an idiot could see *The Mousetrap* twice? When Tony Palmer claimed that the Beatles were the greatest song-writers since Schubert, he had unaccountably forgotten (among very many others) Schumann, Tchaikovsky, Berlioz, Brahms, Wolf, Strauss, Duparc, Mahler, Mussorgsky, Mendelssohn, Liszt, Borodin, Grieg, Fauré, Ravel and Janáček, and for that matter practically all of the creators of American musical comedy from Gershwin to Sondheim, but his claim would have been ridiculous even if none of these had ever been born, and for a very good reason.

For the reason, I return to Mozart's Prague Symphony. If Mozart were to come to life and take up writing symphonies where he left off, I would listen eagerly to each of the new ones as it was performed; but I would also go on listening to the forty-one we already have. Would anybody but the *Mousetrap* idiot or his cousin go on listening to last season's output of McCartney after this season's had appeared?

The world has always been full of ephemera. And since it is in the nature of mankind to err, from time to time some example of it has been thought of permanent value, though there have almost always been a few to point out that the Emperor has no clothes (read Shaw on Parry or for that matter me on Pinter). It is easy, and comforting, to say that it doesn't matter, that nobody much is harmed by these mayflies whose genius is born at breakfast-time and buried before tea. As the bankrupt pop singer showed the other day ('When you reach a period when you're being wined and dined all the time it's difficult to come down off that pedestal when it ends'), the victims are usually those who initially profit from the swelling of the bubble reputation; drink, drugs and suicide have claimed far more of them than can be accounted for by coincidence, and at the moment not a week passes without another set of revelations about the horror of Elvis Presley's brief life. But I believe that art can be damaged as well, or at least – since art itself is imperishable – the effect of art can be.

If enough people are fed for long enough on a diet of bread

and milk – and, moreover, mass-produced sliced bread and sour milk – they will cease to believe that there is more robust fare available, quite apart from the danger that their teeth will fall out, thus making it impossible for them to eat meat even if they could be persuaded to try it. I could, of course, declare that since *I* know the difference between art and rubbish I don't care how many people are unaware of it; but I do not like to think that all the yelling and lies and public relations and˙salesmanship and fiddling and puffing are making it impossible, or at least very difficult, for millions to reach out for art who might otherwise do so.

Art has the rare property, shared only with love, of providing an infinite supply no matter how much is consumed; but even art cannot work its effect on those who pass it by without a glance. That is why, though I do not rejoice at the fall of the pop singer, I do not think it likely that his 'classic *Out of Time*' was really a classic at all, for all that it was top of the charts for ten minutes eighteen years ago. Incidentally, when did anybody last listen to it? My guess is that it was about four days after it ceased to be top of the charts.

*The Times* September 27th, 1984

# Hold your tongue

THERE IS SAD NEWS from Ireland, though on this occasion
it has nothing to do with the now usual reasons for
Irish-inspired sadness. Somebody has proposed that the Irish
language, at present a compulsory subject for all children in
all state schools, should now be optional for those studying
for the Leaving Certificate (the standard senior examination).
Who has proposed it, and what status the proposal has, is by
no means clear; the Minister of Education professes to know
nothing about it, and there is much talk of sub-committees,
recommendations and for all I know composite resolutions
and the reference back. In short, it is so far no more than a
transient gleam in an apparently fishy eye.

But that was enough, apparently, to set knees jerking
throughout the Republic. The two leading organizations
concerned with the Irish language – one official and one
voluntary – have leaped into the fray, and the fact that there is
no fray for them to leap into has made no difference to the
vigour and enthusiasm of their leaping. My old Irish friend
A. O'Spokesman has already declared that he is 'very
alarmed about the proposal', that it is 'of crucial importance'
that Irish shall remain compulsory throughout the whole of
the Irish school curriculum, and that 'the necessity of
teaching Irish to all children at all levels stems not only from
its educational value but also from State policy'; he added, in
words that I would describe as Irish if it were not for my fear
of being reported to the Race Relations Board, that 'Real
freedom of choice in language can only exist if all pupils at all

levels are taught Irish . . .' (As in 'Compulsion is Freedom'.)

Wherein, though, the sadness? It is fourfold. First, there is the display of that tragic Irish propensity to perform a double back-somersault if anyone suggests, however tentatively, that change might occasionally be contemplated, and that the fact that something has been done for a long time does not in itself constitute proof that it must go on being done for ever.

Next comes the apparently inevitable contest among Irishmen to demonstrate, if necessary by breaking one another's heads, that each is more Irish than his fellows.

The third cause of regret is the one that chiefly concerns me today, even though the fourth, when we come to it, will be seen to be the most important.

For many years now, Irish governments of all political complexions have sought to encourage the love and knowledge of their beautiful language. It is a wholly commendable desire; nothing, not even its geography or its mode of government, so defines a nation as its language, and I have always been sorry that so few Irish people speak their ancient tongue. But that is rather the point, isn't it? The Irish governments which instituted, and have maintained, compulsory Irish in schools fell into one of the oldest traps in history; they believed, and the present government no doubt still believes, that you can make a nation speak a language by compelling it to learn it in school. The fact that the first thing most Irish people do on leaving school is to stop trying to talk in any language other than English ought to have demonstrated fairly conclusively that there was a fallacy about, but no government, Irish, British or anything else, has ever been much given to noticing fallacies, particularly when they are the government's own.

You do not have to cross the Irish Sea to see the fallacy demonstrated; Offa's Dyke will do quite as well. The great majority of the Welsh people do not speak Welsh and make it plain that they do not wish to; that is why some organizations claiming to further the interests of the Welsh language have had to resort to violence, and why a succession of feeble Secretaries of State in the Welsh Office have behaved as though the Welsh-speaking minority have rights which supersede those of the rest of Wales. (The Welsh television channel is probably the most ridiculous result of this attitude.)

I think that the slow dying of the Welsh language, which will be a much quicker dying if the violent extremists go on trying to thrust it down Welsh throats by force, is as great a pity as the dying of its Irish cousin. I shall never forget a train journey I took many years ago in Wales; it was a remote branch line (no doubt long since Beechinged to death), and the train itself – it had only one coach – looked like a toy one. I was the only Sais aboard; all my fellow-passengers were middle-aged Welsh ladies, and they all spoke Welsh throughout the journey. Without understanding a word of it (the only thing I can say in Welsh is 'Arses to Englishmen'), I was bathed for three-quarters of an hour in the music of that strange, ancient tongue, and I got off the train feeling as though I had been wallowing in Mozart. I doubt very much whether the children of those ladies speak Welsh today, and I will confidently wager that even if they do *their* children won't. And that saddens me, as I feel it ought to sadden any inhabitant of this kingdom.

Only the Scots seem to have got this thing right (I don't know about the Manx, let alone those Cornishmen who want to speak Cornish); very few of them speak Gaelic, but those who do show no sign of wanting to force their fellow-countrymen to learn it, nor is there anything to match the pitiful insistence, in Wales, on bilingual signposts and similar flapdoodle.

Which brings me to the fourth, and most important, reason for sadness at the news from Ireland with which I began; I have touched upon it in my discussion of the other three, but I think I ought to make it clear. A language, as I have said, defines a nation. The silly modern fashion for decrying the force of nationalism, indeed for denying the existence, let alone the validity, of it, is about as sensible as would be a campaign to abolish the Equator. The strength and cohesion of the people of an ancient country depends on their recognition of themselves as citizens by blood as well as passport. When the bonds of language begin to fray, that recognition begins to fade, and the fact that there is little we can do about it (and nothing that governments and laws can do about it) makes it all the more regrettable.

For what exactly is it against which national feeling stands as a rock? It is, surely, the deadly, centripetal wearing away of all differences between people.

There are those who welcome this development, and urge its furtherance. They are fools, the same kind of fools as those who would break a drum to find out what, inside it, is making the noise. The most conspicuous and melodious drum in the world is that of language, and that is why we should all feel sad that the Irish and Welsh languages are being spoken less and less, and that those who seek to halt this decline are, by their actions, only encouraging it, for such a wish must and can come only from within. I have no doubt that the Irish government, now that the row has started, will insist on keeping the study of Irish compulsory for all its schools and for all children in them, and I have no doubt that the speaking of Irish will nonetheless – no, not nonetheless, *therefore* – continue on its slow, melancholy path to extinction.

*The Times* November 26th, 1984

# Going to extremes

I HAVE ALWAYS MAINTAINED that those of an idealistic tendency who argue that a crisis, emergency or disaster always brings out the best in people and those, more cynical, who insist that it brings out the worst, are both wrong; extremely unusual happenings, as far as my observation goes, tend to bring out only the *most*. That is, everyone behaves in character (though sometimes in a character not normally visible), but in the most extreme form of it.

Take the Prime Minister's conduct in Brighton. Anyone who has even the slightest understanding of her would have been able to predict, with the utmost exactitude, what would be the first thing she would do after escaping death from a bomb by two minutes and/or three feet; she would make sure that her hair was tidy. Where she is concerned, the cliché 'not a hair out of place' sheds its banality and comes to life; it is even possible to analyse in detail the instinct that led her to make sure that her coiffure was flawless before leaving a building which for all she knew was about to collapse on her, coiffure and all.

To start with, as indeed is demonstrated by the very first words she spoke in public after the explosion ('Business as usual'), Mrs Thatcher's whole personality is suffused with her belief that *events* are inferior to *people*; she tidied her hair before emerging because she would have tidied her hair before emerging in normal circumstances, and to omit the automatic adjustment, merely because she had just narrowly survived an attempt to murder her, would have been to allow

herself to be dominated by something impersonal and outside her own will.

In the second place, her professionalism, which is more
complete and more deeply grounded than in any other public
figure of the day (perhaps of any day), told her that the public
would expect her to show visual as well as verbal defiance,
that to accede to that expectation would be the best way to
serve her cause, and that an instinctive and symbolic but very
visible sign of her acknowledgment of those truths would be
the gesture of smoothing her hair. I swear that if the ceiling
of the room had fallen on her, covering her in plaster, she
would have changed her clothes before emerging as well.

In the third place, she is an extremely feminine woman;
you do not need to know much about women in general, let
alone this particular one, to know the role that clean and tidy
hair plays in that sex as a strengthening of femininity, a raiser
of morale and an assurance that all is well within.

From the moment she arrived at the police station, of
course, the conscious mind took over, and from then on – in
her statement, her demeanour and her speech – she was fully
in command of herself. But in the first few minutes after the
bang, her character expresses itself without the aid of her
intention, and she *was* what she *is*.

Exactly the same, in his different way, can be said of her
consort. Mr Thatcher's first public words were: 'There was a
tremendous thump, and the bathroom looked as though it
had been through the wringer.' Nobody, asked in the course
of an after-dinner game to guess what Mr Thatcher would
say if someone attempted to blow up the entire Conservative
Party, starting with its leader, would choose those words,
because they would think them too extravagantly appropriate, too implausibly in keeping. But that is the point; the
frightfulness of what had happened, and the much greater
frightfulness of what might have happened, brought out the
essence of what may be termed the Denisness of Denis. If he
had had time to think, he would have made some fittingly

grave comment, of the kind that anybody might have made; since he had not had time to think, his *semper idem* asserted itself, and he came out with a remark far more splendidly characteristic of himself, and incidentally far more helpful all round in the calming nature of its demotic simplicity.

The same is true of Mr Norman Tebbit. As soon as he began to recover in hospital, his visitors began to report that he was making a string of jokes, and I dare say he was; but by then he was in a position to *think* of the jokes. When he was lying under the rubble, hardly knowing whether he was alive or dead, the jokes his character made as opposed to those made later by his mind, were first, as the rescuers approached, 'You're standing on my bloody foot, Fred', and second, as a doctor with a life-saving hypodermic asked him whether he was allergic to anything, 'Yes, bombs'.

There was also Sir Keith Joseph, whose contribution was to sleep right through the bomb and its sequel, then, when awoken and informed that there had been an untoward incident, to don an elegant silk dressing-gown (from Sulka, by the look of it), and to remember (the only minister who did, apparently) to take his dispatch box with him; the combination of unworldliness, meticulousness and adherence to rules was exactly what would have been expected of him, just as Lord Gowrie's first action on emerging from the hotel into a crowd of shell-shocked refugees was typical of *him*; he ran down to the beach and brought up three dozen deck-chairs for them to sit on. And far away from Brighton, Mr Dafydd Thomas, the Welsh Nationalist MP, sank to the occasion; the man who spoke at a meeting to commemorate Bobby Sands was asked to comment on the Brighton bomb, and replied that the Provisionals should stop doing such things. And why? Because they only strengthened the hands of those opposed to a solution to the problem of Northern Ireland.

Catastrophe, then, does not alter people; but it makes the highlights and darknesses of their nature more pronounced.

You cannot, I think, read Walter Lord's *A Night to Remember*, about the sinking of the *Titanic* (Mr Tam Dalyell probably blames Mrs Thatcher for that, too), without sensing this truth.

On that tragic occasion, the cool and the brave behaved more coolly and more bravely than ever before, the weak and cowardly more like weaklings and poltroons. Lightoller, the second officer, who saved many lives and would have saved more if the incompetence of others had not prevented him, plainly had no idea of the resources of bravery and selflessness in him, but he displayed both in exceptionally great measure, which – to put it with positively excessive moderation – Sir Cosmo Duff Gordon did not. But I do not suppose Sir Cosmo, either, knew his own full character until it was tested under such extreme conditions.

War, obviously, is the hottest crucible of all; there are countless well-authenticated stories of timid, colourless men suddenly becoming heroes in battle; I am convinced that the heroism was already inside them, even though they might otherwise have lived and died in bed without anyone – particularly themselves – ever suspecting of what they were capable. But this truth is by no means confined to questions of courage and cowardice; it is character I am speaking of, and it is that, the stamp which we all bear in a shape different, however slightly, from all others, that is forced, like seedlings in a greenhouse, when something tremendous and terrible takes place.

It is tempting to spend an idle minute in speculation on what might have happened if someone had attempted to blow up the Labour Party. I would back Mr Kinnock to come out smiling, and Mr Kaufman to do Lord Gowrie's sensible deck-chair act; Mr Healey, beneath the rubble, would be heard calling for a large gin-and-tonic in place of an anaesthetic, Mr Hattersley would be calculating the effect of the catastrophe on the chances of his becoming leader of the party, and Mr Benn, who would in any case have contrived to be somewhere else when it happened, would be issuing a press statement claiming that the Special Branch was responsible for the outrage.

During the Spanish Civil War, there was a hotel in Madrid, while the city was under siege from the Franco forces, in which the foreign correspondents were staying. At one point, Franco's artillery began to shell the city; the pressmen gathered in a room to discuss whether they should pull out of Madrid, and Hemingway, already the *doyen* of the corps, read them a lecture. With a relief map of the city and its surroundings on a table before him, he explained, logically and lucidly, that since the Franco troops were *here*, the hotel *there*, and the configuration of the landscape *like this*, the trajectory of the guns could only be *thus*, which meant that it was quite impossible for a shell to land anywhere near where they were. His exposition convinced and relieved his comrades, but just as he finished it, one of Franco's shells scored a direct hit on the hotel and the ceiling of the room they were in descended upon them. Amid the dust and smoke and cursing, Hemingway was heard to say coolly: 'Well, gentlemen, how do you like it now?'

*The Times* October 17th, 1984

# French connection

*Huguenot Heritage* by Robin D. Gwynn[*]
*A Family From Flanders* by John Peters[†]

IN THIS YEAR OF round-figure anniversaries, from Bach and Scarlatti to the safety-bicycle and – ahem – *The Times*, rejoicing must be tempered in one instance; 1985 marks the tercentenary of the Revocation of the Edict of Nantes, a bloodstain on the history of Europe.

Yet even that act of darkness, and the persecution of French Protestants it unleashed, brought light elsewhere, in the enormous contribution to the life of this country made by the Huguenot refugees and their descendants; apart from anything else, if it had not been for the Revocation we should not have had Winston Churchill (his mother was of Huguenot descent), Sir Henry Tizard, Sheridan LeFanu, Sir Samuel Romilly, David Garrick and Laurence Olivier, Roget's *Thesaurus* or Bosanquet's googly.

Of course, persecution across the Channel did not start with the Revocation; the first Protestant martyrdom in France was in 1523 (the last was in 1762) and the Massacre of St Bartholomew in 1572. Moreover, the *dragonnade*, a kind of rudimentary pogrom, was raging in France before Louis XIV picked up his pen, and the Edict had been a dead letter for some time.

Nevertheless, it was the Revocation that convinced French Protestants that there was no future for them in their native land. As Mr Gwynn says:

[*] Routledge, 1985.
[†] Collins, 1985.

During the 1660s and 1670s there was a growing trickle of refugees; from 1679, as oppressive edicts increased sharply in number, a stream; in 1681, with the onset of the *dragonnades*, the stream became a river. After the Revocation . . . the river turned into a torrent.

It is what happened to the torrent when it swept up the beaches of England that is the stuff of Mr Gwynn's book; rarely does anyone, let alone a reviewer, wish that a book were twice its length, but this one is so informative, balanced and crisply written that it leaves the reader hungry for more.

As is usual with successive waves of refugees, the later arrivals found their predecessors well organized to help them settle, and soon the moribund English weaving trade sprang to new life. The weavers among the Huguenots were most numerous, but there were also gardeners, tailors, hair-dressers, jewellers, gunsmiths, architects and milliners; these last must have rejoiced exceedingly when they found themselves with the monopoly of making cardinals' red hats.

The Huguenots in England founded schools and taught French; less obvious were the origins of their success in insurance, science and trade. And the immigrants brought irony with them; thousands of trained soldiers, driven from France, fought for England against the French – so well, indeed, that Marlborough might have lost at Blenheim without them, and at the Battle of the Boyne the aged General Schomberg cried to his French troops: 'There are your persecutors – forward, lads, forward!'

With the obvious exception of Mary, all the English monarchs from Edward VI onwards were surprisingly help-ful to the refugees, though James II helped as little as possible and that grudgingly. Even so, their religious practices faced difficulties at times, and the ice became dangerously thin when native-born Nonconformists were being penalized; when Laud fell and went to the Tower, one of the Huguenot pastors forgot the requirements of Christian charity long enough to say 'It is merry with lambs when the wolf is shut up', and they could breathe easily only when the Glorious Revolution brought a Calvinist to the throne. They have had no religious trouble since.

Social opposition was also light. There were waves of antagonism and some outbreaks of violence, but in general the Huguenots had a better reception from their host country than any other group fleeing to these shores from persecution; certainly the Jews had a much harder time of it. The usual complaints were heard: the immigrants were taking jobs from Englishmen, they spied, they had unpleasant habits in dress, food and gestures, they were responsible for the Great Fire and other misfortunes. What kept hostility restrained was the fear and hatred of Catholicism; Philip of Spain and the fires of Smithfield had not been forgotten, and the horrors that the Huguenots themselves related on landing helped to turn the tide.

Among the odder achievements of the Huguenots chronicled by Mr Gwynn is the invention of oxtail soup. Ox tails at that time were discarded as useless; the poorest immigrants, near to starvation, gathered them up and cooked them. (Campbell can't be a Huguenot name, though I suppose Heinz might be.)

Mr Gwynn includes, as an appendix, a guide for those who wish to search for Huguenot ancestors. Mr Peters' book is an account of how the author sought, and found, his own. Inevitably, he covers much the same ground as Mr Gwynn, but he has no pretensions to historical scholarship or for that matter literary graces. But he tells the story of his quest lightly and lucidly.

He has also fished up a quotation that has escaped Mr Gwynn's net, a complaint about unfair Huguenot competition from some English clothworkers, who explained that the foreigners were able to take the bread out of native mouths 'by reason they do live 5 or 6 in one tenement, the rent whereof is daily paid and causes them to take money when Englishmen cannot'. Mr Enoch Powell could hardly put it better.

The story of the Huguenots is a heartening one; their persecution was an ill wind that blew this country much good, but it also illustrates Britain's long and admirable record of accepting those whom others reject. Today's Huguenots are Mr Patel of the corner-shop and his cousin Mr Patel the millionaire; yesterday's were my own grandparents, from the Pale of Tsarist Russia. I hope that tomorrow's, too, whoever they are, will be able to say 'I was a stranger, and ye took me in'.

*Observer* March 3rd, 1985

# Tell me the old, old story

AFTER TOMORROW'S PERFORMANCES, the Cottesloe
auditorium of the National Theatre will close for a few
months, the closure being Sir Peter Hall's dramatic way
(better one honest murder, as Shaw said in a somewhat
different context, than half a dozen furtive mutilations) of
drawing attention to the stringencies forced upon his company by the difference, in the matter of public funding,
between expectation and reality.

Possibly Sir Peter has forgotten the Chinese proverb which
says that it is a false economy to burn your house down out
of a desire to inconvenience your mother-in-law; but I come
to praise Caesar, not to bury him. The work with which the
Cottesloe will ring down the curtain is *The Mysteries*, a
conflation, in three parts, of the English medieval craft plays
on the life, death and resurrection of Christ; they have been
adapted under the respective titles of *The Nativity*, *The
Passion* and *Doomsday*, and they will play tomorrow in
sequence from elevenses to bed-time. So they did when I saw
the three performances a few Saturdays ago and was as
enthralled, exhilarated and moved as I have ever been in a
theatre in all my life.

The adapter, Tony Harrison, and director, Bill Bryden,
have sought an equivalent of the atmosphere and technique
which must have informed the originals; these were staged
by unlearned men using the texts of poets whose names are
now mostly undiscoverable, and were played upon carts
drawn from place to place through the town (notably

Wakefield, York, Chester and Coventry) as the day, and the story, wore on. Harrison and Bryden must have realized early on that any attempt either to archaicize these works or to make them overtly theatrical would instantly drain the life out of them; what they have done, and done consistently throughout, is to turn the entire drama into an affair of men and women taking time off from their earthly trades to rejoice in the glories of heaven. For consider: the original actors (who were the craftsmen themselves, of course) would have been known as friends, colleagues, neighbours or relatives to the audience, and as the tableaux moved through the streets and the cycle, the distinction between player and audience must have vanished, *along with the distinction between player and character.* That man up there in the funny clothes is Tom the Baker as well as John the Baptist, and the bugger has owed me fourpence since Michaelmas; as for Christ, considering the amount of ale he put down last night he'll fall off the bloody Cross if they don't nail him to it pretty tight.

Men who thought and talked like that were not blaspheming, nor were they indifferent to the spectacle unfolding before them; they had staged these plays to bear witness to the reality of their faith, and the faith was strengthened, not weakened, by the homeliness of the proceedings.

The gap between a modern audience and modern actors was the easier one to bridge; Mr Bryden realized that he had to stage the plays as promenades, undermine self-consciousness with what I suppose must be called community dancing and by moving the action in and out of the crowd, and make the players mingle with the spectators at every possible opportunity. (I was reminded of Peter Brook's final, overwhelming *coup de théâtre* when, at the end of his *Midsummer Night's Dream*, the cast left via the stalls, shaking hands as they went.)

The other bridge was far more difficult to create, and far more rickety; it swung perilously over the gulf, and must have looked likely to dash all concerned to pieces on the rocks below. How do you turn a late twentieth-century audience, whose religion (if any) has been filleted, denatured and sterilized, into a body of men and women to whom Mary the Mother of God is as real as Mary the mother of that little red-headed pest who I'll beat the living daylights out of if he pinches any more of my apples?

Well, you cannot do it by hypnotizing the audience, any more than by asking them to clap if they believe in fairies. You do it by working with the actors until they are freed of the bonds of artifice and elocution, until the sword of technique is beaten into the ploughshares of truth, until they fuse into the words and the characters in the terrible furnace of what and whom they are portraying. You could see the audience, responding to the stupendous energy the cast were imbued with and expending, almost literally catching it, like a fever, until they ached to be given a part themselves and play it, gradually realizing, with wonder and visible joy, that they *had* been given a part, and *were* playing it.

At the risk of being invidious, or causing embarrassment, I must particularize. Take the young actress who initially plays Eve; towards the end of the day she is part of a group which performs a dance of celebration, in form something between Sir Roger de Coverley and a Morris dance. As she came round each time, I saw her face clearly; she was illuminated from within, rapt with the tremendousness of the story now moving to its climax. Don't tell me – I wouldn't believe her if she told me herself – that the look on her face was the result of the director saying 'In the next bit, sweetie, you have to look happy'. Or take the young man who plays, among other parts, Isaac. He, in turn, was part of a chorus at the funeral of the Virgin; as he, too, came round again, he was singing the hymn of triumph in such roaring ecstasy that I thought the heart would burst out of his body, and I will not, likewise, believe that that was in response to the director saying 'A bit louder, please, darling'.

The language of the verse is rich with alliteration, bright

with colour, wonderfully real with its directness. It is not like Chaucer, but it is reminiscent of Chaucer; there is not a line anywhere to suggest that the original poet had momentarily forgotten the nature of his audience, or that the adapter has forgotten the nature of his. Again and again, the simplest tricks of staging open an entire realm of effect, so natural is their conception, and this naturalness is the tone of the whole thing. (Sometimes the actors laugh, not as part of their performance, but because of some tiny mishap, or some movement or comment from the audience. They have clearly been told to go ahead and laugh whenever they feel like it, because it won't matter. And it doesn't.)

This principle is carried to extraordinary lengths at times, though the confidence of all concerned brings them through. In the uncanonical story of Mak the bad shepherd, Mak is caught stealing sheep, and is sentenced to the pillory. The pillory is one of those seaside joke-photograph devices; the actor puts his head through a hole; and the children in the audience (there are many of them) are invited to pelt him with wet sponges. Most of them enter into the game with zest, but one or two hang back. 'Come on,' says Mak, encouraging them; then he mutters, 'You won't get a chance like this at *Coriolanus*, I can tell you.'

It is this welding of actor, audience, play and story into one whole that gives the performance its unique quality – and I wish there were another word for performance, for it diminishes the thing that has been created, which far transcends any idea of a theatre as a place which we visit to see a play, and of a play as that which we visit a theatre to see.

What a way to go! But while the Cottesloe is closed, performances of this mighty achievement will be given in the Lyceum, and when it reopens it is inconceivable that *The Mysteries* will be dropped from the repertoire. In the prefatory pages of the First Folio, there is, as well as the Droeshout portrait and Jonson's well-known eulogy, a verse, 'To the memorie of W. Shakespeare', signed only by the

initials J.M. It is a fitting epitaph on the Cottesloe as it closes
its doors, and a no less fitting prologue to its reopening:

> . . . Wee thought thee dead, but this thy printed worth,
> Tels thy Spectators, that thou went'st but forth
> To enter with applause. An Actors Art,
> Can dye, and live, to acte a second part.
> That's but an *Exit* of Mortalitie;
> This, a Re-entrance to a Plaudite.

*The Times* April 19th, 1985

# Persian roulette

THOSE DEAR OLD-FASHIONED THINGS, the gossip columnists, have recently been getting excited about a treasure hunt which is to take place among the *jeunesse chromée*; no doubt if it is successful their next adventure in nostalgia will be a trip on the maiden voyage of a new transatlantic liner called the *Titanic*. But I was reminded, by all the breathlessness, of a tale about a treasure hunt that I heard many years ago, and which I think is worth preserving in print.

The hero was the late Geoffrey Keating, around whom amazing stories constantly formed, apparently out of nothing, like galaxies after the Big Bang. He had some kind of path-smoothing post in BP which involved knowing everybody – a post for which he was perfectly fitted, as he knew everybody already – and giving them lunch from time to time. Once he was at the Savoy Grill, his guests being King Hussain and Margot Fonteyn, and as they were being ushered to their table, they passed a group already seated, consisting of Geoffrey's opposite number in Shell, giving lunch to Prince Rainier and Princess Grace. As Geoffrey passed the table, he paused for a moment to murmur in his rival's ear 'I'll raise you'.

Geoffrey was the greatest fixer I have ever known. If you wanted a hotel room or flight reservation when there was none to be had, and both the President of the United States and the Pope had tried to help and failed, a telephone call to Geoffrey would bring what was wanted in a quarter of an hour; if you were one of his friends he could find the unfindable, open locked doors, arrange introductions, spring you from jail, have you met in Pago-Pago by the British ambassador (accompanied by the band of the National Guard), beat down art dealers and have bypasses re-routed if they were going to spoil your view. And unlike all other fixers, he *never* wanted anything for himself, not even the credit – all he asked was that when another of his friends needed something that you could help provide, you should, mindful of the help you had received, do whatever you could in return. He died some years ago, and I, like all his friends, miss him still.

One night after dinner he told me the treasure hunt story. He had been in Tehran, where his oil business naturally took him often, and somebody in diplomatic or social circles (this was in the days of the Shah, of course) thought it would be rather a lark to get up an old-fashioned treasure hunt. The organizers listed twelve objects that the hunters had to get within a single day, reckoned from midnight to midnight; the winner would be the first to come back to base with the entire dozen, or – if no one managed to find all of them – who got the largest number by the deadline. The prize was a case of champagne; all the players could easily afford such delights, but the organizers felt it would psychologically sharpen the competitiveness among the anyway exceptionally competitive bunch who were playing.

The objects were not acquired and hidden by the committee; they were all things that every hunter with sufficient ingenuity, not to say *chutzpah*, could find. Geoffrey told me the list, but I have remembered only two; one of these, which was the hinge on which the tale turned, was 'Any document signed by any member of the staff of the Soviet embassy'. The other was 'A hair from the head of the head of any diplomatic mission'.

The hair, which might be thought by you and me to provide some difficulty, was nothing to Geoffrey; he sailed off to see the British ambassador (who was, of course, a close friend of his) and demanded a hair from his head. The Ambassador's first thought was to pick up the poker and call the police, but Geoffrey explained, and His Excellency said he would be delighted to help, though since his hair had been thinning for some time, he begged to be excused plucking a fresh one from his crown, led the way to his bedroom, and there took a hair from his hairbrush. He signed a note guaranteeing its authenticity (this was one of the stipulations of the competition), and another *objet trouvé* was in Geoffrey's bag.

Back and forth across Tehran he sped as the day climbed to its zenith and then declined towards evening; the back seat of his car began to look impressive with the finds, and the list of hunted objects bore more and more ticks. Finally, Geoffrey had bagged eleven of the twelve; the only one remaining – which he had deliberately left till last, deducing that it would be the most difficult – was the Russian signature.

It was now getting towards midnight and deadline; Geoffrey was in a dilemma. He could gamble on the chance that nobody would have got all twelve, go back at once with his eleven and hope to win on a tie-break by returning earlier than other players who had managed to get all but one; or he could try for the impossible at the Soviet embassy and be virtually sure to win if he got back before the chimes of midnight with the precious document. Any reader of these words who knew Geoffrey knows also which choice he took.

He arrived at the Soviet embassy, which was dark and shuttered. He rang the bell, expecting that Siberian wolves would instantly burst from concealed traps in the pavement and devour him; they did not, but nothing else happened either. He plied the bell again, and again, and again; a long pause and he heard a slow step within. The door opened a crack, on a chain, and an eye peered out at him. Until that moment Geoffrey had still conceived no plan at all (he did not speak Russian) for getting what he wanted; when he saw the eye peering suspiciously at him he instinctively put his hand in his pocket, with no conscious intent, and felt a piece of paper. It was the list of items he had had to collect, now no longer needed; he took it out and thrust it through the gap. The eye took it, nodded and made to shut the door; Geoffrey shook his head violently and mimed writing. The eye nodded and shut the door; Geoffrey heard the shuffling step disappear.

Geoffrey waited; he waited long. Eventually, however, the eye was heard approaching, the door was opened again a few inches, and the eye's hand thrust out a piece of paper. Geoffrey took it; it was clearly on official Soviet embassy stationery, and subsequently proved to contain words to the effect of 'Received, one document', with the date and time *and a precious signature*, no doubt obtained from a sleepy Third Secretary.

Geoffrey got back just in time, and had correctly surmised that nobody else in the game had got all twelve objects; being Geoffrey he naturally opened all twelve bottles instantly, so that his midnight victory could be celebrated by all the losers.

He told me the story, as he told all his stories, with wit and drama, but he added a footnote, an item which, he said, had intrigued him at the time and intrigued him still. When day broke upon the Soviet Embassy in Tehran, somebody in the mission was in possession of a list of apparently unrelated and indeed meaningless objects. Soviet diplomatic staff are not notorious for their sense of humour; somebody must have been given the job of working out the meaning of Geoffrey's midnight visit and of the mysterious document. There could be no explanation other than that the visitor was a Soviet sympathizer who was providing top-secret information, possibly the disposition of the Nato forces, news of a forthcoming pre-emptive strike on Soviet nuclear installations, or even the formula for a new, more powerful, American secret weapon. Geoffrey envisaged an office in the KGB, staffed by the service's leading cryptanalysts, working year after year to crack the fiendish code, and regularly being taken away and shot for failing to do so, to be replaced with further code-breakers who would in turn suffer the same fate.

It was a long time ago, and the carnage among KGB cipher-crackers must by now have accounted for a substantial proportion of Smersh's personnel. I cannot be expected to grieve for them, but I think it is time to let bygones be bygones, which is why I have told the story today, to enable the now yellowing scraps of paper to be interred in peace in a file marked 'Capitalist sense of humour'. *Izvestia*, please copy.

*The Times* August 28th, 1985

# The body-snatchers

THERE IS SOMETHING exquisitely symmetrical in the fact that, while debate rages over the question of changing the method by which trade union members contribute to Labour Party funds from 'contracting out' to 'contracting in', Parliament should have discussed a proposal to change the method by which the organs of dead people are made available for transplant from 'contracting in' to 'contracting out'. My own trade union has no political levy, so I am not directly affected by the trade union question; on the other hand, my own kidneys have been with me for a long time now, and before I am willing to contract them in, out or sideways I would like not only to examine the existing and proposed safeguards against my bits and pieces being subjected to a process of transplant *inter vivos* rather than *post mortem*, but also to think that before legislating for the change Parliament might rise to a level of debate considerably higher than it did earlier this week.

What is surprising is that the leading advocates of the change were Sir John Biggs-Davison and Mr Tam Dalyell. Sir John has shown himself to be a man who thinks much and deeply about ethical problems, presumably through his religious convictions, while as for Mr Dalyell, he may be barmy (come, come, Levin, you were not wont to be so mealy-mouthed – he *is* barmy), but however irritating his campaigns may be, they have always been motivated by moral principles; his obsession with the *Belgrano*, after all, was derived not from a thrifty horror at the thought of all that irrecoverable scrap metal but from a different kind of horror at the thought of all those irrecoverable human beings.

Yet they both spoke as though the question of what is, or should be, done with the bodies of the lately dead were of little more moment than that of what should be done with hair cut off at the barber's.

It is, of course, possible to take that very view, and it is clear that many in our society today do take it, though it is even more clear that ours is the first era in which it would have been taken by more than a very few, who would greatly have astonished their fellows. When we are dead, the argument runs, we have no more use for our bodies; if we have souls, they are independent of the earthly clay in which they are temporarily housed, and the clay itself, once the breath is out of it, might as well be recycled in the interests of those who need it. What is wrong with that?

First, and most obvious, there is the double problem of the safeguards and of what I have called, when discussing euthanasia, the Fallacy of the Altered Standpoint. The debate over the definition of death is by no means concluded, and it is hard to see how it ever will be, yet until we can say 'this man is dead' with a certainty that is beyond even semantic dispute (let alone beyond the possibility that he may sit up and say 'Oh, no, I'm not') the safeguards will always remain beneath a cloud, however small, of doubt. This is not just a matter of a mistake by the doctors; it concerns the very nature and meaning of death, and the fact that modern medical science can ensure that patients may remain *in articulo mortis* for months on end makes the importance of that nature and meaning greater, not less.

Now for the Altered Standpoint. Some of my best friends are doctors, and as far as I know very few of them are practising vampires. I do not envisage, should the controls on transplants be weakened, a sudden rush of ghouls in white coats to cut the hearts out of living bodies like so many Aztec priests. (Mind you, Ferdinand Sauerbruch was one of the greatest surgeons of modern times, but he ended mad as a hatter in a welter of butchery like a horror-film, protected by his august reputation.) But, difficult as it is for any man to say how he will behave in conditions he knows about, it is far more so for any of us to say how we would behave in conditions of which at present we have no experience. I do not believe that advocates of the legalization of euthanasia, and especially doctors who advocate it, would feel anything but revulsion at the suggestion that, were euthanasia available, they might start to see in a sinister light those incurably ill or senile whose lives are nothing but a misery to themselves as well as others. But that is the problem about altering standpoints; the view from the new one cannot be predicted and may contain sights previously undreamt of except in nightmares. And as with euthanasia, so with transplants; we simply do not know what an accident victim with extensive and irreversible brain damage will look like on the operating table when the attitude to transplants has been reversed in the manner proposed in Parliament. *Facilis descensus Averni.*

But that leaves the most important aspect of what has been proposed. It was argued on all hands that, since the number of those making a direct commitment to the medical use of their bodies (by signing and carrying a 'kidney card') is insufficient for those whose lives could be saved or prolonged by such use, a new method of increasing the number of bodies available must be introduced. But if the MPs had been talking about increasing the production of sugar-beet by providing low-interest loans for farmers willing to change the balance of their crops they could hardly have shown themselves more oblivious to the colossal weight that all peoples have always given to reverence for the dead.

The MPs did take into account the grief of the abruptly bereaved, but only in terms of the difficulty or embarrassment of asking them for permission to extract the tastiest morsels from the remains of their loved ones; nobody stopped to think that that difficulty and embarrassment are directly connected with the instinctive horror so many people feel at the thought of the offhand disposal of a body they once loved, let alone that the instinctive horror is grounded in something deeper than did ever plummet sound. 'There is evidence', said the Minister, 'that people are strongly opposed to an opting out system.' There is indeed; about 30,000 years of such evidence, and it is not to be dismissed without consideration of what it must mean for the nature of human beings and their most important beliefs.

There was another example of lack of imagination among the MPs who debated this subject. Many people, it was pointed out, do not bother to carry a kidney card, even though they would have no objection to their bodies being used, because they are unable to envisage their abrupt death: 'It is a human failing', said Mr Dalyell, 'to imagine that other people are going to be killed, not oneself.'

A human *failing*? That is no failing; it is an instinct that enshrines one of the most glorious truths about mankind, which is that our faces are set towards the sun of life, not the darkness of death. We do not go about the streets wondering whether we are going to be run over, though we know the figures for road accidents; even the soldier in battle does not believe that the next bullet has his number on it.

This life force is inseparably bound up with the feeling that a dead body must be handled with care, precisely because it once contained life. Those who think of dead bodies as no more than a repository of spare parts, like a carbreaker's yard, have failed to gauge the strength of that feeling and, in their very proper zeal for helping those whose suffering could be alleviated if more of their fellows would assign their bodies for alleviation have made a profound mistake.

*The Times* February 17th, 1984

# Out of battle

## 'The Good War' by Studs Terkel*

WHEN, CENTURIES FROM NOW, archaeologists from Alpha Centauri are trying to discover what sort of people we earthlings were, and in particular what animated the ones who lived in America, they could not do better than to study the works of Studs Terkel and ignore entirely those of more orthodox historians.

Mr Terkel specializes in 'oral history'; he goes about his own country, and many others, with a tape-recorder, a basilisk eye and an ear as acute as Mozart's, and instead of talking, he switches on his machine and listens. He listens to the famous and the unknown, the rich and the poor, the happy and the unhappy, the fluent and the inarticulate; he prompts them rarely, and then only with a very few words. Then he has their words transcribed, cuts them to manageable length (but never rewrites them – everything from swear words to grammatical errors are left as they were spoken), puts the narratives into a cunningly arranged order, and publishes the result.

Easy, is it? Just a lot of interviews cobbled together? Then why do such books as his *Division Street America* and *American Dreams, Lost and Found* not only carry complete conviction but make the reader understand so comprehensively the varied attitudes of a whole nation? And how, beyond that, does he manage to convey a feeling that we are hearing, in the hubbub of the voices he has collected, the

---

* Hamish Hamilton 1985.

authentic tones of humanity itself, telling us what it means to
be human?

His *Working* told us what it means in terms of the way we
earn our living; *Hard Times* answered the question in the
language of poverty and the threat of despair; now, in this
book – his most ambitious and most successful yet – he holds
up the mirror of Mars and bids humanity look into it and tell
him what it shows.

'*The Good War*' (the quotation marks are his, used to
emphasize the incongruity of the coupling) is World War II.
Most of his interlocutors are American, but we hear also
voices from other Allied nations, including the Russians, and
from Germany and Japan. The range is astonishingly wide;
his 120-odd subjects include men and women from every
theatre of war, from the General Staff and the PBI, from the
home front, from the Manhattan Project, from those who
were too young and those who were too old, from the
broken in body or mind or both, from the PoWs who
escaped and the PoWs who did not, from those who became
cynical and those who remained idealists, from those who
didn't want to fight but did and those who wanted to fight
and weren't allowed to.

Themes emerge, too strongly to be random, let alone
coincidental. There are those who found a personality
through war, and more who gained their first income. There
were the ignorant who learned, the selfish who shared, the
frightened who were brave, the intolerant whose minds were
opened. Strongest of the currents that flow through the book
is the realization, which came to some abruptly, to others
slowly and painfully, that the enemy armies were also
composed of individual human beings. A fine discrimination
shows; men who now say that they would go again, freely,
into such a war of the just, are recorded, over and over, as
saying also that the bombing of Dresden and Nagasaki was
unjustified. Humanity bursts forth; those who saw the
concentration camps are still in pain, forty years later, from

the realization that there could be such wickedness in the world.

Courage is repeatedly defined in the same way: 'you couldn't let your buddies down'. Emotion flows with memory; Mr Terkel's stage directions are mostly limited to (*Laughs*) and (*Cries*) but both occur many times. The confusion of war is painted vividly; camaraderie is stressed, lost innocence regretted, the uncertain future feared.

Sometimes, it seems as though centuries have passed since the events described, rather than decades. Racial segregation in the American forces was still strictly enforced long after 'The Good War' broke out, and some of the indignities (and worse than indignities, up to and including murder) that black soldiers suffered are recounted in words all the more effective for their restraint; indeed, there is little bitterness among the blacks who tell their stories.

There are some amazing people here. Dr Drude, for instance, a German schoolmaster who thumbed his nose at the Nazis in exquisitely fashioned metaphors that his classes readily understood; the chaplain who gently dissuaded a young private from collecting gold teeth from dead Japanese; the conscientious objector so insouciant, self-composed and impudent that he drove his persecutors crazy; Patton, half hated and half worshipped.

Curiously, the professional writers come off worst; the war correspondents on the whole convey less feeling than those untrained in the use of words, while the artless contribute some of the most moving passages in the book, not least the account of their work, as troop-entertainers, by one of the Andrews Sisters.

There are unconsidered trifles that remain in the mind. A girl who was twelve when war broke out says: 'After Pearl Harbor, I never played with dolls again'; the worldly-wise ex-soldier who chooses his words with painful care says: 'We do believe, on the whole, it was worth it'; the American who meets the German submariner he sank says: 'There's a maturing with thirty-eight years'; the black soldier, ill-treated by his white officers, who returns home thinking he is embittered, discovers, when he sees the Statue of Liberty, that he is not:

> There's a great outburst. I'm down below and I'm sayin', Hell, I'm not goin' up there. Damn that. All of a sudden, I found myself with tears, cryin' and saying the same thing they were saying. Glad to be home, proud of my country, as irregular as it is.

That last sentence could be Studs Terkel's motto. So could this:

> I learned something about men. I learned something about racism. I learned something about values. I learned something about myself.

Observer March 24th, 1985

# Find the lady

I FIRST BECAME INTERESTED in politics when I was a
schoolboy. I used to read the Parliamentary Reports in *The
Times*, and kept an annotated register of MPs. I think I
classified them according to their distance from my own
views, which at that time were roughly those held today by
Mr Kinnock – that is, based on the assumptions that would
be made by a rather naïve fifteen-year-old. (My excuse is that
I *was* a rather naïve fifteen-year-old: what is Mr Kinnock's?)

A few years went by, and I was a fellow-student of Sir
Alfred Sherman, who was the leader of the LSE Communist
Party; I always knew he would go far. I had had ambitions
for a political career, but at the university I shed them pretty
quickly, together with the naïve fifteen-year-old's views.

Another few years and I had become a journalist, and
began to write about politics, among many other subjects. I
had first voted in a general election in 1951; I voted Labour.
A certain amount of disillusion with Labour set in shortly
afterwards, but I certainly voted for them in 1955 and 1959.
In 1957 I became a parliamentary correspondent; Gaitskell
became my hero, not only for his own qualities but also by
way of reaction from my contemplation of the malignant
shadow dogging his footsteps. I may not have been the first
man to take the full measure of Harold Wilson, but I am sure
I was the first to proclaim that measure regularly and
frequently, and a fat lot of good it did. I voted Labour, I
admit, in both 1964 and 1966, when he was leader, but by
then I had known for many years that in a democracy it is

frequently necessary to enter the polling booth holding one's nose. More years rolled by; I voted Labour in 1970, despite feeling strongly that it was a mistake to do so.

I have not done so since. As more years passed, Labour began to stampede not just towards the left, but away from sanity; worse, away from liberty. My recoil from them was largely based on that, but there was another element, my growing conviction that what governments could do was far more limited than most of them profess most of the time. At the feet of Sir Karl Popper, I had learned to distrust the past as a guide to the future; now I had to learn that the present was not much help either. I have quoted Michael Oakeshott's splendid metaphor before; it will endure another airing:

> In political activity, then, men sail a boundless and bottomless sea; there is neither harbour for shelter nor floor for anchorage, neither starting-point nor appointed destination. The enterprise is to keep afloat on an even keel; the sea is both friend and enemy; and the seamanship consists in using the resources of a traditional manner of behaviour in order to make a friend of every inimical occasion.

It was in that sceptical frame of mind that I watched Britain's retreat through the Seventies; the withering of enterprise, the increasing reliance on the state (and the increasing greed of the state for those willing to be reliant upon it), the general political decay, best symbolized by the rise of Solomon Binding, though we should not forget Mr Heath's invention of 'comparability' to get him off the miners' hook.

Suddenly, there was somebody else. Mrs Thatcher, from the moment she threw her hat in the ring (she had sewn rocks into the lining, which is why it hurt Mr Heath so much when it hit him), began not only to talk a different political language, but to behave as though she meant what she said. I sat up sharply to watch the fun, and voted for her in 1979 with considerable enthusiasm, and in 1983 with even more. Now read on.

All this autobiography has a point. *Tempora mutantur* . . . I have moved restlessly through the political landscape of my time, and though it is not difficult to portray my journey as a continuous progress from left to right, it would be misleading; you will find nothing like the *abjuro* of Paul Johnson in my writings. The sceptical stance in politics, which I adopted (or which adopted me) decades ago, still serves me well in monitoring political activity anywhere on the spectrum, but it means that I could never drop anchor; whatever happens, I remain, and always will, a floating voter. But there is one, and only one, political position that, through all the years and all my changing views and feelings, has never altered, never come into question, never seemed too simple for a complex world. It is my profound and unwavering contempt for the Conservative Party.

That is much more remarkable than it may at first appear. The Conservative Party, after all, has not remained the same; there have been several Conservative parties in my time. When that schoolboy pored over *The Times*, for instance, the Tories in the House of Commons were the pre-war vintage. Most of them had supported Chamberlain, and never stopped hating Churchill; Harold Nicolson looked round the room at Chips Channon's end-of-the-war party, and saw 'the Nurembergers and the Munichois celebrating *our* victory over *their* friend Herr von Ribbentrop'.

Well, it was not difficult to despise that generation, and to rejoice when they went down in 1945. But then, as I looked at the Tory ranks in the six years of the Labour administration, together with the new intake when the Tories returned to power, an amazing truth dawned; the next generation was actually worse than its predecessor. It was characterized chiefly by meanness of spirit; they hated the welfare state, not at all (except for a handful of the old guard, like Sir Waldron Smithers) because they foresaw the Nanny State that eventually grew from it, but because it took money from the 'right' people and gave it to the wrong; I suppose one of the most formative political episodes of my life – formative far more widely and deeply than its effect on my politics – was the contemptuous jeering from the Tories at the thought that the National Health Service was giving people teeth and spectacles.

It became a kind of expletive; 'teethandspectacles, teethandspectacles', they chanted, enraged by the thought that the poor might live a better life. If it had not been for R. A. Butler and his patient, careful work in nursing a new breed of Tory MPs and officials, the party would have descended to a level of *Schweinerei* from which it might never again have risen.

But what actually happened was no better. Under Macmillan, who offered nothing but his cynical '*Enrichissez-vous!*', all principles, even vile ones, were abandoned by the Tories, as they fought to get their bread in the gravy. Going to the Tory conference in the Macmillan years provided a unique insight into the furthest reaches of fatuity, complacency and selfishness attainable by the human race. I remember overhearing a middle-aged woman delegate, with husband in tow, talking to another such couple. One pair had installed a television set at home, the other were thinking of doing so. 'Yes,' she said, 'I suppose we ought to have a television, to know what the ordinary people are thinking.'

I can see her now if I close my eyes; dowdy, vacant, overweight. I never saw anything so ordinary in my life (her husband matched her perfectly), and *she* wanted to know what the ordinary people were thinking. I believe, and I always will, that the premature death of Hugh Gaitskell was the single most damaging political event in Britain in the postwar world, for he left his party to face that Tory attitude, and the Tory attitudes that grew from it later, in the hands of Harold Wilson, an experience from which Labour has never recovered and the country only to a limited extent.

At the Labour conference there were and are people very much worse than that silly woman. There are people who want to destroy this country's freedom, and who work implacably, and with a good deal of success so far, towards that goal; there are also the massed ranks of union delegates, devoid of all energy, understanding, magnanimity, largeness of character or imagination – the visible, tangible incarnation of Britain's industrial failure; and up on the platform men are jockeying for power, lying about their beliefs to gain favour with one group or another, pretending to love colleagues whom they hate, willing to go to any lengths in damaging the country's interests if it will help them to get their behinds on the government benches. And yet their veins are full of blood, not Babycham, and the visitor does not want to go out into the corridor to quell his shuddering stomach, whereas I truly believe that I have not spent a full day at any Tory conference without at some point longing, in Cassandra's famous words, for a quiet corner, an aspidistra, a handkerchief and the old heave-ho.

It is only very recently, with the rise of Thugdom Triumphant, with the Scargills outside Parliament and those who have taken to practising physical intimidation inside, that it has become possible for me to despise the Labour Party as I despise the Tories, although for different reasons. Yet still, one look at the other side and the devout will be inclined to start praying, the superstitious will finger a rabbit's paw, and the wholly materialist will call for brandy.

For today, difficult though it may be to believe, the party's condition is worse than ever. The old guard condemn Mrs Thatcher as a lower middle-class swot who has never read any history, and the newer ones, who have never read any history themselves, or anything else either, are so busy selling their services to bucket-shop proprietors in need of an MP on their letterhead to impress the punters that it is as much as they can do to remember to have their Herbie Frogg shirts monogrammed.

I once described a prominent Conservative – never mind which one – as having the vision of a mole, the passion of a speak-your-weight machine and the oratorical eloquence of a whoopee-cushion. But I did so in the course of urging support for him, and the reason for my urging was that he wanted to change this country for what he thought was the better.

*Not the better off; the better.* Today, if you lined up the Tory MPs, the conference representatives and the entire staff of Central Office, you could throw coconuts at them for an hour and a half without hitting one who knew the difference. Where among them are more than a handful who dream of *changing* Britain, of offering her citizens an aim beyond a bigger car and the suppression of football hooliganism, of believing that there is a moral content to national life, of building cathedrals and pulling down Victoria Street?

That is a lot to ask, is it? Then let me ask less. How many are *not* hankering for a return to 'consensus', for the tiniest increase in inflation (5 per cent, say), for a programme of artificial job creation that will make the figures look better until after the next general election, for leaving the rating system alone, for just a little expansion of the money supply, for an increase in parliamentary allowances for secretarial help, research help, transport, pension arrangements, entertainment of constituents and travel?

Now the most significant aspect of this state of affairs lies in the fact that an astonishingly high proportion of Conservative leaders have despised their followers quite as much as I do. Obviously, Churchill did; more subtly, though no less deeply, Macmillan did; Heath would have been mad, or almost incredibly generous, if he hadn't, and not only after they removed him from the leadership; above all, our present Prime Minister does.

And so she should. For she is the one post-Churchill prime minister of either party who actually has a vision of this country's transformation and future, who has offered that

vision to the nation, who has seen the nation beginning to
respond to it, and then finds that the moment the opinion
polls show a blip on the screen, fully two and a half years
before there is the least likelihood of an election, blue funk is
running through her party like Aids at an orgy.

When Mrs Thatcher makes it clear that she wants to
destroy the class structure of Britain, she means it. When she
insists on returning to private ownership concerns like the
telephone system, British Aerospace, the Gas Board, British
Airways and I hope many more, she makes sure that the
public, and not just the City friends of some of the spivs on
her back benches, can obtain a share in the country's potentially profitable assets. When she decides that council-house
tenants should have the right to buy their homes, she
introduces legislation to that end.

What do you suppose it was that first gave Mrs Thatcher
her appeal to the country? To find out the answer to that
question, you only had to stand still for ten minutes and
listen: you could hear it all round you, and from those who
disagreed with her policies as much as those who believed in
them. It was that in Margaret Thatcher the country had
again, after many a summer, got a leader who knew her own
mind, spoke it, and acted upon it. And what was, what is,
her mind? It is nothing less than the transmogrification of
Britain into a nation of self-reliant, prospering individualists.

She will change the way people see the world and the way
they think. She will make us all see that to save for our old
age is not only a morally commendable thing to do, but is
also likely to make our old age much more comfortable than
relying on the state pension. She will persuade us that it is not
wrong that those who can afford more than a token contribution to their medical care should be obliged to pay it, and
when she has taught us that lesson, we shall teach ourselves
to make better and more careful use of such facilities.

She will make trade union leaders responsible to their
members, and if she lives long enough she will go on to make

the members responsible to the industry that will make them better off if they will allow it to. She will make it easier for entrepreneurs, big and little, to start or extend businesses, she will encourage innovators, she will make the country once again respect those who produce the wealth ('when the water rises, all the boats rise with it') of nations.

I am joking, of course. She will not do such things, though she would dearly like to, because her own party will prevent her. She won the 1979 election for them single-handed; she had rather more support from her colleagues in 1983, but that was only because the party started as the clear favourite, so they were putting their money on the leading horse. (Even then, Mr Pym drew attention to the dangers of a landslide majority, and then seemed astonished when she hastened to get rid of him as soon as she was back in Downing Street.) Now a couple of parliamentary seats have been lost, the local elections have proved a serious disappointment, and the opinion polls are adverse; the standard of revolt has therefore been raised and U-turns are demanded. Come; cover the country with factories in which a million men may be found employment in extracting moonbeams from cucumbers, and don't be so *abrasive*. Be like Mr Julian Critchley; *he's* not abrasive, and look where he's got – writes regularly for the *Listener*, he does, and the ladies of his constituency association positively adore him.

And why doesn't she lower her voice? And give up confrontation? *And above all, save our seats.* Save our seats by hook or by crook, or by both; save our seats by the abandonment of the vain (and anyway far too abrasive) hope of changing the country; save our seats by a liberal distribution of Danegeld; save our seats by what *we* would do in similar circumstances – that is, save our seats by fudging and smudging and nudging, by pretending that Britain's problems can be solved without pain to anyone, by seeking the Middle Ground, the Middle Way and the Middle Ages. Let us lean neither too far to the right nor too far to the left, neither excessively forward nor exaggeratedly back, neither too much up nor superfluously down. That way we shall save our seats; we know that many of us in the new intake of 1979 and 1983 look, sound and behave like so many used-car salesmen who do a bit of safe-blowing on the side, but we wouldn't want to earn our living that way if we could help it.

Have you noticed that some people *hate* Mrs Thatcher? That, I dare say, upsets Denis more than it does her. But it dismays me not at all. For it means that the medicine, nasty though it tastes, may yet cure the patient. Who hated Macmillan, Home, Heath? Who hated Wilson, Callaghan, Foot, and who hates Kinnock?

They say they hate her for her 'manner', her 'ruthlessness', her 'obstinacy', above all for her 'lack of compassion'. They lie; they hate her because they are afraid she might succeed, and transform Britain into a country where endeavour thrives, where merit advances, where the invaluable uniqueness of each individual is promoted and made much of, where success, not failure, is commended. To sum up in terms as offensive as I can find words for, Margaret Thatcher wants Britain to be a country in which nobody has power and influence *either* because he went to bed at Eton with a future Cabinet minister, *or* because he commands at the Labour Party conference hundreds of thousands of votes half of which were rigged and the other half bought.

That is the kind of country I, and many others, want too. Shall we have it? Or shall we let the Conservative Party ensure that we do not?*

*The Times* May 21st, 1985

---

* When this book closed for press, it seemed as though the answer to the first of those two questions was going to be No, and to the second Yes.

# Hell on earth

*The Diaries of Sofia Tolstoy* Translated by Cathy Porter*

'HOW GOOD OF GOD', said Samuel Butler, 'to let Carlyle and Mrs Carlyle marry one another, and so make only two people miserable instead of four.' The same could be said, with considerably more emphasis, about the Tolstoys, whose forty-eight-year marriage resembled at its best a state of armed neutrality enforced by the threat of Mutual Assured Destruction, and at its worst (which was most of the time) the behaviour of a pair of berserk cannibals, each intent on devouring the other.

Three things made certain that this almost uniquely ill-matched pair would together create a life that was unendurable for them both.

First, Sofia never got over the shock she sustained when Tolstoy, on the eve of their marriage, insisted that she should read his diaries, with their full record of his youthful debaucheries; innocent and romantic, she was almost destroyed by her abrupt discovery that such things could exist at all – a discovery made much worse by the unbearable knowledge that her husband-to-be had sunk himself deep in such shame. (To the end of his life she would continue to fling the record in his face.)

Second, Tolstoy's gradual conversion to his form of simplified Christianity not only offended her straightforward Orthodox faith, but drove her almost literally insane when she measured his claims of spiritual rebirth against the reality

* Cape, 1985.

of his monstrous and innumerable hypocrisies. He preached celibacy and practised lust (by no means only on her); he insisted on vegetarianism and ate meat, and on teetotalism and drank wine; he called for humility and had hundreds of photographs of himself taken in every conceivable pose; he lauded the ideal of the family and took no interest in most of his children; above all, he demanded that none should benefit by the labour of others and was waited on hand and foot not only by servants but by his family.

Third, Sofia was by nature suspicious, insecure and resentful, while her husband was incapable of considering anyone's feelings but his own; a vast proportion of this appalling record consists of her claims to consideration and his uncomprehending indifference to them.

Now here, in fuller form than ever before, is her side of the story. (The diaries are not, as is claimed, complete; there is mention of cuts in the 1978 Russian edition from which this version was translated and Sofia's second running account of her life, called her 'Daily diary', is published only in selection. Nor are matters much helped by the fact that the first of the two enormous indexes is largely useless, and the second entirely so.)

However much of her misery Sofia brought upon herself, her sufferings were atrocious. She sank herself in her husband's life and work as gladly and completely as Cosima Wagner; but unlike Cosima she always wanted something else, though she could never make up her mind what it was ('I long to read something really worthwhile, by some really great thinker, but I cannot imagine what'). All the drudgery of fair-copying, proof-reading, business dealings, fell upon her; she accepted the burden with joy, but got no thanks, and she was gradually pushed out of the work she loved, particularly when the horrible Chertkov (the Ralph Schoenman to Tolstoy's Bertrand Russell began to worm his way into control of the household. Some of the children became dissolute, others took sides and sniped across the no-man's-land of the marriage; day after day, she recorded the pain and humiliation. (There are gaps in the record, some of several years; if these represent horrors she could not bring herself to describe, God knows what they could have been, considering the things she *does* write down.)

Withal, she has bursts of manic happiness, convincing herself that all is well ('Who could be happier? Could any marriage be more happy and harmonious than ours?'), but she got it right early in the story: 'It is always the way – the richer the imagination, the poorer the life.' Later, even the happiness is accepted fearfully: '. . . I threw myself into his arms . . . he embraced me and wept, and we both decided that henceforth everything would be different, and we would love and cherish one another. I wonder how long it will last.' (In this instance, the answer was three paragraphs, after which she is complaining of her husband's 'attempts to abase and destroy me'.)

There are some welcome changes of tone; she gives a wonderfully vivid description of a muster of troops, including one of her sons, leaving for the Russo-Japanese War, and when she gets Tolstoy's sister in her sights Sofia's aim is faultless:

> She talks only of monasteries, Father Ambrosius, priests and nuns, John of Kronstadt and the holy powers of this or that icon, but herself likes to eat well and frequently loses her temper, and seems to have no love for anyone.

But most of these half-million words are words of woe, and they get madder and madder towards the end, as she snooped in his room ('dusting a cobweb . . . from which fell a key') and eavesdropped when he had visitors ('I could not help hearing their conversation from the hall'). She was constantly rushing out of the house to commit suicide, and he no less frequently doing so to go to America for ever; then they would both slink back and continue the war. And one cry from the battlefield pierces the heart with its agony and truth:

If he had one iota of the psychological understanding which fills his books, he would understand the pain and despair I was going through.

Inevitably, she fell in love, innocently, regretfully, romantically and platonically, none of which adverbs prevented Tolstoy from going half-mad with jealousy. The truth was that they could live neither together nor apart, and the story ends in a welter of hate: '. . . this diary of mine has pushed him off the pedestal he has spent his entire life creating for himself.' The only possible conclusion is the old riddle: 'What is a martyr?' 'One who lives with a saint.'

*Observer* September 15th, 1985

# Stone dead hath no fellow

THOU SHALT NOT KILL. So, at any rate, it has long been supposed; now, however, it seems that the principle is being called into question. After the two Welsh miners who killed a taxi-driver, David Wilkie, had been sentenced, there were emotional scenes in and near the court. The killers' families were understandably distressed (I dare say the late Mr Wilkie's family were also distressed when they learned that he was a corpse), as was the third miner who was on the bridge with the other two, but who was acquitted of all charges; he spoke, clearly affected, to television reporters, denying (what nobody had asserted) that the two convicted men had *intended* to kill the man they accounted for.

In circumstances as extreme as such a trial ending in convictions, he would be an inexcusably harsh moralist who rebuked those closely involved for words, however unseemly, uttered under such pressure. But when days have passed, a different standard of judgment is required for men, not themselves connected by family ties, who speak, and do, evil publicly.

Perhaps some of my readers may stir uncomfortably at the word evil; it is certainly not a word to be used lightly, and I have always been careful to avoid it unless I really mean it. But in this case I cannot see how a lesser word would suffice.

A few days after the end of the trial, a demonstration and march of miners was organized in Rhymney, the town in which the two killers lived. A newspaper photograph of the march was dominated by a placard, being held aloft, reading 'Rhymney – A town in mourning'. Now what word will you use, if not 'evil', when I tell you that the mourning referred to was not for the victim, but for those who killed him?

That was not all; indeed it was nothing very much compared to what followed. First, the marchers had to be prevented from going to the house of Mr David Williams, the miner who had been travelling in the taxi driven by the dead man, and who was therefore very lucky to escape with his life. The chairman of the local NUM lodge, Mr Ivor John, one of the leaders of the march, said that no one would speak to Mr Williams when he returned to the pit (he had been off work during the trial), but it seems that ostracism was not quite enough for some of Mr John's colleagues, so to avoid more – well, er, more *vigorous* action, the police felt it best to put a guard on Mr Williams's house and (with the stewards) divert the march. Thus balked, the marchers contented themselves with yells of 'Scab', presumably uttered at the closest point to Mr Williams's home they were able to reach.

The march ended with a rally at the ground used for the local Eisteddfod, where there were several speeches. Let us consider first the report of what was said by Mr Ray Davies, a member (Labour) of the mid-Glamorgan County Council: 'When that despicable verdict was announced there were shock waves of horror and revulsion that went through the valley.'

Now I believe, and I doubt if I am in a minority, that when killing is toward, shock waves of horror and revulsion are more appropriately felt for the deed, together with the person killed and his family, rather than for those who killed him. I have written before about the atrophy of the moral judgment that is the characteristic disease of our time, and the symptoms of which are the inability to see evil and the willingness to condone it when it is too lurid to be ignored as invisible. What else but that disease, in an acute form, is at work here?

The meeting continued. Next up was the local Labour MP, Mr Edward Rowlands. He started with a pat on the head for morality: 'We are not saying', he declared (ooh, the courage of the man!), 'that a terrible act was not done . . . But what we are saying is that the two lads in our community are not murderers and should not be branded as murderers.'

Note the two carefully-placed weasel words: 'Lads', especially ones belonging to a 'community', cannot be murderers; a trifle too high-spirited at times, perhaps, and over-fond of horseplay, but murder? Come, come; you'll be accusing them of secondary picketing at this rate.

Ignorance of the law is no excuse. But I do not believe that Mr Rowlands is ignorant of the law. He is a highly educated man, he has been a Minister of State, and he knows perfectly well that at the heart of our legal system is the principle that a man is presumed to intend the consequences of his actions, whether he actually desired those consequences or not. Mr Hancock and Mr Shankland, the two convicted miners, clearly did not set out with premeditation to kill Mr Wilkie. But it must have been, *and was*, obvious to them both that what they did was practically certain to cause death or frightful injury, and armed with that knowledge they went ahead and did it. (There was, incidentally, a Welsh jury.)

But we have not finished. Let us consider next Mr Llew Smith, the Labour MP for the area. He said that the sentence was 'political . . . a warning that anyone who decides to take on the government will not be tolerated'. Just measure *those* words against what happened; for Mr Smith, the killing, in a particularly horrific and brutal manner, of a wholly innocent man, apparently constitutes 'taking on the government'. And that, I may say, is milder than what Mr Peter Heathfield, the general secretary of the NUM, said elsewhere. For him, the killers were 'the victims of legislation designed to indicate to working people "That is your lot if you choose to rebel against the establishment".' Well, some might feel that the dead taxi-driver was more of a victim than the killers, and that his lot – as in 'You've had your lot' – fell upon him (literally, too) because he chose to rebel not against the establishment, but against the NUM.

And finally, there was Mr Kim Howells, an official of the South Wales NUM, who insisted that the 'first act of a Labour government should be to review the case'. He also claimed that 'I am as choked as everyone else here' (well, not quite as choked as Mr Wilkie, surely), that 'This government set out with its whole parliamentary paraphernalia to defeat us as a class', that the two killers 'were the sacrificial lambs of the system' (again, Mr Wilkie seems to me to fit the role of sacrifice rather better), and that 'They will never be alone, our communities will always be with them, and we will do our utmost to ensure that this absurd decision of the court is reversed'.

But Mr Howells said something else: 'Any one of us that took part in active picketing in the strike could have thrown those rocks because we were forced to protect our communities.'

It does not take much knowledge of the case to see that Mr Howells is a liar; the killers did not 'throw rocks'; they dropped a forty-pound block of concrete, and a concrete fence-post, off a bridge on to a car passing below, having first made sure that it was the car carrying a miner to work. But that's a detail; the substance of Mr Howells's words is clear, and they mean, if they mean anything at all, that what the killers did was justified, and would have been justified whoever did it, because the NUM was 'forced to protect our communities'.

A taxi-driver, pursuing his trade; a miner, wishing to follow his; these were an army, were they, advancing with tanks and flame-throwers, to destroy 'our communities' and put all the inhabitants to the sword? They were fair game, were they, at least as the target of 'rocks'? They had come, had they, to offer the Lord a burnt offering of two 'sacrificial lambs'? With people like Mr Howells about, it's a mercy the two killers weren't persuaded to plead self-defence.

It is, of course, pointless to expect a Christian bishop in this country (of either the Anglican or Roman rite) to express moral outrage at the condonation of a foul killing done in the course of a political strike; one or two of them, if they were moved to comment on it at all (in, say, a passing reference at the end of a sermon otherwise entirely devoted to the wickedness of any suggestion of amending the Earnings-Related Pension system), would probably murmur that it was all most regrettable but that, after all, the late Mr Wilkie's action was something of a provocation. So I had better say it for them.

Those that live by the sword shall eventually take life by the sword. The growing organized violence on picket lines, which has nothing to do with 'defending our communities' (there were no 'communities' round Mr Shah's Warrington printing plant), is an instrument of intimidation designed to weaken, and ultimately destroy, the foundation of a democratic society, by denying the duty to respect the rights of others, and thus to settle political differences peacefully and by democratic methods. No limits were set, in the miners' strike, to what might be done in the furtherance of that intimidatory end, and it was therefore obvious to any intelligent observer that, sooner or later, someone would be killed; indeed, when the bridge siege began, the senior police officer in the area said precisely that.

The 'deep damnation of his taking off' is not to be dismissed or trifled with; it is the integument that binds societies of imperfect human beings that might otherwise fly apart under the centrifugal force of greed, intolerance or cruelty. Go and read (in the Authorized Version) the fourth chapter of Genesis, and if the hair does not prickle on the back of your neck, you are already deep in the swamp of the moral relativism that in the end leads to men saying that the conviction of killers is 'despicable', that the killers themselves are 'sacrificial lambs', and that it is appropriate for a town to proclaim itself 'in mourning' for two killers who are alive in prison rather than for the man they killed.

Men who make such comments on such deeds are as far beyond shame as they are beyond sense. But the rest of us must choose between Cain and Abel, and this case is as good a test of the difference as we are likely to have. God knows it gives me no pleasure to contemplate two young lives (both killers are twenty-one) immured in prison for years, particularly since the law's reach is apparently not long enough to touch those who led them into iniquity. But if we allow ourselves, because of that feeling, to feel also that what they did was *not* iniquity, then we are on the road to hell. One way of getting off it would be to pay a visit to David Wilkie's grave.

*The Times* May 27th, 1985

# The hollow man

EVER SINCE THE FALL, there has been in the world a vast quantity of cruelty, hate, pain and fear; it is likely that that state of affairs will continue to the end of time itself. On a less abstract level, the world at any moment contains ample reserves of excrement, vomit and spilt blood. Meanwhile deformity and madness seem to be forever ineradicable.

No one, I think, will dispute those claims; most of us, however, would say that they were not worth making. They are not worth making because they are so obviously true, just as no one goes about insisting that the sun is hot and the moon cold, though no one would challenge such assertions.

But now let us make it, ostensibly at any rate, more difficult. Suppose there were a man of enormous gifts, penetrating vision and ruthless single-mindedness of purpose who had conceived his role as saying, day in and day out and with overwhelming force and conviction, that the night is usually dark, and certainly darker than the day, that to be tortured is almost always a very unpleasant experience, and that sometimes a small child plucking a flower is bitten by a poisonous snake and subsequently dies in agony. Now let us take a vote: are these things more worth saying (taking into account that they are said very forcefully and with a wealth of expression) than my own list? Those who say yes should hasten to the Tate Gallery for the Francis Bacon exhibition; those who say no should not trouble themselves to do so.

The puffing and booming of Francis Bacon seems to me one of the silliest aberrations even of our exceptionally silly

time. Here, summing up the silliness, is the director of the
Tate, Mr Alan Bowness, in his foreword to the catalogue (a
particularly sumptuous catalogue, incidentally, with every
picture reproduced in colour):

> His own work sets the standard for our time, for he is surely the
> greatest living painter; no artist in our century has presented the
> human predicament with such insight and feeling. The paintings
> have the inescapable mark of the present; I am tempted to add
> the word alas, but for Bacon the virtues of truth and honesty
> transcend the tasteful. They give to his paintings a terrible
> beauty that has placed them among the most memorable images
> in the entire history of art. And these paintings have a timeless
> quality that allows them to hang naturally in our museums
> beside those of Rembrandt and Van Gogh.

'The greatest living painter; no artist in our century . . .'
Let us leave the living painter theme; the world is not exactly
awash with genius in painting at the moment, and anyway
we do not want to get into an argument about the precise
meaning of 'greatest'. But 'no artist in our century has
presented the human predicament with such insight and
feeling'? Here is a short list of artists in our century (taking
that to mean artists who did at least a significant proportion
of their work after 1900) whose insight and feeling in
understanding and presenting the human predicament are
manifestly greater than Bacon's – manifestly, at any rate, to
anyone less silly than the director of the Tate and less
*parti-pris* than the seedy throng of Bacon groupies; Bonnard,
Braque, Chagall, Chirico, Derain, Ernst, Gris, Grosz, Kan-
dinsky, Kokoschka, Magritte, Matisse, Matta, Miró, Moore,
Munch, Picasso, Rivera, Rouault, Soutine, Sutherland,
Utrillo, Vlaminck and Vuillard.

Note that I have been strict with the definition. The
slightest stretching of 'human predicament' would have
enabled me to add Arp, Dufy, Klee, Léger and Mondrian,
and a slightly more generous treatment of dates would have

brought in Degas, Monet and Renoir (who, after all, lived to 1917, 1926 and 1919 respectively). Nor have I seized on Mr Bowness's distinction between 'painter' (Bacon the greatest living) and 'artist' (Bacon unrivalled at presenting the human predicament); if I had added the sculptors the list would have swollen substantially.

My objection to Bacon is the same as my objection to those clever young playwrights who finally drove me to give up the job of a dramatic critic; what is the point of being good at saying things if you have nothing to say – or at least, nothing other than that the world is rotten, human beings are rotten, love is rotten, society is rotten, life itself is rotten? In the first place, the claim is obviously untrue; in the second, it runs counter to some thirty centuries of human experience distilled in art – thirty centuries, moreover, in which the world was by no means free, any more than it is today, of envy, hatred, malice and all uncharitableness, nor of battle, murder and sudden death, nor of war, famine and pestilence.

Wandering through the huge Tate exhibition, I looked for evidence that Bacon had ever read *A Winter's Tale*, listened to the G minor Symphony of Mozart, seen *A Nous la Liberté*. There is no such sign. But there is much else.

There is a baboon, also a chimpanzee; both are screaming, as are a very large proportion of the human beings, man and animal – not to be distinguished, anyway – trapped alike in endless torment. (There is a dog which is *not* screaming; it is, however, tugging at its lead because it wishes to inspect a drain it is passing.) There are those endless deformations of faces and bodies which are this artist's most intense obsessions, and which suggest a degree of misanthropy verging on madness. There are the Velázquez variations, those Bacon Popes burning in their own hell (I wonder what Velázquez would think of Bacon – for that matter, I wonder what Bacon thinks of Velázquez, if indeed he ever thinks about Velázquez at all), and there is another parody of a well-known work, which seems to me very significant.

It is based on the Ingres painting of *Oedipus and the Sphinx* in the Louvre. Bacon has imitated the pose of Oedipus, with one leg raised on a rock; but Bacon's Oedipus is a simian figure, and the raised foot is covered in a filthy and blood-stained bandage. There is an indefinable figure in the background, part bat, part jellyfish, part bird; it, too, is blood-stained. An essay in the catalogue says that Bacon sees the creature as one of the Eumenides; if so, he must have forgotten how the *Oresteia* ends – in Bacon's mythology there is neither Apollo to plead for the sinner nor Athena to win over the Furies.

Bodies couple, in hate not love; other bodies writhe on beds, one of them swelling with the effects of the hypodermic embedded in its arm; naked men squat at stool; carcasses of beef hint at human carcasses; 'Reclining Woman' reclines, significantly, more hanging than lying; 'Woman Emptying a Bowl of Water' is accompanied by 'Paralytic Child on All Fours'. Disgust is kept at bay by the feeling that there is nothing sufficiently real in all this waste and folly to make disgust an appropriate reaction.

Bacon is not a charlatan; he feels everything he expresses. Nor has he invented or imagined the darkness in man's soul; Auschwitz and Kolyma are not fairy-tales, nor is the Crucifixion. But Bacon's version of the latter illustrates perfectly the fatuousness of Mr Bowness's claim that Bacon's paintings would 'hang naturally in our museums beside those of Rembrandt and Van Gogh'.

What is the second most noticeable, striking and important fact about the Crucifixion? That it is a story of shame, degradation, failure and death. What is the *most* noticeable, striking and important fact about it? That it is a story of shame put to shame, degradation raised incorruptible, failure turned to overwhelming triumph and death transmuted into eternal life. What is wrong with Francis Bacon? He has not noticed that, half-way through, the Crucifixion turns into its opposite. Tintoretto did; and Rembrandt; and even Dali.

It is much too late to turn the tide. The received wisdom among the *bien pensants* is that Francis Bacon is a great artist, and his work a series of imperishable masterpieces; my claim that the received wisdom and his work alike are very great nonsense will convince nobody except small boys who notice that the Emperor has no clothes. True, those who live for another fifty years will be able to acquire Bacon's paintings for about £2 a hundredweight, but the puffers and boomers will be safely dead by then. All the same, we have a duty to the present, and one part of that duty is to distinguish constantly between the true and the false. And in art, perhaps more than in any other category, those distinctions are necessary and important; which is why I have chosen to draw a few today.

*The Times* June 28th, 1985

# Take the money and stay

Tito's widow has been claiming (unsuccessfully) her inheritance; he had got rid of her a few years before his death, no doubt to instal something more agreeable and up-to-date in her place, and they clearly parted very non-speaks indeed – so much so that she seems to have lived under conditions not far removed from house arrest ever since.

The marital relations of Tito do not concern me; what caused me to twitch an eyebrow when I read of the dispute over his property was the list of the said property. It included cars, motorboats, horses, yachts, jewellery, paintings, a score of villas, orchards, a safari park and vineyards; and the value amounted to millions of pounds.

You see the point immediately, no doubt. What was this noble, selfless, upright, honourable, caring, moral, austere, heroic, truly socialist figure – the Stafford Cripps of the Balkans, the Keir Hardie of the non-aligned, the Nye Bevan of small nations – what was he doing with millions of pounds' worth of luxury goods, disappointed widow or no disappointed widow?

Not everybody can answer that question, and some who can answer it will be reluctant to do so. Yet the answer, however distasteful it may be thought, is surely a very straightforward one: it is that mass murderers are very unlikely indeed to jib at theft. Moreover, when the mass murderer in question is not part of the private sector, but the unchallenged and unchallengeable despotic ruler of an entire state, he can loot the public purse with impunity, for none of the mice will be willing to bell the cat, or even to admit that there is a cat to be belled.

It is easy to see this in the case of Ceausescu, who is *nothing* but a thieving scoundrel, or in that of the Emperor Bokassa, Giscard d'Estaing's *cher ami*. But it is hardly more difficult to see it in the case of some rulers who have committed few, if any, murders, but have concentrated entirely on providing for their old age or overthrow. There must, for instance, be banks in Zürich desperate for space in which to accommodate the savings of President Mobutu of Zaire; it seems that Washington estate agents have been buying whole neighbourhoods on behalf of President Marcos of the Philippines; and one of the few good laughs the people of Poland had when Jaruzelski took power was the sight of those he had supplanted being accused of widespread peculation.

But Tito was supposed (though not by me) to be above all that. Mass murder, yes; the dead'uns were obstructing progress towards socialism, and you can't make a real Yugoslav omelette without breaking a bottle of *slivovitz*. But a taste for luxury, and robbing the public in order to indulge it? Even unreconstructed Stalinists, willing to believe anything bad about the man who defied their hero, will surely be astonished to learn that Tito collected jewellery, country houses and vineyards.

Lord Acton did *not* say 'All power corrupts', and he would have been a prize fool if he had. Did power corrupt Gandhi? Or Clement Attlee? Or Pope John? Or his present successor? Or Florence Nightingale? Or Vespasian? Or, ahem, Hannibal? What Acton said was 'Power *tends to* corrupt'; inevitability was brought into it only in the form, 'Absolute power corrupts absolutely'.

And so it does, and always will. Nor, as my roll-call suggests, is the corruption of power limited to one end of the political spectrum. It is true that supporters of left-wing regimes, and of left-wing insurgents against right-wing regimes, invariably claim that the defeated or beleaguered forces of the right are financially corrupt, and those making the claims proudly contrast their own side's scrupulous purity in money matters, to such an extent that it sometimes seems as though Marxism is not an ideology but an anti-biotic, with the miraculous property of cleansing the patient's blood of avarice, dishonesty and a taste for *grands crus* and caviar.

But apart from the fact that it almost always turns out, even if only after some years, that the Marxist power-brokers were not in the least averse to sleeping on feather-beds, dining off gold plate and exercising every variety of *droit de seigneur*, there is no evidence at all that a belief in commun-ism, even if it is genuine rather than cynically professed, is in any way a guarantee of financial probity and moral uprightness.

How could it be? The potential corruption of power is within us, not external; the reason most of us never succumb to it is that we have no power, and the wiser among us take good care never to acquire any, precisely because we are not certain that we could resist its heady fumes. But even if we have power, or seek it most assiduously, it can never, in societies like ours, be absolute, or even very substantial. It is otherwise with the Titos and Bokassas.

As it happens, I knew that Tito was a crook as long ago as 1977, when, on a state visit to France, he stopped at Michel Guérard's place at Eugénie-les-Bains (to judge by that waist-line I bet he didn't go for the *cuisine minceur*) and skedaddled without paying the bill; Guérard complained loudly, and the French Foreign Office turned as pink as mine host's roast lamb and forked out for what Tito had forked in.

I remember remarking at the time that Tito had been so accustomed to bilking restaurateurs and shopkeepers in his own country without being challenged (because none, back home, would dare to challenge him) that he had altogether forgotten that elsewhere a bit of give is expected to accompany the take.

'We brought nothing into this world,' says the Prayer Book, 'and it is certain that we shall carry nothing out of it.' No, but in between, if we are in a position to do so, we can collect quite a lot, and enjoy it for quite a long time. And when we have the power of life and death over our subjects, how easy it must be to believe that if their lives are ours to command, to regulate and even to destroy, then their property is as nothing, and can be diverted to our use without any feeling of unease, let alone guilt.

And in time, such tyrants come to believe that not only their subjects but the very soil of their country belongs to them (literally – among Tito's inventory was an entire island in the Adriatic), and may be gathered in to make their lives still more comfortable.

Here I pause to make a prophecy. The Widow Mao was accused, when after Mao's death his faction was overthrown, of countless crimes; among these was a taste for luxury, indulged at the expense of the toiling masses. The most bizarre of the charges was that she used to eat hot melon; well, tastes differ and I certainly prefer mine *frappé*, but that is not the point. The point is that the new rulers of China fingered her as corrupt, diverting to her own use that which was the property of all.

Now for my prophecy: within five years of where we sit, Mao will have been condemned by his successors for precisely the same crimes, only to a far greater extent. We shall learn that he had a vast collection of precious jade, golden armour, silk underwear, whores, crocodile-skin shoes, jewelled cigarette-holders. Fabergé knick-knacks and a dozen more varieties of extremely unproletarian comforts; with any luck it will be revealed that he went on the Long March in a Rolls-Royce, with a Fortnums hamper in the boot.

That will be disconcerting to Mr Neville Maxwell (Felix

Greene has died)* but it will not surprise me in the least. Absolute power corrupts absolutely, and when a man is worshipped as a living god (I never tire of pointing out that when Mao died there were *seven hundred million* extant pictures of him in China) he would have to be of a remarkable diffidence and modesty to insist that he was only *primus inter pares*.

Mankind is not yet perfect, and it is my sad task to announce that perfection is most unlikely to be achieved by the week after next, and that meanwhile greedy swine like Tito will take what they can get, and none shall say them nay. The solution lies not in trying to hurry the perfection, but in devising a system that takes the imperfection into account. And there is only one way to achieve that: a form of government which prevents any man from having great power, let alone absolute power, over the governed.

There are, of course, better reasons for democracy than that it prevents its leaders amassing yachts, villas, safari parks, paintings and vineyards, but that is a very good reason none the less. I don't know whether Tito ever read Montaigne, but if he did I wonder what he thought when he got to the bit which says, 'Sit we upon never so high a stool, yet sit we but upon our own tails'. I dare say that all he did was to rearrange the silk cushions and call for some more Bollinger. And woe betide any serf who brought him the non-vintage.

*The Times* January 24th, 1986

---

* These two were the most assiduous of those who extolled in the West the beneficent rule of the all-wise, freedom-loving, miracle-working Mao Tse-tung.

# Darkness at noon

*The True Confessions of an Albino Terrorist* by Breyten Breytenbach*

I F THERE IS A READER of this review who is contemplating any kind of clandestine activity against South Africa, whether peaceful or violent, he would be well advised, should Mr Breytenbach approach him with an offer of advice or assistance, to abandon the enterprise forthwith, and thereafter devote his energies exclusively to raising funds for the Elderly Nurses' Home or the United Society for the Propagation of the Gospel.

No other course of action would be prudent. Mr Breytenbach, who is Afrikaner born, was living abroad when he became involved with a shadowy organization called Okhela, which was working against the South African Government and its apartheid policies. He returned to his native country to further the organization's aims, and he set about his preparations, his journey and his activities within South Africa with such monumental incompetence, such neglect of even the simplest precautions against discovery, such a combination of egregious folly and vanity, that he was shadowed by agents of the South African security services from before he even left Europe to the moment when, at Jan Smuts Airport, he was about to board a plane out of the country.

The reason he had not been arrested as soon as he arrived was that the authorities thought that if they just let him run loose he would lead them, in his criminal innocence, to his

* Faber, 1985.

associates. He did; God knows how many brave men and women were ultimately imprisoned and tortured because of him.

Nor did he stop even when the handcuffs were snapped on his wrists. His policy, first in the course of his trial and then when he was inside, was to believe anything that was obviously untrue, and to trust anyone who was manifestly untrustworthy; this led to his being used repeatedly for pro-government propaganda without ever learning, apparently, from experience. In his book he takes his revenge upon his betrayers – notably Dr Christiaan Barnard – by painting their portraits in merciless acid, but that does not undo the damage he did, and the temptation to say that he deserved his fate is strong.

The temptation is overwhelmed by two counter-arguments. The first is that *no one* could deserve what he endured in the seven years of his imprisonment. The second is provided by the quality of his book.

Mr Breytenbach is, among other things, a poet. He includes a selection of his poems as an appendix, and as a matter of fact they are not very good; but the savage rhythms and psychedelic colours of his prose constitute poetry of a very high order indeed, making the book sing in the mind and leaving the reader with a palimpsest of horrors designed by a man consumed by twin necessities – of voiding himself of the evil he was crammed with merely by breathing the air of a South African political prison, and of making us, his readers who live in civilized safety, see and hear and smell, taste and feel, what it is like to dwell, as long as Jacob served Laban, in the tenth circle of Hell.

His technique is to alternate exact description of the details of prison life – the sadism and stupidity of the warders and interrogators, the precise nature, weight, taste and texture of the rations, the tricks used by the prisoners to outwit their jailers – with a kind of philosophic context for this photographic reality, in which he speculates, to good purpose, on the nature of evil, on the symbiotic bond that links interrogator to interrogated, torturer to tortured, even hangman to hanged man, on the trap of insanity in which the rulers of South Africa have immured themselves.

The author was not himself physically tortured, though the psychological tortures inflicted on him were such that the distinction becomes erased; the reader can be in no doubt at all that if the gas-chambers of extermination are ever set up in South Africa, there will be no lack of personnel, from the staff of Pollsmoor Prison alone, to turn the taps on, and watch, laughing, through the spyholes. ('I believe', says Mr Breytenbach, 'that the torturer is as depraved by his acts as the one who is tortured.')

He is perhaps a little too much given to assuming that every evil effect had a cause originating in a consciously evil intent; ignorance and inefficiency must have contributed much. But even as I write that lofty sentence, I recognize how easy it is for me to do so, how hard for one who has seen, as Mr Breytenbach has, South African prison warders strip a prisoner naked, take everything out of his cell, soak floor and walls with water, and then throw through the bars an object connected to a powerful electric current. (For fun, incidentally, not to extract information.)

He pays tribute to those who still resist (unnecessarily grudging in the case of Helen Suzman), and he is devastatingly honest about the control exerted by the South African Communist Party over the African National Congress and anti-apartheid organizations abroad, though he is no less honest when he adds:

> All of this I do not trot out as criticism or as 'red-baiting' . . . I believe that a communist party is by its very nature and by definition a power machine . . . if it wants to guide the revolutionary struggle . . . it should work within the framework of the liberation movement.

He sees no hope at all, not so much as the tiniest glimmer, of any reform, from within the ruling group, that will avert the inevitable catastrophe; South Africa will change only when its rulers are overthrown. He has no hope, either, that that will be soon. Those who disagree, on either count, should do so tentatively in the presence of a man who has spent seven years in a place where

> it even happened that a prisoner would catch and tame a mouse, and using bread or some other delicacy as bait, the little animal would be taught to go from one cell to the other, again with some *dagga* or tobacco strapped to its body.

No wonder that the name he has coined for the country of his birth is No Man's Land.

*Observer* October 20th, 1985

# Who He?

IT IS NOT GENERALLY KNOWN – indeed, he is probably unaware of it himself – that the birthday of Mr Jeremy Isaacs, the head of Channel 4, falls on the Feast Day of St Eustochium, who inspired St Jerome's *Concerning the Keeping of Virginity* (she was much given to the practice). The significance of this apparently unremarkable coincidence may not be readily apparent, but when I reveal that she died of shock after the community of maidens and widows which she directed was pillaged and burnt by a mob the parallel will, I feel, strike Mr Isaacs at least as being almost uncomfortably clear.

Any day now a mob is likely to storm down Charlotte Street and sack the premises of the television service over which he presides with such controversial distinction; if so, the immediate cause of their fury will be Channel 4's series of three programmes about Christ under the title of *Jesus: The Evidence*. The first of these was transmitted last Sunday, but long before it was shown the blood and bones of Mr Isaacs were being demanded with ever-increasing stridency; those who follow such things will hardly need me to tell them that the most strident of the demanders had not seen the programmes and showed all the *stigmata* of men implacably determined not to do so.

The holy ire was provoked by rumours (themselves inspired by the programme's makers) that the programmes would subject the Gospel accounts to the most rigorous scholarly examination, of the kind applicable to any historical

event; the implication was that such an approach would end
by demonstrating that there was probably no such figure as
Christ (sorry about that, Jesus), but at the most an itinerant
street-corner speaker without any special qualities, powers or
family antecedents, deplorably lacking in sympathy for the
World Council of Churches and quite unfit to be interviewed
on television by Mr Melvyn Bragg. It was also hinted that
the series would touch upon the possibility that Christ was a
homosexual, which would suggest that those who devised
the programmes suffered from a serious lack of imagination,
for ordinary homosexuals are today ten a penny; had they
insisted that Jesus was a Single-Parent Black Lesbian Against
the Bomb they would almost certainly have been eligible for
a grant from the GLC.

I watched the first episode, and I have to say that I came to
the conclusion that Mr Isaacs should certainly be burned, not
at all because of heresy, blasphemy or *scandalum magnatum*,
but because of the almost unbelievable awfulness of the
programme *as television*. There was no known cliché, verbal
or visual, that was omitted; my favourite was the reference to
the nineteenth-century biblical scholar David Strauss, who
was dismissed from his teaching post for his writings. As the
sepulchral tones of the presenter said 'dismissed', there was a
thump, and a stamp fell diagonally across the screen, exactly
like 'Con gain from Lab' on election night, reading DIS-
MISSED: so help me, they did it again ten minutes later,
when we were told of two Catholic scholars who were
excommunicated because of their arguments: another
thump, and up comes ('Lib hold') EXCOMMUNICATED.

The 'historical reconstructions' were wonderfully,
memorably, funny. Luther, for instance, is seen nailing his
theses to the church door. Bang, bang, bang, and he turns
away and strides purposefully into the camera; behind him, a
monk puts his head out, presumably expecting the laundry,
and is puzzled to find nothing but a petition against rate-
capping. The problem of Albert Schweitzer and Rudolf

Bultmann, which was that they were foreigners and might therefore be expected to talk foreign, was solved in the traditional way; they talked English, but with 've haf vays of making bloddy dretful programmes' accents, though those were nothing to the two comic Egyptians who found the Oxyrhynchus papyri in a cave and jabbered over them with so uncannily lifelike an impersonation of the late Peter Sellers playing two comic Egyptians that millions of viewers must have been instantly converted to a belief in the Resurrection if nothing else.

I take it, however, that the makers of the programme (London Weekend) did not intend it to be judged as a contribution to the art of television. Presumably, they intended a serious investigation of who and what (if anyone or anything) Christ was, based on the available historical evidence tested by the methods that would be used by anyone seeking the identity and character of, say, Homer or Tamerlane. And at this point I must insist that Mr Isaacs should be snatched from the stake just as the fire is being kindled; the fright will be quite enough to punish him for the television, and he deserves no punishment at all for the theology, though as a matter of fact it was as clumsy and insubstantial as the television itself.

I had better make my usual disclaimer before continuing: I am not a Christian, and I realize that I meddle with Christian matters at my peril. All the same, I don't suppose anyone, of any denomination or none, could have watched the programme without reflecting on the nature and witness of the central figure, and such reflections on my part lead first of all to the conclusion that those Christians who protested in advance about the very making of the television series, let alone its content, must have a very pessimistic notion of the strength of the case for the defence.

Let us suppose that, sooner or later, incontrovertible evidence should turn up which proves the most disintegrative thesis about the historical Jesus, so that Christians can no longer support the case for a miracle-worker, a Redeemer or a Son of God. What would Christianity have lost, and what would it retain? To answer those questions, answer another: how has Christianity, with its human–divine centre, survived for twenty centuries, despite persecution, deviation, institutionalization, fragmentation and even the New English Bible? The answer, surely, is that Christianity has seized upon a massive truth about man and his relations with the universe, which truth, though it is crystallized around and symbolized by the particular figure whose name it bears, is yet ultimately independent thereof.

Come; let us be particular. Convince Beethoven that Christ was not the Messiah, that indeed there is and will be no Messiah. Then put the manuscript score of the *Missa Solemnis* into his hands, telling him that he will now no doubt want to tear it up, starting with the *Et resurrexit*. When he has stopped laughing and sent you about your business, do not be disheartened; try the same technique on Mathias Grünewald, standing in front of the Issenheim Altar at Colmar. If there was no Christ, it follows that St Antony could not have been sustained by the Christian faith in his hour of trial; will not the artist therefore wish to paint out the figures in the picture as it is now, and replace them by, say, a group portrait of the Executive Committee of the National Secular Society? I think his answer would be much the same as Beethoven's.

We do not have to think of Thomas More, going to the scaffold for disapproving of divorce, of all things (*nous avons changé tout cela*) for I, at any rate, can think of that merry Christian gentleman Father Corbishley, with whom I used to find myself, from time to time, on television and radio programmes, or that other merry fellow Lord Soper (who once rather pertinently observed that before regarding all men as his brothers he would rather like to be sure that they all had the same Father), or that fiery man Donald Reeves, struggling day and night to make his fashionable church (St

James, Piccadilly) unfashionable, or Archbishop Joost de
Blank, or Alexander Solzhenitsyn, or that Rock of Ages Dr
Beyers Naude; devilish difficult it would be to convince any
of these that the Christ of the Gospels was part human, part
mythological and part mushroom, but I cannot see any of
them, should they in the end be convinced of it, transferring
their allegiance to M'Shimba-M'Shamba.

Once upon a time, the makers of such television programmes would have been DISMISSED or EXCOM-
MUNICATED, or WORSE. It is good that that no longer
happens, and it is certainly not bad that the programmes
should be made and shown. And I think that Christ will
somehow survive them and the people who protest at them
alike. For two millennia that figure has inspired adoration,
worship, wonder, holiness, purity, sacrifice, art and love.
However many comic Egyptians find however many
ancient manuscripts in however many caves, I think
Christians can count on at least another two millennia of
the same inspiration.

*The Times* April 13th, 1984

# A credit to the trade

*A Journalist's Odyssey* by Patrick O'Donovan*

IF THIS IS Patrick O'Donovan's memorial, it is an inadequate one for a man who was among the very finest journalists of our time, or of any time. A mere thirty-eight pieces (and shoddily bound at that) out of the many hundreds he wrote in the *Observer* and elsewhere are enough to sharpen the appetite but not to satisfy it, and although the range of the selection is wide, it is far less wide than it would have been at twice the length. Still, it is better to have thirty-eight of his articles than none, better indeed to have thirty-eight than thirty-seven.

The conventional phrase that I used to describe him – 'among the very finest journalists' – tripped easily out of the typewriter. But what does it actually mean? What exactly did his achievement consist of?

First – not most important, but first – is the way he wrote. On page after page of this anthology his hard-edged prose conveys his meaning with images that instantly illuminate the scene. From an account of a Trooping the Colour: 'the band wheeling like a great melodious mob which had found a purpose'. From a description of a ceremony in Westminster Cathedral: 'the monks poured in as if a black and white tap had been turned on'. From a contemplation of the diplomatic round: 'at vast expense, the Ambassadors offer up their livers almost every night in the service of their country'. From a glimpse of a cocktail-party: 'a drawing-room crowded with

* Esmonde, 1985.

hot people holding cold drinks'. From an essay on, of all things, allotments: 'the ferocious vegetable-shows where onions, like severed heads, are laid out on dishes and marrows shown as fat, smooth and useless as Byzantine eunuchs'.

These images are not decoration; they serve like the knots on a parcel, to hold all firm. What they were holding firm was the second of O'Donovan's qualities: the clarity and vigour of both his description and his analysis, combined here in a hymn to nurses (he could have written an immense monograph on hospitals out of his own experiences over the years of his infinitely prolonged fatal illness):

> Illness can be an insult and a degradation. Pain can reduce a man to the level of an animal creeping into a corner. Nurses practise the sort of naval discipline that is fundamentally reasonable and which is designed to sustain humans faced with horror and filth and inhumanity. They have, like sailors, to face an unnatural situation and love itself is insufficient in such a predicament . . .
> As long as I was conscious someone told me all the time what was happening. Someone gave the right degree of believable reassurance. Someone touched me with just the right sort of unsentimental and affectionate respect for a body in a vile predicament.

Next comes his ability to rise to the occasion, which is much rarer in our trade than it should be. Many journalists can write fine descriptive pieces on great ceremonies like coronations and public funerals; O'Donovan realized that that is not enough, that the writer must also take the measure of the ceremony's meaning. He was one of the few who consistently did so, who possessed the necessary understanding and insight to find and convey that meaning.

Two perfect examples, at opposite ends of his spectrum, are the accounts of the enthronement of an Archbishop of Canterbury and the annual Game Fair at the Duke of Wellington's home. Both the sacred ceremony and the secular one are described with colour, charity and wit, yet those who read the descriptions will realize that the writer has not only conjured up the scenes with memorable vividness, but explained something important about the place of the Church of England and country pursuits in Britain.

Which brings me to the last, and most important, quality of O'Donovan's writing: its moral integrity, which shines out of such pieces as the one in which he tries to make up his mind about hunting, or those – particularly 'A Tale of two Englishwomen', with its hideous final twist – about Mao's triumph in the Chinese civil war, or his ostensibly detached 'Short history of Ireland', which is merciless in its pursuit of truth. But his integrity did not float in the air: it was rooted in the soil of his Catholic faith, which gave meaning to both his life and his journalism. Some of the very best items in this book are from the regular column he contributed to the *Catholic Herald* and other Catholic publications, and although these are by no means all on religious topics, they include his most intimate thoughts on his beliefs, culminating in 'God and I', in which he recites his humble and beautiful creed.

My own favourite memory of O'Donovan's journalism is not in this book, but I think deserves to be saluted here. It was during his time as the *Observer*'s Washington correspondent, and recorded his visit to the Library of Congress, the American equivalent of the British Library. Mindful of the rigorous tests that anyone wishing to use the latter must pass, he approached the attendant on the door of the American version, and asked diffidently, 'How do I become a reader?' The custodian looked at him in amazement, shrugged, jerked a thumb at the door, and said 'You just walk in and read, bud.'

*Observer* October 21st, 1985

# The best is not good enough

THE ROYAL ACADEMY OF MUSIC is in trouble, but the trouble is of an exceptionally unusual kind. Moreover, the trouble is not only unusual, it is extremely modern; so modern, indeed, that it was unknown a mere twenty-five years ago.

Well, well; so was Aids, and we must learn to move with the times. In the one case, the brimstone rains down upon the Cities of the Plain; in the other, the RAM is threatened with a like fate because it has a plan to turn itself into – well, into what? What proposed transmogrification of this ancient and honourable seat of musical learning (it was founded in 1822) has so aroused the anger of other musical colleges in this country that they have got together to mount a massive campaign against a proposal which one of the leading campaigners has called 'short-sighted, divisive and harmful to the profession'? Is the Academy going to be sold for a McDonald's? Is it to be pulled down and replaced by a multi-storey car-park? Is it planning to become a cinema for pornographic films, a betting office, a massage parlour, or a supermarket selling nothing but South African oranges, Chilean wine, Northern Ireland tea-towels and South Korean bicycles?

No, nothing like that. An appeal for very substantial private funds is to be launched, and the number of students admitted is to be reduced (so that the state grant will go further), all in order to attract and help, through scholarships, the most promising students, who will find themselves being taught by the highest quality of teaching staff. Thus, it is hoped, the RAM will in time become 'a centre of excellence'. And that is what has upset the other people of the music education world, who 'fear that the Academy would attract the best professors and most talented students'.

*Fear!* The Royal Academy of Music may become an orchard in which green musical talent can ripen into the finest fruit, a school worthy to be compared with the world's finest, its teachers the country's leading musicians and its pupils Britain's brightest and best, and instead of the plan being greeted with fanfares, anthems and stirring choruses in C major, the only sounds to be heard are those produced on the very lowest register of the tuba.

Once upon a time – and, as I have suggested, the time was no more than a quarter of a century ago – excellence was that which was to be striven for, sought out, cherished, admired, considered as a model to emulate or at least aspire to. Now, it is despised, made mock of, looked askance at, *feared*. Take but degree away, untune that string, and hark! what discord follows!

Has not the cultivation of mediocrity, under the name of equality, gone far enough? Or will it go further, so that it will presently be made a crime for one person to be cleverer than another, to run faster, to paint or write better, to sing more melodiously, nay, to be nicer or – *anathema sit! anathema sit!* – prettier? Must everything and everybody be ground into a uniform and indistinguishable powder, lest we begin to remember that some qualities are innate, among which genius, and even talent, are emphatically numbered? Must we live in a society whose god is Procrustes and whose patron saint Tom Thumb? Has the palpable lie that all men are equal so cowed, so weakened and so rotted us that we acquiesce when we see the best cried down *because* it is the best?

Under a Conservative government led by Mrs Thatcher, the Department of Education is at this very moment busy fudging the system of school examinations and certificates of proficiency so that it shall appear that no pupil, however lazy, indifferent, loutish *or stupid*, can be recorded as having failed. Apart from the dishonesty of the whole process, what kind of preparation is it for the real world? True, there are those who are hard at work trying to make the real world into one as imaginary as the world of failure-free school, a world in which there is no pain, no cause for regret, no hardship (and most certainly no *deserved* hardship), above all no penalty for those who will not strive.

> This is the impostume of much wealth and peace,
> Which inward breaks, and shows no sign without
> Why the man dies.

But the world *is* real, and cannot, unlike school, be made unreal; with our schools, we shall eventually give every child passing through the system a handsome decoration called the Gold Star for Conspicuous Merit. But life will, sooner or later, shake the sieve, and a lot of people are going to be unpleasantly surprised by the size of the holes.

A few years ago, some splendid lunatic declared that what Britain needed was a symphony orchestra that could stand comparison with the world's best – the Vienna, the Berlin, the Chicago, the Boston, the Amsterdam. The plan was to raise a million pounds and collect and train the hundred best players in this country, to put the resulting orchestra on a sound financial footing with every member of it in a position as permanent as a member of the Comédie Française, and then to challenge the world.

Nothing happened, because it became clear that the money could not be raised;* but long before hope was abandoned I

---

* Mr Peter Heyworth, the music critic and author, wrote to *The Times* after this appeared, saying that I had understated my case; the money *could* have been found, but the scheme was abandoned because all four London orchestras rejected it instantly.

had moved my bed into the cellar and piled sandbags all round the walls, because I knew that the inevitable uproar, if the orchestra wheeze *had* got off the ground, would have been virtually indistinguishable from the outbreak of the Third World War in the form known as Mutual Assured Destruction.

Wherever you look, the depressing story is the same, right down to those local authorities who wish to forbid the schools under their jurisdiction to organize 'competitive' games (such as football!), lest the children should come to believe that life is inevitably competitive. But life *is* inevitably competitive, and a great disservice is done to the young by telling them that it is not.

And at such a time, when excellence is needed more desperately than ever in our history, in order to offer something worth striving for, it is at its lowest point, consciously rejected by those who long to turn Britain into a suburb of Karl-Marx-Stadt, and abandoned out of resignation, indifference, dullness of spirit or fear by those whose highest duty is to cultivate every form of it as a dyke and rampart against the encroaching barbarians.

The barbarians are at the gates; the Royal Academy of Music proposes to man the walls with a volunteer army of highly-trained warriors, and when those brave defenders of the faith look round for allies, what do they find?

> The North is full of tangled things and texts and aching eyes
> And dead is all the innocence of anger and surprise . . .
> The walls are hung with velvet that is black and soft as sin,
> And little dwarfs creep out of it and little dwarfs creep in.

I have left the choicest morsel to the last. The rival musical colleges which have combined to oppose the plan of the RAM complain that if the Academy succeeds in its aim of attracting the best among staff and students alike, the other colleges would 'become second-rate institutions'. It might with justice be said that educational establishments which can take such an attitude are already second-rate institutions. There is, however, another comment to be made upon their claim. It is that if they fear the Academy's competition there is nothing to stop them announcing their own hunt for excellence, their own plans to raise funds, their own determination to engage and keep the best teachers, to invite and inspire the most eager students.

But the suspicion grows that it is not the Royal Academy of Music which they fear; it is the very idea of taking part in such competition. Why, I'll wager that they would like to get rid of all the awards for outstanding talent they have accumulated over the years – the Hiram H. Higginbotham Medal for oboe-playing, the Kurt Schweinkopf Cup for the best soprano voice, the Rosie O'Grady Bursary for fugue-writing.

Up goes the price of shoddy! But if we all refuse to buy it, it will come down again. The Royal Academy of Music has defied the spirit of our time in striking a blow for excellence. Its rivals, who wish to see the plan fail, are hereby awarded the Levin Lemon for the most egregiously disharmonious wrong note of the year, and I invite them to suck it and see.

*The Times* April 1st, 1986

# Consider your verdict, do

I THINK THIS COUNTRY is going mad. The rule of law, which is the foundation not only of our liberty but of our constitution and our protection against anarchy, has been knocked about a good deal in the last couple of decades: by governments (particularly their law officers); by trade union leaders who choose which laws they will obey and which ignore; by civil servants who similarly decide which confidences to keep and which to break; by the *groupuscules* of the far left, playing at revolution but advocating real crime in the furtherance of it; by local councillors who rob their constituents for their own political advantage; by university authorities who curtail free speech at the first threat of violence, and frequently without even waiting for the threat; by the whole tribe of Single Issue Fanatics; by Mr Scargill's Mohocks; by policemen who bring false charges against the victims of their own illegal acts; by Members of Parliament who openly despise parliamentary government; by such infamies as Michael Foot's closed-shop legislation and the present government's indefensibly undemocratic folly of banning trade unions at GCHQ; by juries who have turned the libel laws into an opencast mine for every gold-digger who can raise the price of a writ; and by the steadily engulfing tide of new legislation, most of which is unnecessary, much of which is pernicious, and all of which presents, in its quantity and its incomprehensibility, a monstrous threat to a public no member of which can hope to understand it or indeed to know of its existence.

> . . . The worst is not
> So long as we can say 'this is the worst'.

For the latest assault on the structure and basis of our law is the growing belief – its growth apparently unstoppable – that if anyone is accused of a serious crime, not just by the prosecuting authorities but by the neighbours, the press and television, or any sufficiently disreputable MP in search of a headline, the accused must inevitably be guilty, and if he cannot be put in prison, he should at least be sacked from his employment and delivered over to the attentions of a mob gathered outside his house to shout abuse and smash his windows. Lynching never took root in this country; if some people have their way, it soon will.

I suppose it all began when, amid collective parliamentary hysteria, the law was changed to prohibit the publication of the name of any woman involved as a witness in criminal proceedings against a man who is alleged to have raped her. (After some antiquary who still adhered to notions of even-handed justice pointed out that that was unfair to the accused man, the law was changed to give him, too, the protection of anonymity. Now, to the surprise of no one familiar with the eel-like suppleness of Home Secretaries' backbones, the present one has been dropping hints about abolishing the anonymity rule for the man but not for the woman.)

When the rule of law was thus being bent into strange and unlovely shapes, the louder and more unbridled among the groups demanding more severe punishments for rapists (Lord Denning has just been advocating castration) apparently began to believe that any man accused of rape must, by virtue of the accusation alone, be guilty. That is not much of an exaggeration; we have already come dangerously close to demands for the abolition, in rape cases, of the defence of consent, and voices have been raised to demand restrictions on the cross-examination of women giving evidence of rape.

Rape is certainly one of the very vilest of crimes, for years
made worse for the victim by the lack of sympathy it evoked,
particularly among judges who behaved as though it was a
trivial matter at best, and the fault of the woman at worst.
But as the pendulum has swung, we are in very real danger of
an assumption that no woman ever deliberately encourages a
man's advances knowing where they are tending, still less
that she ever brings a wholly false charge; if rape is alleged,
reason flees.

And when the alleged offence of sexual molestation concerns children, the baying has recently become even louder
and uglier. In the two most recent notorious instances, the
relevant authorities saw, and said, that no prosecution could
succeed, because of the laws which govern evidence by
young children and the corroboration such evidence requires.
Frustrated by the requirements of justice, the hunters, in the
press and in the streets, found that they had at last got two
real targets marked down for vengeance, in the shape of a
doctor and a clergyman, whose homes were promptly
invested by a crowd of amateur executioners eager to demonstrate their skills and with an alarmingly good chance of
being allowed to do so.

I have no doubt that there have been cases in which rapists,
or those who have sexually abused children or treated them
with non-sexual sadistic brutality, have gone unpunished
because of the law's requirements. But that is the inevitable
result of having a system of court law instead of mob law,
guesswork law, party-political law, tittle-tattle law, publicity
law or no law. A man is not to be punished unless he has been
convicted in due form and in a properly constituted court,
according to laws and rules laid down in advance. If he is
acquitted, or not tried because acquittal would be inevitable,
he is entitled to a presumption of innocence, even if the
whole village is united in thinking him guilty, the media have
demonstrated as much to their own satisfaction, and two-
thirds of the House of Commons are either of a similar

opinion or – more likely – think it wise to placate the noisier of their constituents by pretending that they are.

'Hard cases make bad law.' O, but soft ones make far worse! It is a natural and understandable instinct – an almost essential instinct – for human beings capable of empathy to want to mete out retribution to those who have violated women or harmed children; womanhood defiled on the one hand, and the damaging of innocence and vulnerability on the other, naturally call forth feelings of revenge.

But it is a distinguishing mark of civilization that private revenge (and more particularly vicarious private revenge) is not to be countenanced; vengeance is mine, saith the law, I will repay. And if I cannot repay, the law goes on, because my hands are tied by rules made necessary by the require-ments of justice, let no man presume to usurp my function. No feelings, however powerful, widespread and understand-able, are a substitute for the careful processes of law, and of law, moreover, free of all feeling on the part of those involved in its operation.

It is a well-nigh universal rule that in any situation which induces insensate anger among the observers of it, nothing but calm and reason can deal with the situation that has brought about the rage. The present state of affairs demands calm and reason as never before. Yet this is the very moment at which the government proposes to abolish the right to trial by jury in cases involving criminal charges considered trivial (for an innocent man *there is no such thing as a criminal charge that is trivial*), and to abolish also the right of a defendant to make three peremptory jury-challenges and thus ensure that, in compliance with the law and the constitution, he is tried by a jury of his peers. And worst of all, after a third recent case, there is now growing pressure, of exactly the kind governments are keen to give in to, for a change in the law which would enable a jury in criminal proceedings to know of previous convictions registered against the defendant they are trying.

Do I really have to tell *Times* readers why that is a very bad idea? Very well, then, I shall. It is a very bad idea because a jury is not required, or even permitted, to say whether the accused is a villain; they are required to say only, on the evidence before them, whether he has or has not been proved beyond a reasonable doubt to have committed the crime with which he has been charged; we do not convict a man for being the kind of person who would be likely to break the law, only for actually breaking it.

This hideous rush to judgment must be halted. We are in great danger of losing our footing on a slope at the bottom of which lie things that have no place in a civilized nation, yet there are people, not all of them unimportant, without influence or foolish, urging us all to slide faster. If the law is inadequate to punish people whom the multitude wish to see punished, the argument goes, let the multitude be given the power of punishment. If there are rules of evidence to ensure a fair trial, let the rules be altered until the outcome of a trial is not so much fair as pleasing to the multitude. If the law of contempt prohibits pre-trial discussion of the guilt or innocence of the accused, let a new contempt law be framed, by the workings of which the multitude may condemn in advance a man whose face or demeanor they find displeasing.

Alternatively, let us remember what Plato called it: '. . . that golden and hallowed drawing of judgment which goes by the name of the public law of the city'. There has been precious little such judgment these past few weeks, as the public law of the city has been trampled in the stampede to establish a new kind of justice, in which the courts are ignored, the rule of law rejected, the necessity of proof dispensed with, and the right to determine whose head shall fall given to those who can shout the loudest.

But those who can shout the loudest do not necessarily have justice on their side, as one of my ancestors pointed out to Barabbas. I think it is time for voices to be lowered. It is important for us to reflect upon the damage already done to our rule of law while those who profess or aspire to lead us have so often acquiesced in the damage, and in some cases applauded it. But first, let quiet reign. If it reigns long enough, we might be able to hear this exchange, between More and Roper, in Robert Bolt's *A Man for all Seasons*:

> *The law, Roper, the law. I know what's legal, not what's right. And I'll stick to what's legal . . . What would you do? Cut a great road through the law to get after the Devil?*

> I'd cut down every law in England to do that!

> *Oh? And when the last law was down, and the Devil turned round on you – where would you hide, Roper, the laws all being flat? This country's planted thick with laws from coast to coast – Man's laws, not God's – and if you cut them down – and you're just the man to do it – d'you really think you could stand upright in the winds that would blow then?*

*The Times* March 28th, 1986

# Index